Quakers and the Interfaith Movement

A Handbook for Peacemakers

Edited by

Anthony Manousos

Published by Quaker Universalist Fellowship

To make a contribution, subscribe or for further information, contact: universalistfriends.org

Cover design and layout by Anthony Manousos.

ISBN-10: 1461176670
ISBN-13: 978-1461176671

Second printing 2013 in the United States of America.

TABLE OF CONTENTS

INTRODUCTION

A Quakerly Approach to Interfaith Peacemaking and Dialogue in the Twenty-First Century

by Anthony Manousos

During this era when religion has become an excuse for terrifying violence and endless wars, we need to take to heart the words of the Catholic theologian Hans Kung:

> There can be no peace among the nations without peace among the religions. There can be no peace among religions without dialogue. And there can be no dialogue without a common ethic.

Quakers have had a Peace Testimony for 350 years, but it has become clear we cannot achieve our dream of world peace unless we work in concert with those of other religions who share our vision. As the British Friend Sylvia Stagg put it:

> When I joined the Quaker Committee on Christian and Interfaith Relations (QCCIR), interfaith work was of general interest. Now in 2005... interfaith relations has become an over-riding necessity in all our community relations. It is no longer a choice but an absolute necessity.

This handbook consists of writings by Quakers who have played significant roles in the interfaith movement and have helpful advice and insights to offer. While this book is mainly intended for Quakers, we hope it will be useful for all who are concerned about interfaith peacemaking and dialogue.

5

The book begins with "Advices and Queries," the traditional method used by Quakers to stimulate reflection through pithy quotations and open-ended questions. Quakers feel that before considering the ideas and opinions of others, it is important to reflect upon one's own experiences, motivations, and inward wisdom.

The first section deals with reasons why the interfaith movement is important and describes various approaches to interfaith peacemaking. "Friends and the Interfaith Movment" was the first article to be published on this topic by a major American Quaker magazine.

The second section deals with compassionate listening (one of the most important Quaker contributions to peace-making) and offers practical advice on how to organize encounters that can build trust and understanding among people of different faith traditions.

The third section contains essays by leading Quaker scholars/activists who examine interfaith dialogue in depth from various theological perspectives. Michael Birkel is a professor of religion at Earlham College, which was founded in Richmond, Indiana, by Quakers in 1847. A liberal Christian, he worships in an unprogammed meeting and engages in interfaith dialogue both locally and through the World Council of Churches. His colleague, Stephanie Crumley-Effinger, belongs to a pastoral Quaker tradition and is a campus minister. Sallie King, on the other hand, is a Buddhist Quaker who teaches comparative religion at James Madison University in Richmond, Virginia. Finally, Rachel Stacy is a young Friend who recently graduated from the Earlham School of Religion and describes herself as a Universalist Christian Quaker.

The fourth section describes Quaker Universalist Fellowship (QUF) and the Christian and Interfaith Relations Committee (CIRC) of Friends General Conference (FGC), Quaker organizations that promote interfaith dialogue and understanding. It also contains an essay about the Parliament of the World's Religions, which helped to launch the modern interfaith movement at the Chicago World's Fair in 1893. Quakers played an active part in this extraordinary interreligious gathering, which led to the formation of CIRC.

The last two sections deal with how Friends can reach out to Muslims and Jews. It includes my pamphlet "Islam from a Quaker Perspective," as well as my writings on the Qur'an and the Bible. Also included are excerpts from Michael Sells' translation of the Qur'an, with an insightful commentary.

The final section of the book also examines the question of Israel/Palestine, the most divisive issue for those involved with interfaith work. Because a considerable number of Quakers are of Jewish background, and because Friends have had a deep commitment to this region for over a hundred years—since the formation of the Ramallah Friends School—Friends have played a small but not insignificant role in the search for a just, compassionate and lasting peace in this region.

Those who wish to learn more are encouraged to go to the QUF blog—quakeruniversalist.org, or to our website—universalistfriends.org. The QUF blog contains lively and up-to-date information about what Friends and others are doing to promote Universalism and interfaith understanding. The QUF website is an online library of introspective pieces from renowned Friends, historical overviews and incisive book reports, and over 40 pamphlets downloadable for free. As QUF continues to put ever more content online, this Quaker Library will grow to become a great index of contemporary Quaker writings.

Because much of this material has been used in workshops I have facilitated at the Friends General Conference gathering, Pendle Hill, Quaker Center Ben Lomond, and various other Quaker venues, I would like to thank those who have taken part in these workshops,and are involved actively in nurturing what Martin Luther King called "the Beloved Community."

I also want to express my heartfelt appreciation to QUF and CIRC, and to the numerous Friends and faith leaders who have made my interfaith ministry not only possible, but joyful: Stanford Searl, Diane Manning and Kathy Forsman (members of Santa Monica Meeting who are part of my accountability/support committee); George Amoss, Larry Spears, Sallie King, Sally Rickerman, Lynn Cope, Steve Angell, Michael Birkel, Jim Rose, Rachel Stacy, and Mark Kharas (members of QUF); Tom Paxson, Dorothy Walizer, Michael Birkel, Charley Earp, and Brad Oglivie (members of CIRC). I am also deeply grateful to my various interfaith colleagues and friends: Joseph Prabhu, Ruth Broyde-Sharone, Thomas Hedberg, Debrah and Andre Van Zyl, Laura Ava-Tesimale, Linda Groff, Renee de Palma, Zachary Perlman, Gene Rothman, Noor Malika Chisti, Jasmine Hailey, Ian McIvain, Swami Atmatattwananda (Shiva), John Ishvardas Abdallah, Rev. Jeff Utter, Rev. Jan Chase, Rev. Janet Bregar, and Rev. Richard Rose (Parliament of the World's Religions); Milia Islam-Majeed, Rev. Sandy Olewine, Gretchen Krutz, Roni Love, Rev. Moira Foxe, Rini Ghosh, Khalil Momand, Dale Whitney, Duane Moret, Al Albergate, Richard Brehove, Rev. Jerry Stinson, Gila Katz, Patty Lance, Rev. Reinhard Krauss (South Coast Interfaith Council); Steve Rohde, Paul Nugent, Susan Stouffer, John Forney, Carolfrances Lichen, Rev. Louis Chase, Sister Pat Krommer, Ed Fisher, Ignacio Consuela, Veda Veach, Bonnie Blustein, Grace Dyrness, Rev. George Regas, Shakeel Syed, Stephen Longfellow Fiske, Cheryl Johnson (Interfaith Communities United for Justice and Peace); Leland Stewart, Rabbi Haim Beliak, Rabbi Jonathan Klein (CLUE), Arin Ghosh, Jahan Stanizai, Varun Soni (USC), Hussam Ayloush (CAIR), Jim Birklo (USC), Jerry Campbell (President of the Claremont School of Theology), William Lesher, Rev. William Miller, Father Alexei Smith, Gwynne Guibord, Sande Hart, Rebecca Tobias, Joseph Morris, and many others too numerous to name.

Advices and Queries
About Interfaith Dialogue and
Peacemaking

In this time when we constantly interact with people of other cultures and nationalities, the Christian and Interfaith Relations Committee (CIRC) of FGC invites Friends to consider the challenges and opportunities inherent in a world in which the many religions confront each other daily. Religious differences play a role in many contemporary wars. Religion is too often used as a weapon to frighten or a tool to incite violence and hatred. Friends must demonstrate a different way. *–Sallie B. King, Professor of Philosophy and Religion at James Madison University in Harrisonburg, Virginia.*

The only thing that will tip the balance between planting [*olives trees, symbols of peace*] and uprooting is for all peoples—Jewish, Muslim and Christian—to work together in solidarity. We must pray together. We must work together. We must continue to bring light to those from all faiths whose hearts are trapped in darkness. We must all find ways to root ourselves in the creation of peace.— *Tom Fox, Quaker peace activist and martyr, quoted in "Tom Fox Was My Friend, Yours, Too" (edited by Chuck Fager and available through Kimo Press, kimopress.com).*

This is the word of the Lord God to you all, and a charge to you all in the presence of the living God; be patterns, be examples in all countries, places, islands, nations wherever you come; that your carriage and life may preach among all sorts of people, and to them; then you will come to walk cheerfully over the world, answering that of God in everyone.—*George Fox, founder of Quakerism.*

9

The humble, meek, merciful, just, pious and devout souls everywhere are of one religion and when death has taken off the mask, they will know one another, though the diverse liveries they wore here make them strangers.— *William Penn.*

The Inward Light is a universal light given to all men [and women], religious consciousness being basically the same wherever it is found. Our difficulties come when we try to express it. We cannot express; we can only experience God. Therefore we must always remember tolerance, humility, and tenderness with others whose ways and views may differ from ours.—*Pacific Yearly Meeting Faith and Practice.*

"Mutual irradiation" is defined by Quaker ecumenist Douglas Steere as an interfaith encounter in which "each is willing to expose [him or herself] with great openness to the inward message of the other, as well as to share its own experience, and to trust that whatever is the truth in each experience will irradiate and deepen the experience of the other."—Douglas Steere, *Mutual Irradiation*, Pendle Hill Pamphlet #175.

This is not to say that all religions are one. The religions are indeed different. While Friends avoid creeds, our Testimonies—Truth, Nonviolence, Equality, Simplicity— are clear and not to be compromised, as is our practice of submitting to the guidance of the Spirit. These give us the guidance we need in our relating to other religions.– *Sallie B. King (www.fgcquaker.org/library/welcome/fa-otherreligions.html).*

Do your work gladly with other religious groups in the pursuit of common goals. While remaining faithful to Quaker insights, try to enter imaginatively into the life and witness of other communities of faith, creating together bonds of friendship.—*Britain Yearly Meeting.*

Queries/questions compiled by editor

Are you open to Truth wherever it can be found?

Do you look for "that of God" in other religions as well as in other people?

When you engage in dialogue with those of other faiths, do you avoid making assumptions and instead listen with an open mind as well as an open heart? Do you ask open-ended questions, seeking to know and appreciate differences as well as similarities among faiths?

Do you practice the art of listening, even beyond words?

Are you open to what Douglas Steere called "mutual irradiation"—the sharing of inward spiritual truth and experiences?

Are you willing to work cooperatively with those of other faith traditions to promote peace and justice, and to help the poor, marginalized, and disadvantaged?

For meetings and churches to consider:

Do you have a representative in your local interfaith or ecumenical council?

Do you play an active role in interfaith events and activities in your local community, witnessing to our Quaker convictions and practices?

Do you stand up for religious pluralism and oppose religious bigotry and prejudice?

PART I: WHY THE INTERFAITH MOVEMENT MATTERS

"Friends and the Interfaith Movement"

By Anthony Manousos

Ten years ago, our country and the world were shaken to the core by the events of September 11th. During this critical period Americans were given a moral as well as political choice: should we respond with retaliation and revenge, or should we seek to understand the root causes of violence and find ways to bring about a more peaceful and just world? Sadly, our leaders chose the former course. As a result, we have seen an unrelenting cycle of violence, deception, and mistrust in our country and in the world.

But many here in the United States and abroad are seeking a better way. They have created an interfaith movement with the potential for reducing, and ultimately ending, the violence attributed to religion. I believe that we as a Society of Friends are called to play an active role in this vital movement. We are a small group, but we have a long tradition of compassionate listening and of being willing to speak truth to power. As British Friend Marigold Bentley of Quaker Peace and Social Witness writes:

> The lack of dogma in our own faith enables us to open up to those who, for many, have unacceptable beliefs. Quakers have careful processes to enable delicate spiritual discussions. Quakers also have the gift of meeting houses across the country, which are ideally suited to interfaith encounters as they are

unencumbered with religious artifacts. This is used to great effect by many Friends.

This is true in the USA as well as in the UK. Since 9/11 Friends have been eager to become involved in interfaith conversations. When I gave a workshop on "Islam from a Quaker Perspective" at the Friends General Conference Gathering in Amherst, MA, Friends responded enthusiastically and we were warmly welcomed into the local mosque. At this year's FGC Gathering, the Quaker Universalist Fellowship is focusing on the interfaith movement and has invited Muslim, Christian and Jewish speakers to participate.

Friends have also taken part in the interfaith movement at the local level. For many years, interfaith work was primarily carried on by religious leaders and academics. But since 9/11 interfaith work is now seen as a matter of urgency for all people. As British Friend Sylvia Stagg pointed out:

> When I joined the Quaker Committee on Christian and Interfaith Relations (QCCIR), interfaith work was of general interest. Now in 2005... interfaith relations has become an over-riding necessity in all our community relations. It is no longer a choice but an absolute necessity.

Most ecumenical organizations (which were mainly founded in the '50s and '60s) have changed with the times and become interfaith, enabling Christians, Jews, Muslims and other religious practitioners to work together as equals in local communities.

Although we Friends have reached out warmly and spontaneously to Muslims as individuals and as Meetings, we are not as involved as we could or should be in these newly transformed interfaith organizations. Because Friends don't have professional clergy, we have tended to shy away from whatever smacks of "organized religion."

We were also excluded from full participation in many ecumenical organizations because we were not considered Christian.

Times have changed. Today our Quaker voice needs to be heard, and we need to listen, at these newly emergent interfaith gatherings. Those who feel led to do interfaith work need the support and encouragement of our Meetings.

Interfaith work is not without challenges. When we reach out to those who are different, there are apt to be cultural misunderstandings. We need to be tolerant and patient, especially when dealing with Muslims and Jews who have experienced discrimination and have felt under attack over the centuries. There are many hot-button issues that need to be handled with great care and sensitivity, and we need to do our homework in order to be effective. A list of helpful resources is in the appendix of this book.

Types of interfaith work: the healing and the prophetic

Some interfaith groups focus primarily on healing divisions and building understanding. Others advocate for peace and justice. Friends can learn from and contribute to both approaches.

The work that I do for the South Coast Interfaith Council in the Long Beach area is primarily about fostering understanding. The mediation skills that I have learned as a Quaker over the past 20 years have proven extremely useful. One of the high points of this past year's program was helping to organize an "interfaith icebreaker" for around 60 teenagers of various faith traditions—no easy task, but deeply rewarding. This summer I am facilitating "interfaith cafes" utilizing the Sacred Listening techniques developed by Kay Lindahl, a local interfaith advocate. Her approach is similar to what we do when we get together as Quakers and have worship sharing. We even use questions ("queries") to stimulate in-depth conversation in small groups. (Detailed instructions on how to set up interfaith cafes are provided in the second section of this book.)

The work that I do for Interfaith Communities United for Justice and Peace (ICUJP) often involves "speaking truth to power" and standing up to the "powers and principalities." This group was formed after 9/11 by some of L.A.'s major religious leaders in order to promote peace with justice. Besides organizing educational events, vigils, and demonstrations, we have stood in solidarity with the Muslim community when it has come under attack. Since becoming involved with ICUJP, I have visited a Muslim imam named Abdul Jabbar Hamdan who was arrested on trumped up charges and held in detention for over two years. Ironically, in front of the detention center where this man is currently being held there is a statue in memory of the Japanese-Americans who were unjustly detained during WWII. By visiting Hamdan, I feel that I am following in the footsteps of Quakers who visited the Japanese internees during WWII.

I believe that we are called as Friends to support the prophetic work of interfaith organizations such ICUJP, Tikkun, and the Shalom Center of Philadelphia. (A list of such organizations is provided in the appendix.) It is crucially important for Friends to join in the work of these "spiritual progressives."

Grounds for Hope

Interfaith work is not only important, but it is also an incredibly joyful experience. When Muslims, Jews, Christians and others come together to worship and to work on common concerns, there is often a sense of joy and mutual appreciation too deep for words. Many of these gatherings are celebratory: with music, ethnic food, dance, and various types of worship experiences. Youth and community leaders are honored. Stimulating panel discussions take place and one's spiritual horizons are broadened. For those who haven't experienced such gatherings, I recommend either going to one and/or watching the video "God and Allah Need to Talk" by Ruth Broyde Sharone.* Whatever the format of interfaith gatherings, people come away uplifted, and I sense the Divine Presence at work.

These gatherings also offer grounds for hope. I see parallels between the rise of the interfaith movement and the "citizen diplomacy" movement of the 1980s that helped end the Cold War. Reaching out to the Russians during the Reagan era was my first Quaker concern. It still warms my heart to think back on this Spirit-led work, which I described in a Pendle Hill pamphlet called "Spiritual Linkage with Russians: the Story of a Leading" (1991). Although conservatives believe that the Cold War ended because Ronald Reagan put so much pressure on the Russians that they finally gave up and cried "Uncle," there is considerable evidence that "people power" and citizen diplomacy helpe convince both Reagan and Gorbechev that the time was ripe for ending the Cold War. This trust-building movement didn't accomplish miracles overnight, however. It began rather modestly in the '50s when small delegations like those sponsored by British Quakers went to the Soviet Union to begin a dialogue and create friendship.

A similar process of trust building in the Middle East began in the 1980s and '90s with groups like American Friends Service Committee, Fellowship of Reconciliation, and the Compassionate Listening project leading delegations and teaching listening skills.

In 2004 I went to Israel/Palestine with the Compassionate Listening project. It was an incredibly intense and rewarding experience. Our delegation of Christians, Jews, Muslims, and Buddhists stayed at a kibbutz, a refugee camp, Christian retreat centers, and a

*http://www.filmsthatmatter.com/

school in Bethlehem. We dialogued with those in the Israeli/Palestinian peace movement as well as with settlers. One of the most heartrending experiences was listening as parents shared with us the pain of losing their children to the recent violence. I will never forget the Palestinian family who told us how their 16-year-old son, a peace activist, was shot in the head by Israeli police in front of his mother. Nor will I forget the rabbi whose son was murdered by Arabs and who has dedicated his life to helping other families heal from such traumas. I will also carry with me the image of an elderly Jewish man named Steve who invited a young Palestinian man named Asmi into his home in Jerusalem and treated him like a son. Steve became the guest of honor at Asmi's wedding and is now part of this loving Palestinian family. *

These encounters help us to understand the human depths and complexities of today's conflicts. Despite war and terrorism, this work of trust-building has expanded since 9/11 and now includes mainstream groups such as the Rotary Club International. This reconciliation work goes largely unreported in the media, which tends to focus on the sensational. But I am convinced that these efforts on the part of ordinary people will have an enormous impact over the long run. I am also convinced that this is work we are called to do as Friends.

The Legacy of William Penn and Tom Fox

As Friends respond to the call of the interfaith movement, we do well to keep in mind two Friends whose examples speak powerfully to our times. One speaks primarily to the head, the other to the heart.

Let me begin with William Penn, one of the great intellectual as well as religious figures of colonial America. Growing up in an age of religious war and conflict, and

---

*See article on recent compassionate listening project by David Rush in Part 6.

raised in a military family, Penn was utterly transformed by the experience of Quakerism. He renounced violence. He came to believe that the Light of God is present in all human beings, and in all religions. He founded the Quaker colony of Pennsylvania as a place where people of all faiths could practice their religion without government interference. This was a revolutionary idea at the time. Penn's willingness to allow freedom of religion in Pennsylvania had a significant impact on our country's commitment to religious pluralism.

Furthermore, Penn envisioned a world in which nations would settle their disputes by law, not war. In 1693, he wrote a plan for the *Present and Future Peace of Europe* that is considered a prototype of the United Nations.

I believe that as Friends, we are called upon to carry forward the legacy of Penn and to work diligently for a society based on tolerance and a world governed by international law. We are called to support the Quaker UN Office (QUNO) and other efforts to strengthen the United Nations, especially as it comes under vicious attack from the religious right in our country. Sad to say, many in the religious right equate the UN with the Antichhrist. We need to remind our fellow Americans that the United Nations, for all its flaws, is still the best hope we have for a peaceful and just world.

Another Friend whose example calls to us and to our time is Tom Fox. No Friend is better known throughout the world today, especially in the Muslim world. Fox speaks to the heart of our Quaker faith. Like Mary Dyer, Mary Fisher and other early Friends who were called to travel in the ministry, Fox was willing to risk his life to bear witness to the power of love and the Inward Light.

Fox was also part of the interfaith movement. Although he considered himself a Christian, he was open to spiritual insights from other religions, such as Buddhism, Judaism, and Islam. He went to Israel/Palestine and listened to all sides in this tragic conflict. He lived side-by-side with the Iraqi people and took up their cause and their concerns. He showed by his example what it means to "walk cheerfully on the earth, answering that of God in everyone."

When news of Fox's death was announced, he was deeply mourned by the Muslim community, which will always remember and honor him. A young Muslim man I know named Yasir Shah wrote a letter to *Friends Bulletin* when he learned of Tom Fox's death: "I'm heartbroken to say that it's only recently that I've come to find out about such a courageous and dedicated man.... I believe that Tom Fox's family, the American people, and the Iraqi people were blessed to have someone of his caliber to fight for them...Tom Fox embodied the characteristics of the leaders of the civil rights movement....[and] I pray that we increase our unity in the stand against injustice, and continue to strive for the rights of all humans."

Not all of us have the calling or the courage to follow Tom Fox's example. But we are called to honor his memory and to carry forward his spirit as best we can in our Quaker witness to the world.

Tips on Doing Interfaith Work from a Quaker Perspective

by Alex Levering Kern

1) Whatever your spiritual tradition or practice: pray, pray, pray some more. Pray alone, pray with others. Pray aloud. Pray in silence. Pray in new ways, pray in old. Pray for your enemies, pray for your friends. Pray for yourself. You'll need it!

2) Look for God everywhere, but especially among the poor, the outcast, the hurting and the unclean. I have seen God present in the shanties of Brazil, scurrying over the trash heaps of the waste we export. I have seen God present in a homeless woman and child on the streets of Prague. I have seen God present and alive beneath revival tents in Haiti, still singing, still dancing in the face of the most unimaginable catastrophe.

3) Pay attention to young people, and young people, seek out older mentors. Mind the Inward Teacher, and know also that teachers can be discovered everywhere.

Alexander Levering Kern is a member of Friends Meeting at Cambridge, Massachusetts, and has been involved in interfaith work since his student days at Guilford College in the early 1990s. He has represented FGC Friends at the World Council of Churches and done interfaith peacebuilding work abroad, in northern Nigeria and elsewhere. Currently he serves as Executive Director of Cooperative Metropolitan Ministries (CMM; www.coopmet.org), greater Boston's oldest interfaith social action organization, and as Protestant Chaplain at Brandeis University. He cofounded the Interfaith Youth Initiative (IFYI) and the Brandeis University Interfaith Leadership Development (BUILD) Fellows program. Alex's writing appears in various publications, and he is editor of the anthology Becoming Fire: Spiritual Writing from Rising Generations. *Article used with permission of author.*

4) Remember, as we always liked to say as undergraduate Religious Studies majors, everything is interconnected and interdependent: both the structures of violence and injustice, and our struggles to transform them. When we put transformative nonviolent energy out into the universe, my work to end apartheid assists your work to save the planet, and vice versa.

5) Do your activism with Friends or people of your own tradition, but reach out to include other faiths as well. Our witness will be all the more powerful. In this moment in our history, build bridges with Judaism and Islam. As Hans Kung has said, there will be no peace on earth until there is peace among the religions.

Here I want to pause and tell a brief story about the transformative, reconciling possibilities in our world. In January 2009 I traveled to Nigeria with a delegation of peacemakers from Boston. As you may know, northern Nigeria is a faultline in Christian/Muslim conflict, and in the town of Kaduna many have died. One morning our group walked into a beautiful Catholic mass, replete with drums and dancing and powerful spirit. When we were called to introduce ourselves, my friend and fellow traveler said: "*Asalaamu alaikum.* I am Imam Taalib Mahdee from Masjid Al Quran in Dorchester, Massachusetts," and the place went dead silent—not the rich, deep, peaceful Quaker silence, but the "Oh Yikes, this is tense" kind. It was unlikely a Muslim had ever been in that church, certainly not since the bloodshed. Yet in that moment I observed what I can only describe as a Quaker sacrament. There was no bread, no wine, yet there beside the altar, where we were standing, the Catholic priest, Father Matthew, reached over the divide and literally embraced Imam Taalib, as full and generous a hug you can imagine. And in that instant the silence turned to thunderous applause, and I felt heaven and earth reconciling, and glimpsed a sign of powerful reconciliation for all our faiths, and for the US and Africa (in light of the unhealed legacy of the Middle Passage and slavery) and for the US and the Two-Thirds world, with our deep divides. And it all happened in a distant corner of the world, off the beaten path, but was as real and true as anything I've ever seen.

6) Next tip: Remember you have power, but you are not in charge. Activists are prone to think that we should have singlehandedly saved the world by this time yesterday. This is hubris, and unsustainable. As Thomas Kelly reminded us, we are each given a few leadings, a small bundle of concerns, and we are "not meant to die on every cross." Step back and make room for others; or when you step up, always invite others to join you.

7) Anger has its place but is often the enemy. We may be tempted to despair or anger or fear, but as Deborah Shaw always reminded us here at Guilford: Love is the first order of business—love and also joy, which is the first fruit of the Spirit.

8) Wear your leadership lightly, with humor. As one of my friends says, "Don't believe your own propaganda, or anyone else's." Laugh at yourself. There's lots of good material there!

9) Learn from the past and keep an eye on the long haul: Sometimes, as in Egypt, social change is sudden, cataclysmic, but usually it's slow and incremental. As my grandmother used to say, "Most of life is maintenance." Lick envelopes, do the long, hard work of social change. And remember the witness of the ancestors, and stay accountable to your great, great, great great...grandchildren!

10) Remember: for religious folks, it's all about witness. As someone said, most of life is just showing up. Show up, keep watch, be counted. Be present with your bodies, not just online. As important as Twitter and Facebook are, Hosni Mubarak would not have fallen in Egypt had people just decided to stay home and tweet!

11) Love one another, and do no harm. Children and families are often the first casualties of activist work. Ask forgiveness, make amends – early and often.

12) Find those places that sustain you in the work. Look especially to art, to children, to nature: I have a corner of a reservoir on a high rock and I return there as often as I can, to watch the seasons, to sit in silence, to play with my kids. Dorothy Day of the Catholic Worker movement was fond of saying "only beauty will save the world."

13) Remember what Dorothy Day called "the duty of delight." Life is more serendipity than strategy, the pretty ways of providence than hard and fast planning. You'll be remembered for your joy, and how well you have loved.

PART 2: COMPASSIONATE LISTENING

One of the most Quakerly methods for encouraging interfaith dialogue and understanding is to listen deeply to those of other faith traditions, without judgmentalism. Listening is a skill that most Americans have not been encouraged to develop, but because of our practice of silent worship and worship sharing, Friends have unusually rich experiences and a special calling for this form of ministry. One of the pioneers in the "Compassionate Listening" movement was Gene Knudsen Hoffman. Deeply versed in psychology and spirituality as well as social activism, Gene provided an alternative to our nation's compulsive cult of violence. She insisted that the key to overcoming terrorism is through deep listening to another's pain and inner conflict. Her approach is also applicable to interfaith work.

Gene's work inspired Leah Green, a Jewish American woman who lived for several years in Israel and is fluent in Hebrew and Arabic. With help from Gene, Leah started the Compassionate Listening Project. Its purpose is "to teach heart-based skills for peace-building and reconciliation in our families, communities, on the job, and in the world...speaking and listening from the heart, even in the heat of conflict."

Leah takes interfaith groups to Israel and Palestine to hear the many sides of this conflict and to help create understanding. In 2004 I went on a Compassionate Listening tour of Israel and the Occupied Territories with Leah Green, Maha El Taji (a Muslim Palestinian woman), and a group of American Jews, Christians, and others of various faith traditions. We went to kibbutzim, settlements, refugee camps and other sites and talked to Israeli Jews and Palestinians. We met and listened to "ordinary people" and extraordinary peace activists. It was a powerful experience that changed my life and perspectives. You can learn more at the website compassionatelistening.org and also by reading David Rush's article about his Compassionate Listening trip (see Part 6).

Selections from Gene Hoffman's Writings

"The job of the peacemaker is"
    to know there is no enemy
    what we fear are fear-masks
    worn by ourselves
    and the "other side."
    And behind each mask
    —the hooded Klansman
    —the complacent housewife
    —the rich who seek more riches
Is something trembling
to be born:

something pure in eclipse
some love waiting to be released
a person deserving
reverence and faith.

*****

Some time ago, I recognized that terrorists were people who had grievances, who thought their grievances would never be heard and certainly never addressed. Later, I saw that all parties to every conflict were wounded, and that at the heart of every act of violence was an unhealed wound. I began to search for ways we peace people might help to heal these violence-causing wounds.—Gene Hoffman, *Pieces of the Mideast Puzzle*, p. 9.

*****

We peace people have always listened to the oppressed and disenfranchised. That's very important. One of the new steps I think we should take is to listen to those we consider "the enemy" with the same openness, non-judgment, and compassion we bring to those with whom our sympathies lie.

Everyone has a partial truth, and we must listen, discern, and acknowledge this partial truth in everyone—particularly those with whom we disagree. That remarkable saint, Thomas Aquinas, would support this, for he wrote: "We must love them both, those with whom we agree and those with whom we disagree. For both have labored in the search of truth, and both have helped in the finding of it....."

*****

Compassionate Listening is adaptable to any conflict. The listening requires a particular attitude. It is non-judgmental, non-adversarial, and seeks the truth of the person questioned. It also seeks to see through any masks of hostility and fear to the sacredness of the individual and to discern the wounds suffered by all parties. Listeners do not defend themselves, but accept what others say as their perceptions. By listening they validate the others' right to those perceptions.

I'm not talking about listening with the 'human ear.' I am talking about discerning. To discern means to perceive something hidden or obscure. We must listen with our "spiritual ear." This is very different from deciding in advance who is right and who is wrong, and then seeking to rectify it. And it's very hard to listen to people who I feel are misleading, if not lying. Hard to listen to such different memories of the same event—hard! –*Gene Hoffman, A talk given November 25, 1997, at the University of California at Santa Barbara.*

Selected queries on Compassionate Listening compiled by the editor

Do I practice the art of listening to others, even beyond words?

Do I reach out to the violator and the oppressor as well as to the violated and oppressed with courage and love?

Do I make an effort to understand the causes of violence within a community and to help develop just and reconciling ways of dealing with such violence?

Do I help others respond creatively and in a reconciling way to any conflict and hostility which they experience?

Do I help increase understanding and use of nonviolent approaches to the resolution of conflicts?

Website and other resources

www.compassionatelistening.org/ The Compassionate Listening Project, formerly Mid-East Citizen Diplomacy, is a US-based nonprofit organization dedicated to empowering individuals to heal polarization and build bridges between people, communities and nations in conflict. This organization organizes workshops in the US and in the Middle East, and has published videos and books devoted to Compassionate Listening work. Leah Green, director of this program, writes of her experience applying Gene Hoffman's techniques to real-life situations in Israel:

The first premise for Compassionate Listeners is that we must acknowledge that every party to a conflict is suffering. And that our job as peacemakers is to hear their grievances and find ways to tell each side about the humanity and the suffering of the other. We have to find ways to bring conflicting parties to listen to one another—not to dialogue at first, not to argue or debate. Just to listen. We must drop any arrogance of thinking that we know how it is for another.

Recommended:

"Children of Abraham," a broadcast quality video about Compassionate Listening work in the Middle East and *Listening With the Heart, a Guide for Compassionate Listening* by Carol Hwoschinsky. Available through compassionatelistening. org.

www.coopcomm.org/compassion contains an archive of Gene Hoffman's work in PDF format, all free, including a sourcebook of Compassionate Listening material. Especially recomended are:

♦ *Road to Reconciliation,* by Gene Knudsen Hoffman. Published by Pendle Hill Publications, 338 Plush Mill Road, Wallingford, PA. 19086-6099.
♦ *An Enemy Is One Whose Story We Have Not Heard,* by Gene Knudsen Hoffman, Fellowship of Reconciliation, P.O. Box 271, Nyack, NY 10960. Also available as an e-book at www.coopcomm.org/listening

Sacred Listening and Interfaith Cafés

Another important teacher and practitioner of listening skills has been Kay Lindahl, founder of the Sacred Listening Center. She also started The Alliance for Spiritual Community, a grass-roots interfaith organization whose main work is practicing the art of dialogue. An ordained interfaith minister committed to peace among religions, Kay has published books and facilitated workshops nationally and internationally (including one at Pendle Hill, the Quaker center near Philadelphia).

One of her innovative ideas was the "Interfaith Café," which is described in her book Practicing the Sacred Art of Listening. *Interfaith cafés provide a model for how people of different faith traditions can meet and have respectful conversations about religious questions. This model appeals to Friends since it closely resembles our Quaker practice of worship sharing (sometimes called "Quaker dialogue").*

For more information, see www.sacredlistening.com.

Interfaith Cafés*

Welcome to the Interfaith Café. One of the things we have learned over the past few years is the value of small group conversations. When we sit together and talk about what's important to us, our world begins to change, we become more alive, we tap into hope. Sewing circles and committees of correspondence helped birth America. Conversations in cafés and salons spawned the French Revolution. Study circles created the massive changes in economic and social policies in northern Europe.

This café setting invites that kind of conversation and collective reflection. Even though we lead busy lives, with more to do than we can ever get done, something's missing.

*© 2005 Kay Lindahl. PO Box 6805, Laguna Niguel, CA 92607-6805. E-mail: TheListenC@aol.com, www.sacredlistening.com

We still yearn for community. We are hungry to tell our stories. In days gone by this happened on front porches, in pubs, in coffee houses. There were unwritten rules for these conversations. No one wrote them down, and yet everyone knew the boundaries.

Today we live in one of the most diverse nations in the world. We come from all over the world and we practice a multitude of faith traditions. So to make sure that we all know how to be in this conversation, we have created Cafe Etiquette. There are only three guidelines:

1. Speak from your heart. Use I statements. This conversation is a sharing from our hearts, not a debate, so we invite you to own what you say with your language. Speak from your own experience, not from or for anyone else. Watch for: "everyone knows," "we all know," "of course", use of the word "you."

2.: Listen with respect. For understanding, not to necessarily agree with or believe. You don't have to agree with or believe what someone is saying to listen with respect. This also means no cross-talk and one person speaks at a time.

3. Discover and explore. Listen for patterns, themes, new questions. Notice what's being said instead of rehearsing what you are going to say. Keep an open mind. Be curious about the others. Appreciate the differences.

We chose the name etiquette for a reason—it is about good manners, being polite, creating a space for everyone to be heard. So we invite you to take this on in your groups and try them out for the time that we are together.

The format is as follows:

Each group (limit to 4 - 5 people) has a café host, who has a copy of the etiquette and the questions for the dialogue.

You will begin with brief introductions, so you'll know who everyone in your circle is, where they are from and what their faith traditions or spiritual paths are. Then you'll review the etiquette and be asked to take them on for your conversation. Your host will state the questions and invite the dialogue to begin.

You will have forty minutes for everyone to speak. You'll get a five minute warning to complete your dialogue. The next five minutes will be your opportunity to notice what happened during the dialogue. What themes or patterns emerged? What new questions came up? Use post-it notes to write them down. (Have pads of post-it notes in each small group.)

At this point two people from each group will be invited to stand up to be ambassadors to two other groups. Each ambassador will go to a different group. Those who stay will be the hosts to two ambassadors from the other groups. You will have fifteen minutes to share. Have the ambassadors briefly introduce themselves and share what their group learned followed by someone from the host group sharing what they learned.

The final 15 minutes will be spent debriefing the cafés process in the large group. You will have the opportunity to post your notes on the walls, for all to see.

Any questions?

Sample Questions

Part I: Icebreaking questions: religion/spirituality in everyday life.

How do my religious beliefs influence the way I:

Have fun (entertainment, relaxation)

Choose your friends

Pray

Make difficult choices

Part II: Social Dimension: Faith into Practice

How do I define peace?

What beliefs obstruct the achievement of peace in our world?

How do I apply my faith to peace?

How can we learn to understand one another better?

What is the most difficult principle in my faith to practice?

How does my faith impact my stance on current affairs?

As you gain more experience in interfaith cafés, you can develop your own questions to meet the needs and interests of your group.

Varieties of Interfaith Work

by Alexander Levering Kern

The following list suggests the wide range and scope of interfaith activities. For more information, see www.coopmet.org and www.pluralism.org.

a) **Intervisitation to each other's congregations/sacred spaces** (sometimes at times of worship)

b) **Symbolic public/civic occasions and interfaith religious services—** Thanksgiving, King Day, inauguration of elected officials, *seders, iftars*

c) **Dialogues**—between interfaith leaders, congregation to congregation, public forums [and interfaith cafés]

d) **Study groups**—book groups such as Daughters of Abraham, interfaith study tours

e) **Educational, arts, cultural programs—** films, speaker series, dance, etc.

f) **Interfaith spirituality programs—** retreats on contemplative prayer, etc.

g) **Social Action and Activism—** Community service, service learning: Days of Interfaith Service

Alexander Kern is currently executive director of the Cooperative Metropolitan Ministries (www.coopmet.org), an interfaith organization in Boston, MA. Used with permission of author.

Direct human services programs focused on poverty, immigrants, etc.

Community organizing and public policy work

Lobbying days, letter writing/ calling legislators

Delegations and community panels

Candidates' forums

Protests, rallies, vigils responding to injustices, hate crimes, etc.

h) **Partnerships between diverse congregations or groups, one on one**

i) **Interfaith youth leadership programs (IFYI, Camp IF, Interfaith Action, IFYC)**

Interfaith Youth Work

by Anthony Manousos

Preparing young people for a pluralistic world is one of the great challenges of our era. Interfaith youth work, an essential component of this burgeoning movement, has many aspects: service, dialogue, worship sharing, leadership development, fun and games, and of course pizza—the universal sacrament uniting youth of all traditions.

Eboo Patel, founder of the Interfaith Youth Core, has committed his life to bringing together young people of different faith traditions through service projects. He writes:

> What if people of all faiths and traditions worked together to promote the common good for all? What if once again, young people led the way? Across the country, Muslims and Hindus, Jews and Christians, Buddhists and non-religious are coming together in a movement of interfaith cooperation. They are proving that the 21st century can be defined by cooperation between diverse communities instead of conflict. (www.ifyc.org)

I know from experience how important service projects can be in helping young people to form their religious identities and to see the world from different perspectives, including that of the poor and marginalized. In 1992, I helped to start a youth service program jointly funded by the American Friends Service Committee and Southern California Quarterly Meeting of the Religious Society of Friends (Quakers). This program mainly drew Quaker youth, but around ten to twenty percent of the participants hailed from different backgrounds, including a significant number of African American teens. For ten years I took teens on service projects to various sites: homeless shelters, a shelter for wild animals, an AIDS hospice center, and communities in Mexico where we built community centers and homes for workers living in utter poverty, without running water or electricity. These service projects were a powerful learning opportunities for all involved, especially the teens. Many reported having had life-changing experiences.

Today interfaith youth service projects are becoming increasingly common and popular. Greg Damhorst, a young Evangelical Christian, describes how one such project arose after the earthquakes in Haiti. Determined to help, Greg turned not just to his own religious community, but also to his friends of other faiths:

> I brought the idea to a small group of friends – the "executive committee" that organized Interfaith in Action's programs. We were an evangelical Christian, a Catholic, a Buddhist, a Hindu and a Humanist, and we set out to plan an event at which our campus could package these meals for Haiti.
>
> I got a hold of the cell phone number for Rick McNary, founder of Numana, Inc., with whom I discussed the logistics of the project. We started a search for facilities to host the event, the money to fund the event, and the volunteers to staff the event.
>
> We connected with the regional office of the Salvation Army who connected us with the local corps at the same time that a phone call from Washington, D.C., out of the Salvation Army World Service Office confirmed that a federal grant was going to fund our project.
>
> With that, a community-wide, multi-faith endeavor was born. The event was moved to an abandoned Hobby Lobby building on the west side of Champaign, and staff from Numana, Inc. flew in prepare for the event.
>
> In a single weekend, 5,112 volunteers from every walk of life, faith and philosophical tradition passed

through that site to lend a hand. In less than 12 hours, 1,012,640 meals were packaged for shipment to Haiti where they were protected by the 82nd airborne and distributed by Salvation Army humanitarian workers. This is a story of coming together; it's a story of cooperation; and it's a story of interfaith work. As an evangelical, this is a snapshot of how I desire to live out my faith. To do so alongside people whom I desire to show the compassion of Jesus makes it an even more compelling endeavor.

Jesus said, "I was hungry and you brought me something to eat." Consider the significance of inviting others to join in such an activity. If you ask me, this is a simple yet profound way to communicate the compassion of Christ, meet the needs of the world, and build a better community. (www.ifyc.org/content/feeding-hungry)

Another way to enable young people of different faith traditions to connect is through interfaith get-togethers. I helped organize an "interfaith icebreaker" which attracted Muslims, Jews, Bahais, Christians and Hindu youth. We met at a synagogue, played games, sang songs, and shared stories about our faith journeys. It was a powerful experience that was written up in a local newspaper.

We also organized an interfaith café, which took place during the month of Ramadan/Tishrei (October) in 2006. Around fifty youths showed up for discussions about their faith traditions at a local Presbyterian church. Later many went to the nearby mosque in order to partake of *iftar*, the breaking of the fast at sunset. We ate delicious South Asian food, watched the Muslim prayers on closed-circuit TV, and learned about Islam from various Muslim speakers.

Our local interfaith organization created a youth council. We called on youths from different faith traditions to come together to plan their own programs and also to have input into adult programs. This work led to discovering and nurturing youth leaders, some of whom went on to organize programs of their own.

The local chapter of the Parliament of the World's Religions also encouraged youth participation. Youths were involved in planning our pre-Parliament events and took part in panels and organized workshops. They also provided service during our banquets and other events. Several were given financial assistance so they could attend the Parliament gathering in Melbourne, Australia, in 2008. This event, which drew over 6,000 religious leaders from around the world, had an exciting and inspiring youth program.

I am convinced that interfaith organizations are ideally and uniquely suited to do this work. The need for building interfaith understanding among youth is clear: we live in a society that is not only culturally but religiously diverse. We need to appreciate religious as well as cultural diversity in order to get along. Schools have made an effort to teach about cultural diversity, but have been reluctant to focus on religion—a much riskier topic. Interfaith organizations can provide opportunities for youth of different faith traditions to get together, talk openly, and learn from each other in an atmosphere of mutual respect and trust. The goal of this work is to help youth to gain a clearer understanding of their own faith and an appreciative understanding of other faiths.

As my list of sources indicates, exciting interfaith youth work is taking place around the country in small "pilot projects." My hope is that the American Friends Service Committee or some Quaker group will become involved in interfaith youth work. I would love to see "Peace Camps" at local meetings that invite kids from different faith traditions to participate. Some work is already being done (as the following websites make clear), but much more is needed. The possibilities are endless!

Sources for interfaith youth work

Interfaith Youth Core (IFYC) was first envisioned in 1998 by a group of passionate and committed college student to empower young people of faith to be leaders in building a pluralist society. Their website goes on to say:

> We are building a movement that brings together young people of different religious and moral traditions for cooperative service and dialogue around shared values like service and hospitality. Whether you're a young person, a college student, a youth advisor, a faith leader or a civic leader, there's a way to get involved!

IFYC director Dr. Eboo Patel received his doctorate in the sociology of religion from Oxford University, where he studied on a Rhodes scholarship. Eboo is is currently writing a book on the role of religious youth in the 21st Century with Beacon Press. Eboo is an Ashoka Fellow, part of an elite network of social entrepreneurs with ideas that have the potential to change the world. eboo@ifyc.org. (312) 573-8941. See www.ifyc.org.

Interfaith youth camps

www.traubman.igc.org/camps.htm This website lists a dozen camps for Jews and Christians in North America, including Seeds of Peace, Peace Camp Boston, Creativity for Peace (New Mexico), etc.

www.soundinterfaithcamp.org/ Puget Sound Interfaith Youth Camp.

www.interfaithinventions.org. An interfaith youth camp in California run by Rabbi Lynn Gottlieb.

The Interfaith Youth Initiatives

by Alexander Levering Kern

In light of pressing realities in our congregations and the wider world, the need for interfaith leadership training is abundantly clear. Increasingly, our seminarians and emerging religious leaders will be called upon to understand and effectively navigate the changing religious landscape of our nation and world, a reality well documented by our friends and partners at Harvard's Pluralism Project (see www.pluralism.org). The skills of interfaith dialogue and cooperation will be critical in ministry training, if we are ever to transform interreligious conflicts ranging from those we have witnessed in Boston over the past several years to the wars abroad that some have framed as a "clash of faiths and civilizations." Closer to home, younger religious leaders will need to manage conflict in their congregations and communities facing growing economic, social, and environmental pressures. Anyone who assumes the mantle of religious leadership in our day will need new frameworks and skills to effectively engage cultures of violence, social and economic injustice, and environmental devastation. The need is enormous, and young leaders are ready and able to assume responsibility for the work ahead.

At the same time, seminaries, faith communities, and religious leaders will need to comprehend and respond to youth within and beyond our walls: their cultures, their economic insecurities, their relationships with new technologies, and their powerful gifts and callings. New generations are struggling for meaning and survival, often without the support structures that organized religion has provided previous generations. Seminaries and congregations must journey with them, and equip new leaders who will harness the energies and imaginations of the disenfranchised and disillusioned young.

The IFYI program is addressing these needs, helping our seminarians, young religious leaders, and teens to develop skills for transformative leadership in a multicultural, multifaith world. Our young IFYI leaders are at the vanguard of a new generation of spiritually grounded, culturally equipped individuals who can build community and find common cause with those whose faiths and cultures differ radically from their own. If we are to survive and flourish and reclaim relevance in the public square, we must support these young clergy and lay leaders as they articulate a new vision of what the world might become.

For more information about IYI, contact Alex Kern at akern@brandeis.edu.

PART 3: GOING DEEPER: REFLECTIVE ESSAYS ON INTERFAITH WORK BY FRIENDS

"Toward a Deeper Dialogue"

(Revision of Plenary Talk from Ohio Valley Yearly Meeting, 2005)

by Michael Birkel

We live in an era rich with opportunity for religious dialogue: among different sorts of Friends, among different branches of the wider Christian family, and between different religious traditions. It has been my privilege to have all three kinds of conversations, and in this essay I hope to reflect on how each of these kinds of conversations invites us into deeper dialogue with people of faith. In these reflections I'll be drawing on my experience as a teacher, who seeks to invite students of many backgrounds and persuasions into a community of conversation. In the classroom I don't expect all my students to become Quaker

Michael Birkel teaches in the Religion Department of Earlham College in Richmond, Indiana—a college founded in 1847 by Quakers. A scholar who has written extensively on Quakerism and, most recently, the German mystic Jacob Boehme, Michael has also felt a leading to be engaged in interfaith dialogue as an expression of the peace testimony of Friends. Michael has a particular concern for Muslim-Christian dialogue. He has pursued this in the classroom, in his local community, through the work of Christian and Interfaith Relations Committee of Friends General Conference, and as a member of the Interfaith Relations Commission of the National Council of Churches. This talk used with permission of the author.

or Christian. But we do explore some great texts together and learn how to talk about them. My wish in my teaching is that all of my students who come from a religious community will leave the course stronger and more vibrant in their religious traditions. I come to this work:

♦ as a Quaker who travels among a variety of Friends

♦ as someone who stands in the middle of Quakerism theologically and spiritually (a Christian but not profoundly shaped by the evangelical tradition, even though I have much respect for that tradition) and also can stand at the boundaries of Christianity (firmly Christian in my identity but open to other traditions)

♦ as a participant in interfaith dialogue

My intent is to explore with you some aspects of the inner dimension of dialogue and then to offer some comments on the practice of dialogue across boundaries of religious difference.

The Inner Dimension

Before engaging in conversation with others, it is good to reflect deeply on just what is precious in your own faith, so that you can articulate your own treasures that you bring to the exchange. Dialogue always challenges each side to explore its own faith more fully—just what is the Quaker concept of God, of the Light, of that of God in everyone? It's good to give some reflection to such questions as: just what does Jesus mean to us, why do Friends abstain from external observance of baptism and communion? It's also good to anticipate those questions. What do you believe and why? This doesn't mean that you need a degree in theological studies to do this. It's good to be informed, but this kind of conversation is by no means only for specialists. In interfaith circles, we speak of scholarly interfaith dialogue and also of the dialogue of life. (More about that in a moment.) Before beginning dialogue (though if dialogue has already begun, it is not to late to do this), it is valuable to consider what motivates this interaction. As in most of life, our motives are usually mixed, and that's fine, but it is good to be aware of them. Do I seek this interaction largely out of guilt? An example of this might be a person who is of German descent (as I am) and who seeks dialogue with Jews chiefly out of feelings of guilt with regard to the tragedies that befell European Jews in the Hitler era. If that is my primary motivation, then my words and actions may be centered mostly on myself and my emotional needs rather than on actually encountering the other person. This can pose an obstacle to deep listening. Additionally, I'll be tempted to be less than fully honest, to overlook the historical failings of the other. I'll be tempted to be patronizing, to hold the other to a lower standard of ethical expectation. Generosity is fine when it is based on recognition of the truth, but not when I am deceiving myself.

For example, in a Muslim-Christian Dialogue course that I taught in the fall of 2001, after 9/11 the Christian students were sympathetic to the trials faced by our Muslims participants. They were tempted not to hold Islam to the same standard ethically because the Muslim world was clearly suffering so much, especially in the US, when Islamophobia was so prevalent. Fortunately, a Coptic Christian student in the course would not let the Western Christians get away with this. As a Copt, that is, as a member of the ancient Christian community in Egypt, she knew personally how difficult it was to live as a Christian in a predominantly Muslim society, and she was not going to let us forget the injustices done to her people. She kept us honest.

So it is good to know what role guilt may be playing in motivating my behavior. I believe that God can work through and with our imperfect motivations, so I am not here to say that we cannot move forward until our hearts are completely pure. That could leave us frozen in moral paralysis. But some self-awareness is a good thing. At the very least, it can help prevent us from saying some rather foolish, one-sided comments that in the long run can prove to be rather self-centered.

It's also good to ask yourself: to what extent might I be motivated by a hope to persuade the other that I am right? This motivation is often stronger the closer our conversation partner's tradition is to ours. We may harbor little hope (much less conscious intent) that we will persuade a Buddhist to become a Quaker. It's when we're among different sorts of Friends, those who are closest to us in some ways, that we are tempted to want to change them, to make them like us, so that we can be sure that we are right.

So how do we approach this encounter? Are we rivals? Are we partners? What do we seek?

This brings to mind a passage from John Woolman. In his *Journal* he is on his way through a difficult path to visit a settlement of the Delaware Nation at Wyalusing. The going is tough: it's been raining, their tents aren't waterproof, their sleeping gear is soaked—oh, and did I mention that there is a war going on and their lives are in danger? Stuck in his leaky tent while it's pouring outside, John Woolman asks himself: now why was I doing this? What moved me to undertake such a dangerous journey? He writes:

> Love was the first motion, and then a concern arose that I might feel and understand their life and the spirit they lived in, if haply I might receive some instruction from them, or they in any degree helped forward by my following the leadings of Truth amongst them.[1]

This is what prompts his efforts at a dialogue that moves beyond toleration to the discovery of common spiritual ground. Note how his words show both openness to the other and faithfulness to what he knows most deeply to be true. This is not a debate; it is an exchange of what is truest for each conversation partner. An exchange is a matter of giving and receiving.

So it's good to ask, what drives me to do this?

Here's another question to ask ourselves: what wounds do I bear? Many come to Friends with difficult and painful experiences from other traditions. These wounds bear more power if they are unnamed. Naming them alone may not fix them, but can give us the power to recognize them and so not to be unconsciously subject to them. My monastic friends from the fourth century taught me this long ago. They said that there are patterns to the arising of thoughts and feelings in our soul that can disturb our efforts at inner peace. By careful observation, we can come to recognize these potential disturbers of the peace, and this can disarm them. When I see such a disturbance coming on the horizon, I have time to respond mindfully: "Oh, I know you! We're old acquaintances. Look, I'm busy right now. I promise I'll get back to you later, but at the moment I'm engaged in a challenging conversation with someone whose theology is rather different from mine, and that task requires my full attention. So stay on the line and I'll get back to you. Your call is important to us."

Do honor that promise to get back to the disturbing thought, but don't let it dominate the dialogue that you are striving to have. If I only notice such a feeling or thought when it's right in front of my nose, then I tend to react out of habit or panic or anger. That doesn't help with the conversation that's before me.

So it can be good to consider, what wounds do I bear? Have I suffered pain in the past from the group with whom I am seeking dialogue? Have I once suffered the pain of exclusion from a different group, but something in me now feels the hurt of that pain once again, since this new group defines the blessed community in such a way that I feel left out? Liberal Quakerism attracts many immigrants. That's fine, but, to continue the metaphor from the political sphere, it can leave diplomatic relations strained. If my pain is still great, it may not be my leading at this time to pursue this dialogue. I can allow others to carry on that task, if they are so led. But I really should allow them to carry out that task and not let my old pains sabotage their leadings.

The Practice of Dialogue across Boundaries

Those are some thoughts on the inner dimension of dialogue—questions that I might ask myself. We might think of them as ways of tidying up the house when we've invited guests to come. I'd like to turn now to some suggestions of the practice of dialogue across boundaries of religious difference.

First, listen spaciously. By this I mean a prayerful listening for the presence of the Spirit in what the other has to say. Listen for the treasures, and expect to be surprised.

Learn to listen without agenda, without polemic, without formulating your response as you sit there. Let the other person have her or his turn to speak from the heart. Respect the heart of the other.

This means listening from a centered place where this deeper kind of listening is possible. If love is the first motion or motivation in this conversation, it is important to move out of a place of fear and defensiveness to a place of love.

Listen in a Quaker way, as though the other person were offering vocal ministry. This requires a gentle receptivity. Listen to what comes from God.

This means a risk, a willingness to be changed. It's not that we expect to be converted to the other person's faith. A West African Muslim once described it to me in a wonderful phrase: "The point is not to dilute but to dilate." That requires a deep trust in the God who motivates our desire to engage in dialogue.

This kind of openness makes possible the "dialogue of life" that I mentioned earlier. Our encounters need not be just about theological differences. Life speaks to life: joys, sorrows, births, deaths. This kind of personal contact is essential. As in overcoming our predispositions about race or gender identity, it is through coming to know real people on the other side that we come to new insight. We see how theological conviction takes shape in a concrete life. We see, to borrow from the Gospel of John, how word becomes flesh.

Here we might entertain another metaphor: dialogue across religious boundaries is like good hospitality. The English word "hospitality" has its own interesting story. It comes from the Latin word "hospes," which means both host and guest. This suggests that hospitality is not about who gives and who receives but instead about a relationship of giving and receiving. At times we are the ones who open our home to others; at other times we are the guests in the home of others. Hospitality is about the quality of a relationship.

The metaphor of hospitality also helps us to be realistic about our encounters. It points to the realization that I will not be more than a guest. Our differing groups do not inhabit the same house. They are not the same family, or at least not the same nuclear family. It is useful to recognize that truth. There are limits, boundaries—and these are valuable. Otherwise each group's unique gifts could become extinct, and that would be a loss to humankind. As in the biosphere, spiritual diversity is a good thing. So, even as we approach someone who is different, we must value what is distinctive about our own tradition of faith.

To enter into genuine dialogue, we must sink into our particularity. It's the way to the deeper commonalities. In my experience, it's the only way to those deeper realms. Let's pick a ridiculous example of superficial similarities that do not open the way to those deeper possibilities. Here a liberal Quaker meets a member of the Islamic faith, and we hear the Quaker side of the conversation. Our imaginary, not-too-thoughtful Friend responds to the Muslim with these words:

"Oh, so you're a Muslim. That's interesting."

"You don't eat pork? At our potlucks, it seems most of the Quakers I know are veggies."

"You don't drink alcohol? We have query about that. We don't serve beer at yearly meeting."

"No ordained clergy? Hey, that's us, too."

"In your beliefs, Jesus is not the son of God? Lots of folks in my monthly meeting wouldn't call him that, either."

I hope that the shallowness of this imaginary conversation might amuse you, but I also hope that it might invite all of us to consider how to get beyond such mere tolerance.

If I am to be in conversation with someone who differs from me religiously, and if we are going to attempt to get to that deeper place where we might discover our commonalities, the only way that I know to get to that deeper place is to sink into the particularities of my faith. To communicate effectively, we need to use language, and the mother tongue of my spiritual life is my Quaker and my Christian identity. That's what gives me the vocabulary to describe my experiences. For me, the greatest spiritual realities are described in the language of love—not the language of submission or of commandment or of compassion, at least not in the same way that these words would be central to Muslim or Jewish or Buddhist conversation partners. As a Quaker, the language of leading will be central—rather than magisterium or justification or second blessing, as they would be to a Catholic, a Lutheran or a Protestant in the Holiness tradition.

But by allowing each side to speak its mother tongue, we can come to the deeper realities that can unite us. I remember a conversation with a Muslim when his personal description of *islam*,[2] submission, suddenly sounded a lot like the *Gelassenheit* of my beloved medieval Christian mystics. *Gelassenheit* literally means "yielding," as *islam* literally means "submission," but among mystics such as Johannes Tauler (whom earlier Quakers loved to read) it meant relinquishing, letting go, calmness, the selfless serenity that comes of fulfillment rather than low self-esteem. I encountered this deeper commonality only by permitting my Muslim friend to speak his native tongue in the spiritual life.

This means that we should expect and acknowledge that there will be significant differences that we will have to navigate before we can come to a deeper sense of commonness.

Some of those differences may amuse us. Others may even strike us as repulsive.

Here I remember a story from the first Quaker Women's Theological Conference, held at Woodbrooke College in Britain in 1990. The organizers of this conference worked very hard to see that the list of participants in this gathering would be representative of Quakerism worldwide. Their success made for challenges in theological discussion, in cross-cultural understanding, and in diet. A Friend from the Arctic Circle was having bodily difficulty adjusting to an English menu and was experiencing some real physical discomfort. At one point she was heard to say, "What I wouldn't give for some seal oil and whale blubber right now." As an evangelical Christian, she found that liberal English Quakerism was not the only thing that was difficult for her to stomach. A liberal Quaker remarked, "It's not just that I don't want what she wants. It's that what would help her would make me ill. But, because we have a relationship, I want her to get what she needs"—physically and spiritually, seal oil and evangelical piety.

"I want her to get what she needs." That kind of statement comes of trust, of mutual vulnerability, and of the courage to take risks.

There are practices that help to develop the trust to take risks. One is humor: the ability to laugh at yourself, to take the task of dialogue seriously but to not take yourself too seriously.

Another is humility—a virtue that often seems to be a species of honesty. Here are some examples of the humility that serves these kinds of encounters:

Expect to make mistakes and be willing to learn from them gracefully. Let me offer a personal example of an embarrassing moment in a course that I led on the Bible.

One time, my class was reading a feminist commentary on Genesis, and Genesis includes the story of Lot, the kinsperson of Abraham who was urged by angels to leave the city of Sodom before it was destroyed by fire from heaven. According to the story, Lot and his two daughters are in a cave, and it's raining brimstone and fire. Lot's wife has already been turned into a pillar of salt. The daughters probably think that the whole human race is being destroyed and that they are the only ones left—two females and one male. The daughters think, well, we have to play Adam and Eve with Dad to survive, but we need to get him pretty inebriated first, so they do. He's not even conscious of what happens, but they become pregnant by him.

There and in other parts of the story, Lot doesn't come off as someone who is very thoughtful. He serves as a foil to Abraham, who is clearly the narrator's hero.

In this class, my students came from all different backgrounds. Some were of European descent, some from African descent, some were Christian, some Muslim, some Jewish, some straight, some gay, some out, some not. Whenever I go into the classroom, I assume that the Bible is of inestimable value for some people in the room. It may have literally saved their lives. For other people in the room, this text has been used to beat them up.

So there we were, reading this feminist commentary, and a very reserved female student who'd barely spoken before in the course started really launching into old Lot, letting him have it. I thought, "She is finding her voice; she is participating in discussion. This is good."

But then there was a silence. A Muslim student said,

"Excuse me, but is Lot the same as Lut in the Qur'an?" I mentally slapped my forehead, remembering that, in the Qur'an, Lut is a champion of monotheism. In Islam, Lut is revered as a prophet, and you don't talk about a prophet the way this woman just talked about Lot.

By trying to extend an invitation to some members of my classroom community, I unintentionally ran the risk of offense to other members of the classroom. This all happened near the end of class. I emailed them afterward and said, "Here's the mistake I made." All of the Muslim students wrote back to me. In their replies, each said words to this effect: "You know, people have inadvertently insulted me as a Muslim many times in the U.S., but most of the time no one took the effort to recognize this, and never has anyone made an apology." We all learned from it, and I went off and read the Qur'an more carefully, in the hopes that I could become more sensitive to how a Muslim might read the Hebrew Scriptures.

Dialogue is like dancing in the dark where everyone is barefoot. We don't know where the toes are because we can't see them. What we can try to do in advance is think about where the hurtful places could be.

The lesson of this story, for me, is to expect to get it wrong sometimes and to seek to learn from those missteps. Here are more examples of humility in action.

Self-criticism: admit your group's failures. This goes a long way toward reconciliation.

Develop awareness of the suffering that the other group has experienced, both historically and in the present.

Admit the possibility of self-deception, always the most slippery of temptations.

Don't presume moral superiority. It's good to be a believer, but it's also good to remember that, in general, people don't choose to join or stay in religious groups that they think are dumb or immoral. "How can you stay in a church that has abusive clergy or that oppresses women?" When we Quakers have as many people of color or poor people as, for example, the Pentecostals, maybe we can begin to think about feeling entitled to the moral high ground that we often seem to presume that is ours. Please don't get me wrong. I'm proud to be a Friend. I love our testimonies and our community's faithful practice of them. But I hope to be honest about our collective shortcomings— and my participation in them. It's not my purpose to make any of us feel guilty here (liberals are already accomplished at that) but simply to suggest that it does not serve us to approach conversations with other groups with the assumption that our group is somehow "better."

Related to such honesty is the natural tendency we have to judge ourselves by our highest ideals and others by their worst behaviors. "Jesus preached love, but bin Laden is a terrorist." Don't compare apples and thumbtacks.

Here is a final suggestion under that heading of honesty and humility, and I hope to offer it gently. I mention this behavior because I hear it all the time, and it is usually intended with generosity, but it does not sound that way to those outside your community. Don't say: "That sounds just like (FGC, Quakerism,...) to me." "You're a Quaker (or Christian, or believer in God) and you just don't know it." That may work if the other person is searching for a new community, but otherwise it does not often serve dialogue. It feels like identity theft. The other person may be too polite to say it, but what is on their mind may be something like this: "So, the only good thing about my group is that it looks like yours in some way, and you're trying to take credit for that goodness." It is essential to allow your conversation partners to define themselves in their own terms.

So reach across boundaries, but do not pretend to erase them. Observe boundaries. They allow communities to exist. They give meaning and content to membership. They don't just keep out: they hold together. A boundary binds together those within it.

Here is a story about boundaries, with the moral "Don't

pretend to be what you're not." It is my privilege to teach some courses in the Jewish Studies program at my college. My name is listed with other faculty who *are* Jews, but some of them happen to be converts, so their family names were not exactly common in the shtetl (the Old World settlements of Eastern European Jewry). So, from time to time, a parent of a prospective student will find the web page on Jewish Studies and go down the list to find someone to call or visit in his office and ask about Jewish life on campus. For some reason, they don't choose my colleagues with Anglo-Saxon surnames, but Birkel, hmm, … Berk, Berkovitz, Bikel, these are all good Ashkenazic names…and lots can happen at Ellis Island. As far as I know, there's no *Yiddishkeit* in my background, but these parents of prospective students call me, and I try to answer their questions. "Can they observe the holidays?" "Yes, there's a Jewish cultural center on campus, which celebrates each *yontif* [holiday] and hosts dinner on *Shabbat* [the Sabbath]. And there's a small synagogue in town that always welcomes students, so they can *daven* [pray] at the local *shul* [synagogue]." At some point in these conversations, though, I feel morally obligated to come out as a *goy*, a gentile. I have to tell them that I'm not a Jew, even though I'm warmly welcomed in the Jewish Studies program and I've been richly nourished in the spiritual life by the Jewish tradition. It's just not right for me to pretend to be what I'm not.

Here's another story. Gentile though I am, I love klezmer music, the celebration music of eastern European Jews. I even taught a course once on klezmer music, and to prepare for this I went to a weeklong klezmer camp. There the norm was to be Jewish, of course, and so everyone assumed that I was Jewish. It's not that I was trying to pass off as something that I'm not, but neither was I, as a non-Jewish guest, trying to attract attention to myself. But at one point it just seemed important to tell someone that I was not a Jew. I did not want to deceive anyone. So I confessed to being a gentile, and the response was very generous: "So what? *Du hobst a yiddishe neshome.*" ("You have a Jewish soul.") This was not an occasion of interfaith dialogue. It was an occasion of being a guest in the house of Judaism. So it was a high compliment, and I accepted it with gratitude.

A different story: once I was a retreatant at a Buddhist meditation center—to learn, not to engage in interfaith dialogue. Again, I was a guest. Toward the end of the retreat, the leader issued a Buddhist altar call, inviting retreatants to take the five precepts of Buddhist laity. These are to refrain from killing any sentient life (usually understood to include embracing a vegetarian diet), to refrain from stealing, from sexual misconduct, from lying, and from intoxicants. No one accepted, and he looked quite disappointed. I thought for a moment: *I* could take the five precepts. I already practice them. They are quite close to some of our cherished testimonies. But to take them would have been perceived as becoming a Buddhist, something that I had no intention of doing. It would have blurred distinctions that mattered both to the leader of the retreat and to me. On this occasion it mattered to observe the boundaries between our communities.

Thinking about boundaries can be difficult for us because as liberal Friends we often find it hard to define our own. We're not always sure where our own collective boundary of membership is. That, by that way, is not an affliction unique to us. Nor is it always an affliction. In our Christian heritage, it goes back at least as far as the apostle Paul, who wrestled deeply (and came up with some radical answers) to the question of what it means to be a follower of Jesus. The boundary was no longer restricted to membership in Judaism—gentiles like me were now invited. But was adherence to the full legal teachings of Judaism required? Paul said, "No," and effected a monumental boundary redefinition.

Liberal Quakerism is asking similar questions of itself. Must we identify ourselves as Christian? The individual response has become "That's optional," but the status of the collective answer is an unclear boundary. More recently, it has become increasingly optional that liberal Quakers believe in God, though that seems to be still a minority view at this point.

As you can probably tell, because I've spent a lot of time sitting at the feet of earlier Friends, I tend to value our traditions. I feel that we would lose a great deal if we were to jettison our collective Christian and theistic identity. Yet, my faithfulness to Friends and to the apostle Paul (not to mention Jesus) requires of me that I be open to conversation about where our boundaries might move.

Boundaries are also useful because that is where we can meet others. We travel to our boundaries to encounter others. To have the conversations that I've been talking about, we need to encourage people who operate easily and effectively on the boundaries of their own community and reach out to others with empathy. There are people like this in our meetings, and we should nurture them. At the same time, we need to acknowledge that there are people who will not negotiate. To them, it means betrayal. In their eyes, boundaries are to protect the truth. The rest of us will do well to bear in mind that it serves neither them nor the process of dialogue with other communities if we push such people off the high dive into the deep end. We're not all called to all difficult conversations, but we're each called to some, and discerning those callings can be a delicate communal task.

Gathering together the various threads of this essay, we might summarize like this:

♦ Pursue the difficult conversation, whether they are within your meeting, with other kinds of Friends, other Christian communities, or the interfaith world.
♦ Reflect on what is precious to you.
♦ Seek to be aware of what motivates you to dialogue. Ask yourself: what do I seek in this adventure? What pains from the past do I bring?

♦ Listen to your conversation partner from a deep place, as though it were vocal ministry.

♦ Sink into your particularity, expressed in the distinctive accent of your spiritual mother tongue. It's the way to deeper commonalities.

♦ Walk humbly.

♦ Build trust.

♦ Observe boundaries.

♦ Cultivate and nurture those who can work at the boundaries.

What might we expect from such encounters? We should not expect agreement, nor victory—after all, it's not a contest. Instead we might find the common ground that comes of listening. We might experience growing respect, despite conflict and challenge. Maybe you and your conversation partners will come to agree on *how* to disagree. Articulating that "how" can be wonderfully liberating, even exhilarating. Misunderstanding can be an opportunity to learn rather than a reason to be offended. That requires a kind of generosity based in trust.

You might discover a new dimension of what it means to love your neighbor. Like John Woolman's experience, we can find that our first motion, our motivation, is love, and from there we can be genuinely open to others while being faithful to what is truest in our own tradition.

Being Faithful Friends
in a Multifaith America
God-Talk After 9-11-01 and 12-26-04 (when over 150,000 people died in a tsunami caused by an earthquake off the coast of Indonesia)

by Stephanie Crumley-Effinger,
April 3, 2005, Quaker Lecture,
Wilmington College of Ohio

Introduction

"Who are they, and why do they hate us?"

The poignant questions resounded across the country as we reeled in shock when the Twin Towers of the World Trade Center were struck by planes, exploded in flames, and collapsed into a huge tomb of smoldering rubble, with another plane crashing in the Pennsylvania countryside, and the Pentagon having a gaping wound in its side.

"Who are they, and why do they hate us?"

The questions echoed across kitchen tables, news broadcasts, gatherings of grieving friends and families, school classrooms, and worship services, as television news showed pictures of cheering crowds in far-off places who seemed to be rejoicing over the deaths of thousands of people of our and other countries.

"Who are they, and why do they hate us?"

Some analyzed the questions in light of frustrations with our country's foreign policies, some named as cause foreign jealousy of our freedoms, and others blamed Satan or beliefs they identified with evil.

"Who are they, and why do they hate us?"

Some reacted to these questions with rage and blame,

Stephanie Crumley-Effinger is Director of Field Education/ Student Services at the Earlham School of Religion. Used with permission of the author.

seeking to even the score by carrying out acts of violence towards Muslim individuals and communities in towns and cities across the United States.

"Who *are* these people of this other religion, far away across the world and right here in our own country, whose beliefs and ways are a mystery to us?" Some reverted to stereotypes of a violent religion focused on holy war, while others bought out the Islam section in their local bookstores, flocked to courses on Islam, and reached out in love and compassion to their frightened and besieged Muslim neighbors and friends.

September 11, 2001, was a turning point in so many ways. Perhaps you, too, were visited with this awareness as you sought to take in the enormity of what had occurred. I remember walking over to teach my afternoon class, in grief and shock for the many unknown people suffering and dying, and concern for the safety of my two brothers-in-law who work in Manhattan. I saw the beautiful blue sky, and was struck by the irony of my experience in Richmond of a peaceful, warm, late summer day in such contrast to the smoke, death and destruction occurring seven hundred miles to the east, and struck also by the conviction that in as-yet-undetermined ways things in this country and the wider world beyond us would never be the same again.

Evidences of this turning point confront us constantly— large evidences, like updates on the horrors of the war in Iraq, accounts of the treatment and legal travails of detainees at Guantanamo Bay and Abu Ghraib, stories of families grieving the death of soldier daughters, sons, fathers, siblings. And there are the small evidences, like the Patriot Act requiring extra paperwork for changing signatures on our Meeting's checking account, having to arrive at the airport an hour and a half early to take off one's shoes, coat, and sweater to go through three or four levels of security checks, signs bearing the logo "Department of Homeland Security," and the longer lines and sets of instructions for fingerprinting those entering the U.S. from other countries. And, of particular interest to people of faith, the evidence of the U.S.' increasing awareness of Islam as a major factor in our understanding of the world. Happily, for many people Islam increasingly is no longer seen as a monolithic force, but a diverse, complex collection of practices and peoples with names like Shi'a, Sunni, Wajabi, and Sufi, fragilely connected by their common commitment to God, whom they know as Allah, Mohammed as his prophet, and the Qur'an as the holy book guiding life and faith.

The agonized questions, "Who are they, and why do they hate us?" have become more complex and are being addressed on political, social, geographic and religious levels as the hijackers and their sponsors are, at least by many Americans, differentiated from the religion which they shamed and maligned by associating it with their vicious acts. Claims rashly made in the early responses to the events of that terrible day three and a half years ago are being investigated, historical factors researched, dynamics and issues sorted out, and nuances named and explored.

This is only part of the increasing awareness of the religious world beyond the typical description of the "Judeo-Christian" influence on America. This was demonstrated three months ago in the wake of the devastating tsunami that destroyed many coastal towns in south Asia. The victims represented a wide range of religious traditions. All over the world, we human beings were asking questions about the meaning of a tragedy of such epic proportions, and those who believe in God were wondering where God stood in relationship to it.

Here in the US, journalists interviewed not just the usual suspects of a Catholic priest, a rabbi and some Protestant ministers, but also practitioners and leaders of other faiths. It was fascinating to hear Buddhists, Hindus and Muslims wrestling with these questions and issues, as well as Christian and Jewish leaders. And also fascinating to hear that the responses had a similar range of ideas about God. Using different terms and concepts, each leader articulated one of four basic approaches:

(1) that the tragedy was due to the action of God or to karma, with people having brought about their fate by unfaithful or improper living;

(2) that God does not bring about things like this, but suffers with people and is present to help them deal with it, especially through the care of those who provide help;

(3) that God is all-powerful and therefore made this happen, but we can't understand God's ways or know why this happened and why some people were spared and others were not; or

(4) that it is a mystery but that it serves to call us to turn to God.

With these two events, of September 11, 2001, and December 26, 2004,* the pluralistic religious society of our world and of American society was vividly demonstrated. Anyone who thought that we still live in a "Christian" country, if ever we did, and is paying attention, is aware that there are a lot of folks out there with other beliefs and practices.

We have gathered this afternoon as a group of Quakers and other people interested in hearing (or students shanghaied with the promise of extra credit to attend) a lecture concerning the interplay of Quaker faith and the pluralistic religious culture which US society is more and more becoming. I come as one with more questions than answers, suggesting things I have not attained and

---

*Date of a devastating tsunami caused by an earthquake off the coast of Indonesia, which was the deadliest recorded in human history. Because many of the countries affected were predominantly Muslim, many religious questions were raised, as well as questions about the amount of humanitarian aid provided.—Editor.

inviting you to engage the proposition that we seek to embody faithfully one religious tradition out of which we then relate with people of other religious traditions. I speak not as a scholar of world religions, but as a Quaker called to public ministry, and specifically as a Friend who seeks a life centered in the Living Christ present in our midst, the teachings of Jesus recorded in the Bible, and Quaker understandings of faith and practice. I speak as one who worships in the manner of programmed Friends, and who has been enriched and deepened in this Quaker Christian faith by encounter and worship with diverse kinds of Quakers from this country and other countries, and with people of various faiths—mostly Christians of various denominations, Jews, Baha'is, Muslims, and Buddhists.

I am also speaking as someone who is not interested in religious faith as a phenomenon, but as a focus for life, something to be experienced and not just speculated about. I recently heard someone express this eloquently on a segment of the PBS special *From Jesus to Christ*. A commentator noted that "the Sufis have a saying that there are three ways you can learn about fire. You can hear about it from others. You can see it for yourself. Or you can be burned by it." He went on to say that this third way was how the disciples experienced Jesus.* So the other context for my talk is that I speak as someone who has been "burned" by encounter with the Holy, not in the sense of being harmed or turned off, but in this Sufi sense of experiencing it directly and not solely through observation or others' descriptions. While this is likely also the experience of some of you, I ask the indulgence of those for whom that is a strange or even uncomfortable idea.

There are three main points I hope to make. First, that God is really complex. Second, that people of different faiths are here to stay and can be experienced as friends

*www.pbs.org/wgbh/pages/frontline/shows/religion/

and as "mysteries to be explored rather than as problems to be solved." And third, that we can best approach interfaith encounter by first going deep into the faith tradition that calls us.

God's Complexity

First, there is the matter of the complexity of God [*holding hands some distance apart to indicate bigness*] and us [*holding hands close together to indicate smallness*].Poets may express this best. Quaker poet Sterling Olmsted, a Friend who formerly served as Dean of the Faculty here at Wilmington College and also taught English for many years, put it well in the following poem:

Discovery?

When I consider
the vastness of the ultimate
and the closeness of the intimate
together,

I wonder whether
Grace may not be everywhere,
and the out-there
of space
and the in-here
be the same
undivided place.*

Another poetic expression of the divine-human contrast is in Psalm 8, verses 1, 3 and 4:

---

*(c) 1993 (Sterling P. Olmsted, *Poems from Six Decades*, 2nd edition, 2003, edited by Barbara Dixson with help from Donna Decker, and published by the Friends Association for Higher Education.)

O LORD, our Sovereign, how majestic is your name
in all the earth!
You have set your glory above the heaven.
When I look at your heavens, the work of your fingers,
the moon and the stars that you have established;
what are human beings that you are mindful of them,
mortals that you care for us?

The basic point is that God is vast and we are puny.
And that God cares for us. We human beings are always
trying to figure out the dimensions and specifics of this
dynamic. We long to know what it means that God is
vast and we are not, and how to understand God being so
much more and so far beyond us, and yet also close to us
and directly connected to us. We come up with many ideas
and theories about how God works, and comfort ourselves
with the sense that we can figure it all out and, perhaps,
even control God somewhat through our understanding.

Earlier this winter I spent a few days in Florida
attending a workshop for seminary faculty on ministers
and sexual misconduct. One day when we had a break
between sessions I went outside to look at the ocean waves,
and the opening verses of Psalm 121 came to me.

I lift up my eyes to the hills —
from where will my help come?
My help comes from the LORD,
who made heaven and earth.

It was two or three weeks after the tsunami, and
sitting there watching the waves I was struck by the
contrast between the peaceful ocean scene before me and
the horror-filled one in South Asia. I thought of how people
on that other morning had fled for the hills, certainly many
of them calling on God for help. A flash of rage toward
God came over me, and I said (maybe even aloud), "They
lifted their eyes to the hills, but you sure didn't come
through with help for them." Then suddenly a question

filled my heart in response: "How do you know?" A sense of shame came over me, because I realized that I had no idea of how God may have helped them. It didn't look like what I would consider help—saving their lives–but how could I dare to say that God had not helped them? What do I know about the ways that God can help people, ways that may differ from what I think help should look like?

Once again I was reminded of my finiteness compared to God's beyondness and infiniteness, and startled into awareness of my hubris, chutzpah, arrogance, in thinking that I can truly understand what God can do or has done.

The apostle Paul also wrote poetically of our limitedness in Romans 8:26, "the Spirit helps us in our weakness; for we do not know how to pray as we ought, but that very Spirit intercedes for us with groans too deep for words." God knows us as limited, and makes concessions for this–God isn't dependent on our getting things just right.

A MultiFaith America is Here to Stay

Harvard religion scholar Diana Eck has written a fascinating book that provides a scenic tour of the religious diversity in this country, both its present state and history. Entitled *A New Religious America: How "Christian Country" Has Become the World's Most Religiously Diverse Nation*, Eck's book begins with a quick overview:

> The huge white dome of a mosque with its minarets rises from the cornfields just outside Toledo, Ohio . . . A great Hindu temple with elephants carved in . . . the doorway stands on a hillside in the western suburbs of Nashville, Tennessee. A Cambodian Buddhist temple and monastery with a hint of a Southeast Asian roofline is set in the farmlands south of Minneapolis, Minnesota. In suburban Fremont, California, flags fly from the golden domes of a new

Sikh Gurdwara ... The religious landscape of America has changed radically in the past thirty years, but most of us have not yet begun to see the dimensions and scope of that change, so gradual has it been and yet so colossal. It began with the "new immigration" spurred by the Immigration and Nationality Act of 1965, as people from all over the world came to America and became citizens.

With them have come the religious traditions of the world – Islamic, Hindu, Buddhist, Jain, Sikh, Zoroastrian, African and Afro-Caribbean.

The people of these living traditions of faith have moved into American neighborhoods, tentatively at first, their altars and prayer rooms in storefronts and office buildings, basements and garages, recreation rooms and coat closets, nearly invisible to the rest of us. But in the past decade, we have begun to see their visible presence. Not all of us have seen the Toledo mosque or the Nashville temple, but we will see places like them, if we keep our eyes open, even in our own communities. They are the architectural signs of a new religious America (p. 1).

Eck goes on to note a few statistics: in this country there are more Muslims than Jews, Episcopalians, or Presbyterian Church (USA) members—about six million practitioners of Islam. Los Angeles is the most complex Buddhist city in the world, because it is home to the whole range and diversity of Asian Buddhism including Sri Lankan, Chinese, Japanese, Vietnamese, Cambodian, Thai, Tibetan and Korean (p. 148) with more than 300 temples (p. 142). There are about 4 million Buddhists in the US as a whole, with more than a thousand centers for meditation and practice (p. 149). In addition, over one million persons comprise the wide-ranging and diverse Hindu population of our country (pp. 2-3).

But even though there has been in the past few decades a tremendous explosion in the diversity of American religious practice, many traditions have long roots in this country. In 1830s New England, Ralph Waldo Emerson was exploring and writing on Hindu and Buddhist scriptures (pp., 94-5), and in the 1890s a Hindu teacher named Swami Vivekenanda had an influential two-year visit to this country in connection with his participation in the 1893 World's Parliament of Religions in Chicago. At the Parliament, Vivekenanda told his hearers that the Lord has declared to the Hindu in his incarnation as Krishna, "I am in every religion as the thread through a string of pearls. And wherever thou seest extraordinary holiness and extraordinary power raising and purifying humanity, know yet that I am there" (p. 99).

Speaking and writing widely on yoga and other Hindu practices and beliefs, Vivekenanda founded America's first Hindu organization, the Vedanta Society, which is still active. After he returned to India, other Hindu teachers followed him, and in 1906 the first Hindu temple was built, in San Francisco. A variety of forms of Hindu faith and practice have also taken root in the US in the century since then.

Also present at the World's Parliament of Religions were Buddhist delegates, but the first American encounter with Buddhism had already occurred in the 1850's when Chinese workers emigrated to the West Coast for the Gold Rush. Between the Buddhist, Taoist, and Confucian traditions they brought, by 1875 there were eight Chinese temples in San Francisco. And by 1899 hundreds of Chinese temples and shrines had been built along the West Coast and in the Rocky Mountains (p.165). Japanese Buddhist teachers came at that time to nurture the Japanese immigrant community on the West Coast. They startled Christian neighbors with their "religion without God" (p, 151), since the Buddha is understood to be not divine being, but an enlightened, or awakened, human being pointing the way for others to follow (p. 152). As is Hinduism, Buddhism in America is characterized by many forms of practice, linked to the diversity of teachers and movements which have come to or developed in this country in the past 150 years or so. And America serves as a remarkable crossroads, where Buddhists who would never have met in Asia encounter one another and experience very different cultures of Buddhism (p. 149).

In contrast to Hinduism and Buddhism, Islam was negatively perceived by many Americans even before having many adherents here due to centuries of Christian-Muslim conflict in the Holy Land and Europe (p. 233). Thus the only Muslim speaking at the 1893 World Religions Parliament was an American who had converted to Islam while working in the Philippines in the 1880's. He addressed the stereotype of Muslims putting infidels to the sword and challenged his fellow citizens instead to learn about Islam firsthand (p. 235). Unknown to most people is research from the past twenty years which demonstrates that Islam first came to the Americas through Muslim Africans brought here as slaves. It is estimated that 10% of the West Africans captured and taken to America were Muslim (p. 239). One of them, Omar Ibn Said, described his experiences of being "sold into the hands of the Christians" and brought to Charleston (p. 240).

While these enslaved African Muslims had to practice their faith as individuals, Muslim communities in the US came into existence with nineteenth century immigrants from countries such as Syria and Lebanon (p. 228). The first documented Muslim gatherings for prayer were held in North Dakota in the early 1900s (p. 245), and early mosques were established there and in Iowa, Maine, Michigan, and Indiana. In 1952 a number of Muslim groups came together to form the Federation of Islamic Associations (p. 235). These organizations and new groups founded in the 1990s after the wave of Muslim immigration devote much of their efforts to challenging prejudice through educational offerings for non-Muslims, such as the annual Islam Awareness Week. They are particularly active in countering the seemingly endless array of images linking violence with Islam.

The history of Islam in this country includes African-American Muslim communities, beginning with Moorish Science Temple founded in Newark early in the twentieth century. It and some others, such as the Nation of Islam, later known as Black Muslims, that arose in the 1930's and two decades later drew in Malcolm X, developed their own forms of the religion. While many of these groups have now become part of more mainstream American Islamic society, some remain separate to this day (pp. 253-258.)

Diana Eck notes that "in the U.S., where Islam is too often identified with the Middle East, Muslims continually remind us, and one another, that 'Islam is a universal call. It is not an Arab religion or an eastern or Middle Eastern cult'" (p. 267). There are approximately 1,400 mosques in the US, about 80% of which have been in existence for 25 years or less. These represent a diverse range of Muslim groups, including Sunni, Shi'ite, Ahmadiyya, and Sufi, with both native-born Americans of various backgrounds and immigrants from many countries (p. 264). Like Quaker Meetings of the nineteenth century, many mosques have schools to provide a guarded education that nurtures young people in the values and behavior of their faith communities (p. 284).

It is clear that even if the town one lives in does not have much religious diversity, it is a part of the American experience that is here to stay. We who are Jewish and Christian Americans often don't know quite what to do with this new reality. Especially with Christianity having been the majority religion for so long, it can feel like we have a lot to lose by affirming the increasing religious diversity of our country. Many Christians are unhappy about the increasing loss of Sunday as a time set aside for worship, as nowadays often people are scheduled to work, or athletic and other events are being held. How will we adjust to these new realities? To what extent is our faith dependent on holding a special status in the culture and calendar of America?

Going Deep into One's Faith

In light of her hopes for people of different faiths to relate to one another, Diana Eck opens the section on Islam by citing a verse from the Qur'an: "Do you not know, O people, that I have made you into tribes and nations that you may know each other?" She suggests that "our religious and cultural differences should not be the occasion for division, but, on the contrary, the occasion for the biggest challenge of all: 'that we may know each other'" (p. 222).

At the same time, we also need to guard against thinking that we know each other when it is actually prejudice masquerading as knowledge. This winter a member of our Richmond area ministers' association forwarded the group an e-mail purporting to describe an encounter of an evangelical Christian minister and a Muslim imam. In a condescending and superior tone, it gave an account based on the old stereotype that Muslims are instructed to kill non-Muslims. It ended with the Christian triumphantly asking the imam if he shouldn't worship Jesus, whose followers are to love others, rather than Allah, whose followers are to kill others. Reading this with a growing sense of disbelief, fury and disgust, I sent a confrontational response to the list, challenging the premise of the story as based on falsehood and prejudice, reminding the sender that Christians are not to bear false witness against others, and encouraging ministers to learn about Islam rather than to accept stereotypes about it. I confess that my note was written in less than a fully loving spirit.

Another way in which people can respond to religious differences is by trying to find a "lowest common denominator" of things which various groups have in common, or to pretend that the ways in which we are alike are all that matter. While there are important similarities among groups, there are also important differences, and no one who takes seriously the practice of religious faith is going to be satisfied by ignoring the particularity of their tradition. I am convinced that Quakers and others need to develop their response to religious diversity through being grounded in a deep formation in their own tradition.

What does it mean to be deeply formed in one's religious tradition? For me as a Christ-centered Friend, this means both individual and corporate practice as a disciple of Jesus in a Quaker manner. This includes intentional nurture of my own personal faith and practice through such means as reading, prayer, volunteer work, and spiritual friendship with others, and through regular participation in Meeting for Worship, Meeting for Business, religious education, committee work, and other group opportunities for spiritual practice. It means seeking to know myself fully and to pay attention to others' wisdom about me, both about my giftedness and my brokenness, so as to understand my flaws and offer them for God's transforming work, and to identify my gifts and offer them for God to work through. It means opening myself to holy texts and processes, such as praying the Psalms, so as to come to resemble more fully the image of God in which we human beings have been created, in my case in the particular Stephanie Anne Crumley-Effinger manifestation of that image to which God is calling me. It means making myself available for God's power to work in me, drawing me closer to the Divine source and forming me ever more fully as Jesus' disciple. I know that I have a long way to go, but I can also look over my life and see points of change and growth, which offers hope and encouragement to my awareness of how much still needs God's transforming touch.

Just last Sunday I experienced in a very particular way the blessings of seeking to be deeply formed in one's faith. I had spent the week traveling on a visit to a student with whom I am working this year in ESR's distance education program, and ended up in Brooklyn with my sister for the weekend. When I called home I learned from

Michael the stunning and unbelievable news of the tragic and unexpected death of a young woman in our community of soccer families back home in Richmond. Sunday morning, then, I sat through much of the lovely and meaningful Easter service at my sister's church in tears or on the edge of them. I kept thinking how much it felt like Good Friday rather than Easter but for those of us who were grieving. And at the same time even while there was a sense of disjoint, it was good and right to be in the presence of celebration and rejoicing, to be reminded that grief is not the sole reality even though it was uppermost in my experience at that moment. Such reminder is part of the blessing of participation in the faith community beyond oneself; our personal story is held and caught up in the bigger story of which we are also a part.

The previous Sunday I had been with my student visiting her unprogrammed Friends Meeting. One of the members had asked if, when it came time for me to talk with them after Meeting for Worship, I would explain programmed Quaker worship to them. During Meeting, then, it came to me to use the metaphor of water in discussing programmed and unprogrammed worship. The 42nd Psalm says that "as a deer pants for flowing water, so my soul cries out for you, my God" and in the fourth chapter of the gospel of John, Jesus talked to the woman at the well about worshiping in grace and truth and offered her "living water." Talking about these passages and using this image, then, I told them that I believe that both kinds of Friends in worship are seeking to "get wet with this living water." It is as if in coming to worship we approach a lake and begin to wade in. Unprogrammed Friends walk in, each on her or his own, until going deep enough to be thoroughly soaked and immersed. Programmed Friends walk in and as they do, some take a turn sprinkling water on everyone, so that each person is getting wet not only through their own wading, but also because water is coming at them from other directions. After a time they, too, are thoroughly soaked and immersed in the living water of which Jesus spoke. It is the same water, and both groups are all wet, but it has come about in somewhat different fashion.

To follow this metaphor, then, I believe that "going deep" in my formation as a Friend allows me to "get wet" more readily and thoroughly when I go to Meeting to "go wading." I suspect that this metaphor is applicable to people of varying religious traditions. Our formation will differ, because different practices form persons in different ways, but if it is a religious faith centered in divine reality, I think that one truly "gets wet" with the living water Jesus offered.

Meanwhile, in seeking to know and engage people of other faiths, we who are Christians need to bear in mind that in this country our religious tradition has power and privilege to which other religious groups do not have access. This fall, one of my students attended a workshop on "Pastoral Care in a Multicultural World." Her notes detail a number of important things to consider in relating to people of faiths other than our own. There is power inherent in not having to wonder if one's faith will be accepted and understood, one's holidays will be recognized, one's kinds of food will be available, one's daily religious practices will be respected, and if one will be safe in practicing our faith. We who are part of the Christian majority take such things for granted and assume that they are also the case for practitioners of other religions. We need to identify such assumptions, and to learn about ourselves as well as seek to learn about others. Further, we who are in a majority religion will know less about people in minority religious groups than they will know about us, because while we are free to ignore them without consequence, they will almost always have had to learn about us in order to survive in America (Priscilla Berggren-Thomas, workshop notes, 10/14/2004).

We are challenged to be good stewards of our privilege rather than blind consumers of it. We need to be willing to take risks and listen to other voices. We are invited to learn the words and ideas of other faiths and travel into new and foreign territory so as to come to know each other in this new multifaith America in which we all live. We can learn to make common cause with one another where we can do so, and to negotiate conflicts and tensions where these emerge.

In closing, I would like to emphasize the importance of acting from grounding in one's faith by returning to the theme of getting wet with the living water that Jesus offered to the woman at the well. There is a wonderful song which some of you may know from *Worship in Song*, a hymnal published about ten years ago by unprogrammed U.S. Friends. It goes:

1. Cause us to come to Thy river, O Lord. Cause us to come to Thy river, O Lord. Cause us to come to Thy river, O Lord.
(Refrain) Cause us to come, cause us to drink, cause us to live.
2. Cause us to drink from Thy river, O Lord. Cause us to drink from Thy river, O Lord. Cause us to drink from Thy river, O Lord. (Refrain)
3. Cause us to live in Thy river, O Lord. Cause us to live in Thy river, O Lord. Cause us to live in Thy river, O Lord. (Refrain)

Bibliography

Eck , Diana L. *A New Religious America: How "Christian Country" Has Become the World's Most Religiously Diverse Nation.* New York: HarperCollins, 2001.

A Quaker/Buddhist View of Religious Pluralism

By Sallie King

I am a Quaker and I am a Buddhist. (For those of you not familiar with it, Quakerism, also known as the Religious Society of Friends, is a branch of Protestant Christianity.) In the mid-1990s, I had occasion to give a lecture on Buddhism and Quakerism at an annual Quaker gathering. As I rose to speak, I saw about 1,500 Quakers, or Friends as we call ourselves, in the audience, and I could not resist asking them this: "If you have taken Buddhism into your spiritual life in some way, would you please stand up." About 85–90% of the room stood up. So I am by no means the only one who feels a serious affinity between Buddhism and Quakerism and who has brought the two together. Many have done so, to some degree. However, not many go as far as I in claiming a double religious identity.

I have held this double religious identity for about the last twenty years. As this identity has evolved, my view of religious pluralism has evolved with it, drawing,

Sallie B. King is Professor of Philosophy and Religion at James Madison University in Harrisonburg, Virginia. She is the author of many books and articles on Buddhism, Quakerism, interfaith dialogue, and the cross-cultural philosophy of religion. She is former co-clerk of Valley Friends Meeting, former president of the Society for Buddhist-Christian Studies, and a trustee of the international, interfaith Peace Council. She serves on the CIRC and QUF. The author thanks Orbis Press for granting permission for re-publication of this article, previously published as "A Pluralistic View of Religious Pluralism" in Paul F. Knitter, ed., The Myth of Religious Superiority: Multifaith Explorations of Religious Pluralism *(Orbis Press, 2005).*

primarily, upon the resources of both Quakerism and Buddhism that most significantly shape my religious thinking. I speak today with this double voice.

I begin by reviewing my understanding of the kind of thing that religion is; much of my understanding of religious pluralism is implicit in my understanding of religion.

1. Religions are tools.

This understanding I take from Buddhism. A prominent text in the Buddhist tradition is the "Parable of the Raft" (*Alagaddupama Sutta, Majjhima Nikaya,* pp. 228-229). In this *sutta,* the Buddha compares the Dhamma—i.e., his teachings, Buddhism itself—to a raft, something to take us from this shore of samsara (the realm of ignorance and suffering) to the other shore of nirvana (the realm of wisdom and freedom). A raft, as he points out, does not transport one passively but requires one to make an effort if one wants to reach the other shore. A raft, moreover, is of no use once one actually reaches the other shore; one should leave it aside and go on one's way. Just so, says the Buddha, Buddhism is a vehicle, a tool, for helping us to transport ourselves from our present condition to the condition of enlightenment. It is not the end, it is a means; it is to be left aside when one has realized the goal. That is, Buddhism relativizes itself; it subordinates itself to Truth. It declares categorically that it is not itself the Truth; it is a vehicle or tool for realizing Truth. From this starting point in early Buddhism develop such well-known Buddhist teachings as the Zen Buddhist declaration that all of Buddhism (and, implicitly, all religious teachings of whatever origin) is no more than a "finger pointing at the moon." What we seek is the moon. We are repeatedly advised not to mistake the finger for the moon.

Obviously, on the basis of this premise one could assert that Buddhism is the best tool for reaching the goal of enlightenment and many Buddhists do so. It is rather difficult, on this premise, however, to consistently hold to the kind of exclusivist view that one can hold on the basis of a claimed divine revelation. Certainly the door is open, on the basis of this premise, to a pluralistic view that sees many religions as potential usable vehicles to Truth.

Quakers do not generally explicitly speak of Quakerism as a method. One exception to this generalization comes from a classic study by Howard Brinton, who writes,

> Quakerism is primarily a method, just as science is primarily a method. Quakerism includes also a certain body of beliefs, as does science, but in both cases these beliefs are accepted because they have been arrived at by experts using the proper method. They can be modified by further use of the same method by which they were arrived at in the first place.[1]

While Brinton is one of the few Friends to have thought to put it this way, the reality behind his reference to Quakerism as a method is one that most Friends would recognize: Quakerism is a form of practice that, Quakers believe, opens one to experience of the divine. Quakerism has no creed or particular theology and has, over the centuries, adamantly refused to define itself in this way. Instead, Quakerism is defined by certain core practices, the most important of which is the unprogrammed Meeting for Worship in which Friends gather in silence, still their thoughts, and open themselves to the leadings of the divine Spirit. Other Quaker practices such as Meeting for Business, worship sharing, clearness committees, queries, etc., are all methods by which Friends attempt to open themselves to be in touch with, and guided by, the divine. Thus Quakerism, too, is not an end in itself, not the embodiment of ultimate Truth, but a means, a method, a set of practices, the aim of which is to gain the individual (and, importantly in Quakerism, the group) access to the divine Spirit.

The point here is not to compare Quakerism and Buddhism. The point is to see how each tradition is open to religious pluralism. Inasmuch as both religions see themselves as means to an end, each implicitly relativizes itself. Neither is bound to claim for itself "possession" of ultimate Truth, much less exclusive possession of ultimate Truth. They do not think in those terms. They do claim that they are vehicles to such Truth—good, reliable vehicles. That, in itself, says nothing about whether others also may be such vehicles, but it does leave the door open to such a view. The Dalai Lama, for one, does draw the pluralist conclusion from the view that religions are tools.

In my own case, I am convinced that Buddhism provides me with the most effective framework within which to situate my efforts to develop spiritually through cultivating love and compassion. At the same time, I must acknowledge that while Buddhism represents the best path for me—that is, it suits my character, my temperament, my inclinations, and my cultural background—the same will be true of Christianity for Christians. For them, Christianity is the best way. On the basis of my conviction, I cannot, therefore, say that Buddhism is best for everyone.[2]

For the Dalai Lama, since religions are tools, given that people differ in significant ways from each other, it is easy to see that while some religions will suit some people best, other religions will suit other people best.

2. The universal presence of the Light/Buddha Nature within.

Mahayana Buddhists, such as myself, work with the teaching of the "Buddha Nature," which states that "all sentient beings possess the Buddha Nature." The Buddha Nature teaching arose in response to the question whether all people can and will, eventually, attain enlightenment. The answer that Mahayana Buddhism came up with was:

yes, all people (actually, all sentient beings) can and will eventually attain enlightenment, or Buddhahood, because their true nature is Buddhahood and this Buddha Nature is present in everyone.

This teaching means not only that all persons are *potential* Buddhas, but also that the "true nature" of humankind is a Buddha's nature. We have a Buddha within. That is, while on the surface we may manifest various degrees of ignorance, greed, fear, selfishness, etc., we nonetheless have the nature of a Buddha—compassion and wisdom—concealed within us. Much Mahayana Buddhist practice is designed to get the Buddhist practitioner in touch with the Buddha within him or her. Actualization of one's Buddha nature is enlightenment. The contemporary Vietnamese Zen master Thich Nhat Hanh writes:

> As an historical person, the Buddha was born in Kapilavastu, ... got married, had one child, left home, practiced many kinds of meditation, became enlightened, and shared the teaching until he died at the age of eighty. But there is also the Buddha within ourselves who transcends space and time. This is the living Buddha, the Buddha of the ultimate reality, the one who transcends all ideas and notions and is available to us at any time.[3]

Quakers have a remarkably similar teaching in the idea of the Light Within, or Christ Within. Quakerism heavily emphasizes this "third person" of the Christian Trinity, the Holy Spirit, that part of the divine that, for Quakers, is present within every human being.

The Religious Society of Friends holds as the basis of its faith the belief that God endows each human being with a measure of the Divine Spirit. The gift of God's presence and the light of God's truth have been available to all people in all ages. ... The Divine Spirit, which Friends variously call the Inner Light, the Light of Truth, the

Christ Within, That of God in Everyone, has power to reveal, to overcome evil, and to enable us to carry out God's will. Quaker testimonies arise from listening to and obeying this Spirit.[4]

This teaching is similar to the Buddhist teaching in being a principle of enlightenability and in being universal. However, in the Quaker case, it is explicitly stated that this principle is divine and, moreover, the moral implications of the idea are drawn out.

Most significant for us is the fact that belief in this principle is the root of a prominent strain of religious universalism present in Quakerism since its origins. A famous statement from the early American Quaker John Woolman reads,

> There is a principle which is pure, placed in the human mind, which in different places and ages hath had different names. It is, however, pure and proceeds from God. It is deep and inward, confined to no forms of religion nor excluded from any, where the heart stands in perfect sincerity. In whomsoever this takes root and grows, of what nation soever, they become brethren in the best sense of the expression.[5]

Here John Woolman makes perfectly explicit the implication of the universality of the Light Within: since the Light Within is found in all persons of all places and all ages, it cannot be confined to any particular form of religion. Here the religious pluralism of Quakerism becomes completely evident.

In the ancient Buddhist texts, such explicit pluralism is not found in connection with the idea of Buddha Nature but, again, the door is open to it, since what is needed for enlightenment is within and therefore not the exclusive possession of a religious institution. Some contemporary Buddhist leaders have become explicit in their pluralism. Thich Nhat Hanh sees Jesus the same way he sees the Buddha:

As the child of Mary and Joseph, Jesus is the Son of Woman and Man. As someone animated by the energy of the Holy Spirit, He is the Son of God. The fact that Jesus is both the Son of Man and the Son of God is not difficult for a Buddhist to accept.[6]

For Nhat Hanh, there is a historical Buddha and a historical Jesus, a living Buddha and a living Christ. The living Buddha is the Buddha Nature, alive in us. The living Christ is the Holy Spirit, alive in us. On this basis he draws an explicitly pluralist conclusion:

> When we understand and practice deeply the life and teachings of Buddha or the life and teachings of Jesus, we penetrate the door and enter the abode of the living Buddha and the living Christ, and life eternal presents itself to us.[7]

Nhat Hanh does not hesitate to identify the living Buddha (Buddha Nature) and the living Christ (Holy Spirit), both the indwelling of Truth, of Life.

3. Religious truth is experiential, not doctrinal or dogmatic.

Buddhist and Quaker teachings on the Buddha Nature and the Inner Light are important for the present purpose not only in that they are universal, but also in that they are the foundation of the two religions' view that religious truth is experiential, not doctrinal or dogmatic, much less creedal. In 1648, the founder of Quakerism, George Fox, wrote in his *Journal*,

> Now the Lord God hath opened to me by his invisible power how that every man was enlightened by the divine light of Christ; and I saw it shine through all.... This I saw in the pure openings of the Light without

the help of any man, neither did I then know where to find it in the Scriptures; though afterwards, searching the Scriptures, I found it. For I saw in that Light and Spirit which was before Scripture was given forth, and which led the holy men of God to give them [the Scriptures] forth, that all must come to that Spirit, if they would know God, or Christ, or the Scriptures aright, which they that gave them forth were led and taught by.[8]

In this passage, Fox declares the authority of religious experience, i.e., experience of the Inner Light, to be superior to that of scripture. While he is glad to find what he sees as confirmation of his experience in scripture, it is clear that what he relies upon is his experience. Scripture, he declares, is but an expression given forth from the Inner Light. It is more or less the traces left behind by the living Spirit.

In a similar vein, another early and "weighty" Friend, Isaac Pennington, wrote,

And the end of words is to bring men to the knowledge of things beyond what words can utter. So, learn of the Lord to make a right use of the Scriptures: which is by esteeming them in their right place, and prizing *that* above them which is above them.[9]

What is above scripture, and to be prized more highly than it, is, of course, the Inner Light and the illumination and guidance that it brings. Again and again Quakers declare that it is the Inner Light that is primary, all else being a manifestation of it.

That religious truth is experiential, rather than doctrinal, is foundational in Buddhism. The Buddha himself was a man who became the Buddha because of his enlightenment experience, a form of experience that both discloses religious truth and radically transforms the person. Buddhism is a method or path designed to lead its practitioners into this kind of experience. Buddhism is a religion whose approach is not faith but *ehi-passika*, "come and see"; i.e., come and see in one's own experience. The Buddha clearly differentiated between belief and knowledge, insisting upon the latter. In one famous exchange, a people called the Kalamas told the Buddha that they had heard many different teachings from many different itinerant religious teachers and did not know whom or what to believe. The Buddha's advice was this:

> Yes, Kalamas, it is proper that you have doubt, that you have perplexity, for a doubt has arisen in a manner which is doubtful. Now, look you Kalamas, do not be led by reports, or tradition, or hearsay. Be not led by the authority of religious texts, nor by mere logic or inference, nor by considering appearances, nor by the delight in speculative opinions, nor by seeming possibilities nor by the idea: 'this is our teacher.' But, O Kalamas, when you know for yourselves that certain things are unwholesome ... and wrong, and bad, then give them up ... And when you know for yourselves that certain things are wholesome ... and good, then accept them and follow them.[10]

In short, belief, respect, authority, tradition, inference have no spiritual value; only actual *knowledge* is of value, that is, indubitable knowledge based in one's own life experience. This kind of attitude, while sometimes neglected, has remained important in Buddhism to this day: experiential knowledge is what Buddhism is all about. In Zen Buddhism, Bodhidharma's famous saying that Zen is "not founded on words or scripture" and the famous painting of Zen monks gleefully burning books and scripture are dramatic ways of making the same point: truth is found in one's own experience; it does one no good to rely on the secondhand source of the traces of other peoples' experience, left behind in books. Thich Nhat Hanh writes,

The Buddha did not present an absolute doctrine. His teaching of non-self was offered in the context of his time. It was an instrument for meditation. But many Buddhists since then have gotten caught by the idea of non-self. They confuse the means and the end, the raft and the shore, the finger pointing to the moon and the moon. There is something more important than non-self. It is the freedom from the notions of both self and non-self. For a Buddhist to be attached to any doctrine, even a Buddhist one, is to betray the Buddha. It is not words or concepts that are important. What is important is our insight into the nature of reality and our way of responding to reality.[11]

There is an important corollary to the view that religious truth is experiential and not doctrinal: while both Buddhists and Quakers do, of course, speak, they are, at heart, suspicious of doctrinal formulations of religious truths. A twentieth century Friend, celebrating the good relationship between Quakerism and science, wrote,

Religious creeds are a great obstacle to any full sympathy between the outlook of the scientist and the outlook which religion is so often supposed to require. ... It would be a shock to come across a university where it was the practice of the students to recite adherence to Newton's laws of motion, to Maxwell's equations, and to the electromagnetic theory of light. We should not deplore it the less if our own pet theory happened to be included, or if the list were brought up to date every few years. ... So too in religion we are repelled by that confident theological doctrine which has settled for all generations just how the spiritual world is worked....[12]

The contemporary Zen teacher Thich Nhat Hanh composed a precept stating,

> Do not be idolatrous about or bound to any doctrine, theory, or ideology, even Buddhist ones. All systems of thought are guiding means; they are not absolute truth.[13]

With respect to religious pluralism, if religious truth is experiential, rather than doctrinal, then there will be no impulse to identify the particular verbal teaching of a particular religion as itself Truth, or belief in it as necessary for salvation. If religious truth is experiential, and especially if that religious experience is universally available, then it is not the possession of any religion and not under any religion's control. It is outside of all that, something that is available to human beings simply by virtue of our being human.

Moreover, given that Truth is experiential, another corollary follows: language that attempts to express religious Truth can never be fixed but is, on the contrary, in principle open to ongoing efforts to express the inexpressible. Quakers call this "ongoing revelation" or "continuing revelation." This is the idea that just as, in the past, experience of the Spirit led to the composition of the Bible, Spirit continues to lead people today and throughout time in "ongoing revelation" just as valid and authoritative. George Fox is famous for having challenged the preachers in churches, saying, "You will say, Christ saith this, and the apostles say this; but what canst thou say?"[14]

Thich Nhat Hanh puts together the language of religion as a method, of the divine within, of religious pluralism and of ongoing revelation in the following Buddhist-Christian idiom:

> Jesus said, "I am the door." He describes Himself as the door of salvation and everlasting life, the door to

the Kingdom of God. Because God the Son is made of the energy of the Holy Spirit, He is the door for us to enter the Kingdom of God.

The Buddha is also described as a door, a teacher who shows us the way in this life. ... But it is said that there are 84,000 Dharma doors, doors of teaching. If you are lucky enough to find a door, it would not be very Buddhist to say that yours is the only door. In fact, we have to open even more doors for future generations. We should not be afraid of more Dharma doors—if anything, we should be afraid that no more will be opened. ... Each of us, by our practice and our loving-kindness, is capable of opening new Dharma doors.[15]

With the universal presence of the Spirit/Buddha Nature, ongoing revelation, or the opening of new Dharma doors is the norm to be expected.[16]

4. Epistemological transcendence.

It should be obvious by now, but is still worth making explicit, that in this view, religious Truth is epistemologically transcendent. It cannot be conceptually known in any final or adequate way. There are two aspects to this understanding of epistemological transcendence. First, concepts are tied in with language and culture. But Truth as revealed by the Inner Light or Buddha Nature is not of that nature. Therefore, language and concepts don't fit it well. Second, the Truth of the Inner Light or Buddha Nature is vast beyond our measuring. Whatever we might want to think or say with respect to it would be radically inadequate.

5. Form and emptiness.

The Mahayana Buddhist idea of form and emptiness is a useful tool for expressing the relationship between religious Truth and the effort of religions to express that Truth. When we say that that Truth is "empty" to us, we refer to its epistemological transcendence. The "empty" nature of Truth is its lack of a permanent, fixed absolute form that we can grasp, name or say. Truth transcends our ability to definitively grasp, name or conceive it. This we know. And yet, we believe that we have had a little experiential taste of that Truth. Therefore, we cannot resist pointing our finger at the moon. The urge somehow to speak of it seems innate to us. We must manifest in some form our sense of our relationship with it, our sense of what it means to us. So we always, again and again, express the emptiness in some form, knowing always that none of those forms is adequate or ever can be adequate. This is the dialectic of our religious life. We know that no language, no ritual, no symbol, no form of any kind is an adequate expression of the Truth. Yet without some form we cannot open our mouths, we cannot support each other in our seeking, we cannot even point at the moon. So we do our best, again and again, to express emptiness in form. The danger is that we come to love our forms so much, we become so attached to them that we forget that they are not the Truth, not the moon, only the pointing finger.

As we have seen, both Quakerism and Buddhism see themselves as means to the religious end, not as "possessors" of the ultimate Truth. Maintaining a strong sense of the "unpossessability" of ultimate Truth, they require forms that can express this unpossessability. But does not a form, by its very nature, attempt to "capture" the Truth?

Quakerism's strategy for avoiding this problem is to strip the form down to its barest possible bones. Friends meet for worship in an unadorned room, or perhaps outdoors, in silence. They attempt to still their thoughts and open themselves to the presence of the living Spirit, "waiting upon the Lord." If anyone is moved by the Spirit to speak, he or she may do so; male or female, child or elder, the only stipulation is that no one should come to the Meeting for Worship intending either to speak or not to speak. If someone speaks, the others listen but do not respond. That is the entirety of the form. The idea is to avoid forcing the Spirit to take any particular form. "The Spirit moveth where it listeth" (John 3:8) and Friends would not constrain it in any way.

In his classic history of Quakerism, Howard Brinton describes early Quaker worship. Though he speaks in the past tense, this form of worship is still practiced in Friends Meetings to this day.

> Worship consisted in waiting upon the Lord to hear His voice and to feel His power. Rituals, books, words and songs which were at one time vital expressions no longer for the most part retained their vitality. They were not necessarily expressions of the experience of the worshiper. Quaker worship was designed to prevent the substitution of form for Spirit by omitting forms established in advance of the time of worship and presenting an opportunity, in the silence of waiting, for the Spirit to appear in whatever form it chose to take. What that form would be no one could predict.[17]

Of course, all of this is still a form, but a more bare-bones form is hard to imagine.

Buddhism's strategy is different. In its Mahayana schools, Buddhism has embraced the idea of *upaya*, skillful means. This is the teaching that one should adjust the form of the teaching, the form that Buddhism itself takes, as necessary in order to fulfill the Buddhist goal of assisting people's search for enlightenment. Explicitly devising and embracing this teaching is good evidence of how conscious Mahayana Buddhists were of the relativity of all religious forms, very much including their own, and how intentional they were in making the teaching of the relativity of all religious forms a central part of the

Buddhist message. The *Heart Sutra* famously negates the foundational Buddhist doctrines in its awareness that they, like all religious forms, are only fingers pointing at the moon, only skillful means, not absolute Truth. It boldly asserts that this very act of negation is itself the "perfection of wisdom," thereby reaffirming freedom from clinging to views, even Buddhist views, as part of enlightenment.

Quakers and Buddhists, then, should, and often do, recognize that the words and actions of no religion possess the Truth and take all forms of worship, ceremonies, teachings, etc. with a grain of salt, including their own. Since Truth cannot be contained in any form, what counts is results: does this form of expression help people to actualize or be in touch with the Truth that is within them? If so, it is of value. That is the sole criterion that is consistent with their core affirmations. It follows that they should recognize that in the forms of worship, ceremonies, teachings, etc. of another religion there may potentially be something of value for them, a manifestation of emptiness or Truth that has the ability to speak to them. The Spirit moveth where it listeth; one cannot know in advance where it might appear. As Brinton wrote, we cannot predict the form it will take. It might well take the form of a teaching from another religion. Thus we need to be open to learning from other religions.

Drawing upon this kind of awareness, twentieth-century Friend Douglas Steere urges Friends to engage in spiritual learning from persons of other religions in a practice that he calls "mutual irradiation."

In this practice, each is willing to expose [him or herself] with great openness to the inward message of the other, as well as to share [their] own experience, and to trust that whatever is the truth in each experience will irradiate and deepen the experience of the other.[18]

The Dalai Lama also advocates this kind of thing and

has himself participated in some historic inter-religious spiritual encounters. He writes that

> It is good to meet genuine practitioners of different religions. Here you cannot really say "no" to the value of other religious traditions. According to my own religious experience and through personal contacts, my appreciation and knowledge about the deeper value of Christianity grew. These kinds of meetings can give a really powerful understanding about the value of other religious traditions.[19]

6. Religions are like languages.

I am a Quaker and a Buddhist, but I do not want to say that these religions "say the same thing." They do not say the same thing; their forms—their languages, ceremonies, etc.—are quite different. They are different life-worlds, internally quite consistent but, as forms, far apart. Yet because of their core beliefs about religious experience and religious language, they do not contradict each other in any final way.

Living as a Buddhist and as a Quaker, I have come to see that religions are like languages. The world looks one way within one language and quite different in another. Languages are not really mutually translatable. They are not interchangeable. Something is always lost in translation. Living in the Quaker life-world, one is immersed in a world with a strong flavor of divine and human love; a world of Biblical characters, hymns and symbols; a world in which one lives a kind of secular monastic life very much in the world; a world in which one is challenged to live up to the example of one's Quaker antecedents who spoke truth to power and played major roles in shaping the social and political life of England and America. As soon as one says, "Christ Within" or "Inner Light," all this is implicit. Living in the Buddhist world, one lives in the world of the serenely smiling

Buddha; a world whose vista embraces lifetime after lifetime of countless rebirths held in tension with an invitation to complete selflessness; a world in which one strives to remove all "thought coverings," to erase everything and plunge again and again into vast emptiness; a world in which one feels one's connectedness with all things and has compassion for all beings, the insect as well as the human. Say "Buddha Nature" and all this is implicit. These worlds overlap, but they are not the same. They are two life-worlds, two languages. On some points, they can understand each other deeply; on other points, they elude each other. This is exactly why they can learn from each other.

7. We know the presence of the Spirit by its fruits.

While I do feel a great closeness between Quakerism and Buddhism, and while I do think it right, on principle, for members of the world's religions to learn from each other, I still think it necessary to put some limits on this sharing and mutuality. I don't necessarily want to learn from just anyone, only those that I respect as expressions of the same Spirit that, I trust, is at work in the religions to which I am committed. Since anyone can start a religion for any reason, such a limitation seems to be necessary. Given my, and my religious traditions', mistrust of doctrine, it follows that I will look to the behavior of respected and revered persons in another religion to determine whether it seems to be a manifestation of the same Spirit by which I attempt to be led. We know the presence of the Spirit by its fruits in behavior. What particular behaviors do I look for?

1. **Unconditional love**, by which I mean a deep commitment to the well-being of all others, manifesting spontaneously in acts of gratuitous kindness, playing no favorites, except perhaps favoring the most needy.
2. **Selflessness, or self-forgetfulness**, putting oneself

second and others first, manifesting in acts of generosity and perhaps of courage.

3. Non-violence, gentleness, and kindness as a general rule. Nonetheless, sometimes one still must speak very directly, as when the prophetic voice is used.

4. Avoidance of rigid dogmatism. This is not to say that such a person does not have commitments and beliefs. However, those commitments will be worn with a smile, not a frown; they will not preclude friendship with persons of other beliefs.

In the presence of these behaviors, I know I am in the presence of the Spirit and I hope I am open to learn from the person who manifests them. The major (and, I am confident, many smaller) religions all have saints or the equivalent who manifest these kinds of behaviors. For those of us who believe in the universal presence of the Inner Light, this is no surprise. On the contrary, it is to be expected.

8. The supremacy of Spirit.

I close by letting my Quaker prophetic voice speak.

From a Quaker perspective, religious experience—the Inner Light—is everyone's most direct access to Spirit or Truth. I am greatly suspicious of any religious institution that uses exalted claims of its authority, its wisdom or paternal care, that raises fear, uses rewards or more subtle tools of influence and conditioning to insinuate itself between humankind and our own Inner Light, claiming, in effect, to speak for God. Any religious institution that claims for itself, "we alone possess the Truth; we alone possess access to salvation" errs gravely. The Truth, the divine and the power of the divine cannot be possessed. To make such a claim is, at best, the sin of pride, the sin of idolatry, the sin of confusing oneself and one's human instruments with the divine. *This* is the true original sin. At worst, such a claim is no more than a cynical arrogation of power by a mere human institution putting itself in the place of the divine. What Quakers call the Inner Light and what Buddhists call the Buddha Nature has, in fact, been known experientially by people in all times and places. It is our most inalienable and precious gift as human beings. It is this that gives us our best access to God, Buddhahood, Truth. To interfere in any way with any person's accessing and actualizing that Inner Light is a grievous sin.

Only God is God. Only the Holy is the Holy. We dare not interfere. The divine of which I speak is radically and universally immanent. I can only celebrate it, wherever it manifests itself, in whatever form, under whatever name. I know for sure that it manifests itself in Christian, Muslim, Buddhist, Jewish, Hindu, Baha'i, indigenous, Taoist, Sikh and countless other forms. That is in no way a problem. I can only regret, attempt to enlighten, or perhaps challenge any individual, or any institution— governmental, religious, or other—that attempts to control, stifle, suppress or erase it, in whatever form, under whatever name it manifests itself.

We cannot possess the Truth. We cannot possess the Spirit. The Spirit possesses us. All religions are but forms attempting to manifest the vast emptiness. A religion is most skillful when it manifests in a way that allows the Spirit to present itself but also remembers its own non-ultimacy, its own smallness and non-necessity. With the acceptance of one's own non-ultimacy comes the humility to accept that other religions can manifest Truth, too.

Contemporary Quakerism has several forms. Throughout this essay, I am referring to the form of Quakerism associated with the Friends General Conference. This branch of Quakerism maintains the original Quaker practices of unprogrammed Meeting for Worship and eschewal of paid ministry.

Notes

[1]Howard H. Brinton, *Friends for 300 Years* (Wallingford, PA: Pendle Hill Publications, 1952, 1964), p. xiii.

[2]His Holiness the Dalai Lama, *Ethics for the New Millennium*, (New York: Riverhead Books, 1999), pp. 225-226.

[3]Thich Nhat Hanh, *Living Buddha, Living Christ* (New York: Riverhead Books, 1995), pp. 34-35.

[4]Baltimore Yearly Meeting, *Faith and Practice of Baltimore Yearly Meeting of the Religious Society of Friends* (Sandy Spring, MD: Baltimore Yearly Meeting, 1988), pp. ii, 12.

[5]John Woolman, quoted in *Faith and Practice of New England Yearly Meeting of Friends* (Worcester, MA: New England Yearly Meeting Friends, 1985), p. 91.

[6]Thich Nhat Hanh, *Living Buddha, Living Christ*, p. 36.

[7]Ibid., p. 56.

[8]George Fox, *Journal*, ed. John L. Nickalls (1952), p. 33.

[9]Isaac Pennington, *Letters*, ed., John Barclay (1828), pp. 39-40; Letter XVI, undated.

[10]*Anguttara Nikaya* (Colombo, 1929), p. 115, cited in Walpola Rahula, *What the Buddha Taught*, revised edition (New York: Grove Press, 1959, 1974), pp. 2-3.

[11]Thich Nhat Hanh, *Living Buddha, Living Christ*, pp. 54-55.

[12]A. Stanley Eddington, *Science and the Unseen World* (1929), pp. 88-91, cited in *Faith and Practice of New England Yearly Meeting*, pp. 57-58.

[13]Thich Nhat Hanh, *Interbeing: Commentaries on the Tiep Hien Precepts*, edited by Fred Eppsteiner (Berkeley, CA: Parallax Press, 1987), p. 27.

[14]Testimony of Margaret Fell Fox. *Journal of George Fox*, II, 512, bicentenary edition. Cited in Brinton.

[15]Thich Nhat Hanh, *Living Buddha, Living Christ*,

pp. 38-39.

[16]My readers might still want to challenge my double-voicedness, saying: despite your views on religious language, these two paths are still incompatible, inasmuch as Quakerism affirms that, ultimately, there is something there (that you call Spirit), while Buddhists do not affirm that there is anything there, in any sense; there only is emptiness, an absence of something. While there is plenty here that philosophers, scholars and theologians could discuss, at the end of the day, I do not find an incompatibility here. If one held to a full-bodied Christian theology, there could be a problem. But Quakers have already taken a major first step. Many Quakers already shy away from unreserved affirmation of God as "a being," moving in the direction of a vague "Spirit." Quakers recognize many concepts of God in the Bible. Quakerism makes it possible to leave aside the God of classic theology understood as "a being" (though many Friends certainly accept that theology) and to embrace the God in whom we "live and move and have our being" (Acts 17:28). While Buddhism tends to take a resolutely apophatic path, a reality in which we live and move and have our being, or a reality which could be called Spirit, is not necessarily outside the pale of Buddhist thought, as is evident in the importance in Buddhism of Dhamma/Dharma (which means Truth and Reality, as well as the Buddhist teachings) and the great respect, in some branches, shown to something called Mind.

[17]Brinton, pp. 16-17.

[18]Douglas V. Steere, *Mutual Irradiation: A Quaker View of Ecumenism*, Pendle Hill Pamphlet No. 175 (Wallingford, PA: Pendle Hill Publications, 1971), p. 8.

[19]His Holiness Tenzin Gyatso, the XIVth Dalai Lama, "Dialogue on Religion and Peace" in David W. Chappell, ed., *Buddhist Peacework: Creating Cultures of Peace* (Boston: Wisdom Publications, 1999), p. 191.

Narrative Transformation: The Power of Interreligious Engagement

By Rachel Stacy

Imagine you are a ten-year-old boy living in the West Bank of the Palestinian territories. To get to school each day you have to pass through an Israeli security check point where you and your friends are systematically searched. Your book bags are opened and you are often instructed to lift up your jacket, shirt, or pant legs. Sometimes the soldiers dump all of your school supplies and your homework on the ground. It is worst when it is raining. Your only contact with Israelis is this daily ritual of humiliation.

Many of your friends have been arrested for throwing stones at the soldiers and your hatred for them prompts you to do the same. However, your mother has begged you over and over again not to provoke the soldiers. She wants you to finish your education and get out of Palestine. You cannot imagine what leaving home would be like; while Israel is only a few kilometers away, you are not allowed to cross the border.

Rachel Stacy is a practitioner and scholar of peace-building, alternatives to violence programs, inter-religious dialogue, and community development. She has written and presented on these topics to a variety of audiences around the world. Rachel holds a teaching degree from Towson University and a religious studies degree with an emphasis in peace and justice from the Earlham School of Religion. Throughout her work, Rachel has developed a passion for educating others about the people, culture, and peacebuilding efforts of the Middle East. As her experience in the region deepens, Rachel hopes to continue to facilitate the sharing of ideas, inspiration, and hope. This article was used with permission of the author.

One Saturday you and your father are out on the family's field harvesting olives. When the truck is full you climb into the cab with your father and begin the ride home. On the way you and your father pass by a small group of Israeli soldiers who flag the truck over and demand that you and your father get out of the vehicle. The soldiers begin yelling in Hebrew and you do not understand what is going on. You and your father only speak Arabic. You are motioned to place your hands over your head and you are pushed down onto the hood of one of the Israeli military vehicles. Your father is held down on the trunk of his truck in the same manner.

Your father's truck is searched and your toy gun is found among the olives. Your father tries to explain that it is a toy but the soldiers keep yelling. A crowd gathers near you. The yelling turns physical and your father begins receiving blows from the soldiers. You try to run to him but one of the soldiers continues to hold you down on the front of the military vehicle. Other people try to intervene and help, but the solider uses you as human shield between the locals and your father. At this point you are crying and have wet your pants. Your father begs the soldiers in Arabic to let you go. It feels like everyone is screaming.

Out of the crowd steps a tall white man with a full beard and a Jewish kippa on his head. This man, obviously a Jew, should not be in the West Bank. He moves between the soldiers and your father. He speaks with the soldiers who after a few moments of discourse begin shouting at him too. The Jewish man continues to shield your father from the soldiers' attacks even to the point of receiving a few of the blows. The Jewish man looks at you and says in Arabic, "Do not be afraid." You only start crying more.

News teams begin to arrive to document the incident. The soldiers, uncomfortable with the media attention and the presence of this Jewish man begin to back down and the one holding you releases you. You run to your father who cradles you on the ground. Eventually you and your father are allowed to drive home. When you and your father return home and tell others of the incident you can only talk about the strange tall Jewish man in a kippa who came to your rescue and who told you not to be afraid.[1]

In this story, the cultural narrative is one of humiliation and violence between two groups of people: the Palestinians and the Israelis. For a young child whose only interaction with the 'other' is negative, an experience such as this one challenges constructed biases. While the Jewish man in the story did help in the situation, his lasting effect is on the child.

There is great power in the establishment of new narratives that challenge existing ones. When experiences do not fit within a particular world view, a new synoptic must be created. This story is an example of a child who sees his "enemy" protecting him. While the boy is unlikely to immediately befriend the soldiers who are checking his backpack the next morning, he has an experience with a Jewish man that is different from the rest. This experience creates the possibility for the process of narrative transformation: a three part process of a) dispelling bigotry formed by mythology though interactions with the "other" b) intra/interreligious study to reform ideas about mythology c) community support to enact new narratives in everyday and ritualized life.

a) Dispelling bigotry formed by mythology through interactions with the 'other'

Experiencing the "other" is a complicated and emotionally challenging process. In some cases the "other" is a neighbor of the same religious and cultural background but with whom conflict may have occurred. While groups like the WI'AM Palestinian Conflict Resolution Center focus on intracultural reconciliation, the skills that are taught and learned at this center can be applied beyond cultural boundaries. The Alternatives to Violence Project (AVP) also teaches conflict resolution and community development. AVP has been used effectively across the world in the education of nonviolence.

Seeds of Peace, an organization founded in 1993 and "is dedicated to empowering young leaders from regions of conflict with the leadership skills required to advance reconciliation and coexistence."[2] Seeds of Peace works intraculturally by bringing young leaders from different sides of conflict together during a summer camp program in Maine. By living and learning together, participants establish constructive relationships with the "other."

Another program that attempts to cross cultural lines and bring different people together in dialogue is the Alternative Tourism Project. A conglomeration of several different nonviolence and conflict resolution organizations, the Alternative Tourism Project offers intricate itineraries for visitors of Israel and Palestine that bring outsiders into conversation with many different voices and opinions. Tourists may have the opportunity to speak with Palestinians, Israeli settlers, members of Israeli and Palestinian governments, different non-violence groups and leaders of educational institutions. By offering an experience of hearing many different stories, the Alternative Tourism Project attempts to deconstruct the idea of polarity and construct a sense of intricate complexity.

Teaching and learning the skill of storytelling creates the possibility of authentic interreligious dialogue. However, dialogue is an intricate and dynamic process unto itself. Leonard Swidler, a professor at Temple University, defines dialogue "as a conversation on a common subject between two or more persons with differing views, the primary purpose of which is for each participant to learn from the other so that s/he can change and grow." Therefore, interreligious dialogue is when the conversation between these different people or groups concerns faith and religion.

The image most often associated with dialogue is that of people around a table. There are things that each person or group must do in order to come and sit at the table. Once at the table each participant is expected to conduct themselves in a certain manner. When conflicts arise, the diverse assembly around the table must also know how to proceed. Then, once the dialogue is over, each participant must then proceed through the experience of leaving the table and returning home. This image of dialogue around a table will be used to frame the following exploration of the foundations of interreligious dialogue.

Coming to the table

Each participant who engages in interreligious dialogue must do so willingly. Invitations should be extended without judgment and the participants must refrain from coming to the dialogue with expectations of particular outcomes. In his article "Understanding Dialogue" Swidler expands on these requirements:

> What is needed for dialogue participants then is 1) an openness to learn from the other, 2) knowledge of one's own tradition, and 3) an equally disposed and knowledgeable dialogue partner from the other tradition. This exchange can happen on almost any level of knowledge and education. The key is the openness to learn from the other.[3]

Coming to the table also assumes that each participant is willing to learn and change. One must not enter into dialogue assuming that all the answers have already been discovered. Rather a certain sense of vulnerability is required where each participant is slightly critical of his/her own tradition and willing to seek out new experiences of truth. The process of coming to the table is risky and for that reason a foundation of trust must be built in order for people to feel comfortable sharing their stories.

At the table

Once everyone has arrived at the table, a common community can be developed. Community development models often begin with a period of introductions and pair these activities with work or worship. Sharing a common space and creating a common story engages the participants in an experience that requires each individual to rely on another and to rely on the community as a whole. Trust is formed. This period of community development is essential to dialogue. First, befriend the other as a fellow member of humanity; then engage the hard subjects with your friend (not the stranger). Each of us needs to feel a sense of safety in order to willingly engage the boundaries of our comfort and vulnerability.

Once introductions are complete and a sense of community is developed, dialogue on controversial religious topics can begin. The skill of storytelling keeps the sharing to the personal experiences of an individual or a religious group. Paired with authentic and meaningful storytelling is compassionate and active listening. More often than not, individuals feel in conflict with the other party when they feel that their stories are not being heard.

Active listening is a term created by Thomas Gordon in 1977 for his book *Leader Effectiveness Training.*[4] Since 1977, the methodology of active listening has been used by many different groups including pastoral care practitioners, counselors, and community leaders. Active listening includes the process of verbal summary from the listener back to the storyteller. By summarizing what has been shared, the storyteller is able to hear if the listener has achieved understanding. In this way questions and misunderstandings can be addressed. Active listening also includes eye contact, an engaged physical posture, and verbal affirmations. The listener, therefore, is not a passive object but rather an active participant in the sharing. There are several organizations that teach listening skills, including the Center for Nonviolent Communication and the Compassionate Listening Project, which demonstrates not only the necessity of listening to the dialogue experiences but also its complexity.

Non-violent communication (NVC) is a listening methodology that is a contemporary of active listening. Developed by Dr. Marshall Rosenberg in the 1970s, non-violent communication attempts to teach the dialogue skills needed in peacemaking efforts. NVC has been used all over the world and proven to be effective in resolving conflict. Nonviolent communication presumes that each individual desires to connect with another:

> With NVC we learn to hear our own deeper needs and those of others. Through its emphasis on deep listening—to ourselves as well as others—NVC helps us discover the depth of our own compassion. This language reveals the awareness that all human beings are only trying to honor universal values and needs, every minute, every day.[5]

Nonviolent communication demonstrates that the way we talk to each other affects the way we act towards each other. By abandoning communication dominated by blame, shame, and judgment, listening and sharing can form constructive ends.

The Compassionate Listening Project was founded by Leah Green in 1990 in conjunction with the Earthstewards Network. The Project uses a listening methodology developed by Gene Knudsen Hoffman from the teaching of Buddhist monk, Thich Nhat Hanh. Compassionate listening calls for "peacemakers to initiate humanizing contact and cultivate compassion for those on all sides of a conflict."[6] The project has brought more than 600 Americans to the Middle East to listen to the stories and feelings of Israelis and Palestinians from all sides and perspectives of the current conflict.

Sitting at the table also means staying at the table and when conflict arises, staying at the table can be very difficult. During the beginning period of community formation, it is useful to discuss personal needs in dealing with conflict. Some people need to verbally process anger and frustrations; other people need space and solitude to sort through their feelings. Physical touch may be welcomed during moments of grief or joy, but in some cultures physical touch, in this manner, is intrusive and taboo. The group around the table may find it helpful to come to consensus regarding the actions to be taken in working with conflict. That way, when conflict does arise, everyone will feel supported and respected.

Leaving the table and returning home

The last part of the dialogue process is the journey away from the table. While relationships may have been built during the time and space of the dialogue, social influences, family responsibilities and cultural expectations challenge the continuation of these relationships. Yet interreligious dialogue also consists of telling the story of the dialogue to one's community. In his article "Bringing the Dialogue Home," Jewish scholar Michael S. Kogan tells the story of engaging his students in an experimental Christian-Jewish dialogue. He then continued his "experiments" in activities with his Synagogue, local interfaith communities, the sharing of Thanksgiving and even being a guest preacher at several Christian churches. Kogan's story shows that interreligious dialogue is not a onetime event. Rather, as the dialogue transforms the individual, dialogue becomes a way of life.

b) Intra/interreligious scripture study to re-imagine established narratives

At the end of 2009, a small eighteen-page document was published by Christian Palestinians in both English and Arabic. Called the Kairos Palestine document, its aim was to provide a unified voice of Christian Palestinians against the occupation of Palestine by Israel. The document was named the Kairos Palestine document after the publication of the Kairos document in 1985 by a group of South African liberation theologians. In the original Kairos document, church leaders called for the church to examine its role in apartheid and take a stand against the injustices of South Africa. The Kairos Palestine document calls for a similar action and targets the Christian communities of Palestine, pleading for them to examine how they are contributing to the occupation and offering suggestions of nonviolent resistance.

The Kairos Palestine document is an example of intra-religious scripture study that is attempting to reimagine historically drawn lines between denominations on this topic. For communities such as the Roman Catholic and the Greek Orthodox which have been at odds for many years, the Kairos Palestine document is an example of one successful attempt to find reconciliation.

In addition, the Kairos Palestine document addresses Jewish and Muslim leaders broadening the audience to all the different sides involved in the conflict:

We address an appeal to the religious and spiritual leaders, Jewish and Muslim, with whom we share the same vision that every human being is created by God and has been given equal dignity. Hence the obligation for each of us to defend the oppressed and the dignity God has bestowed on them. Let us together try to rise up above the political positions that have failed so far and continue to lead us on the path of failure and suffering. [7]

While the Kairos Palestine document begins the dialogue, further interreligious study of scripture and mythology will need to be done to bring these religious groups together on common ground. There are many people from all the different sides of the conflict who are willing to search together for a solution but religious extremists from all three religious traditions continue to spin theology away from peace. Studying the scripture, theology and mythology of the various religious traditions may turn up unexpected results.

Another form of interreligious scripture study is the engagement of dialogue through worship. Interreligious dialogue through worship has at least two different forms. Members of different religious traditions can either create an interreligious worship with elements of each participant's tradition or observe and support the worship of a single dialogue participant. Maria Hornung, in her article "Making Dialogue Real," proposes that:

> Remarkable interfaith prayer movements and shared liturgies are more common than ever. The wisdom of experience and some of the findings recorded by theologians mitigate the fear inherent in stepping into these spaces of shared ritual. Where face-based exchanges at the grass roots are happening, the people involved are experiencing warmth, excitement, empowerment and hope.[8]

One example of an interreligious worship project is Fistula Stories.* Fistula Stories is a women's initiative that begun in 2009 out of a conversation of the Women,

---

* A fistula (pl. fistulas or fistulae) is an abnormal connection or passageway between two epithelium-lined organs or vessels that normally do not connect. Fistulas are sometimes caused by difficult pregnancies and lead to uncontrollable urination and other humiliating side effects. Poor women suffering from this condition in developing countries are often ostracized from their community. A documentary called "Walk to Beautiful" depicts how treatment of this condition has redeemed the lives of these unfortunate women. See www.pbs.org/wgbh/nova/beautiful/producer.html

Faith and Development Alliance Breakthrough Summit.[9] The United Nations granted the National Council of Churches a grant to develop educational and worship resources for communities of different ages and faiths on the global issues surrounding women's reproductive health. The NCCC worked with scholars from various denominational, faith, and cultural backgrounds to develop a curriculum for intra- and interreligious dialogue.

The premise of this project is that there is a common experience among all women that through faith communities can be explored and supported. The sharing of stories, prayer, songs, sacred scripture and liturgy among women of many faiths demonstrates the universality of the female experience. Meagan Manas, the grant coordinator of the project explains the choice of the project title "Fistula Stories":

> The title "Fistula Stories" seeks to honor the courage and dignity of women who are obstetric fistula patients and survivors by listening to their stories and hearing the connections to our own lives and the global women's movement. This curriculum also examines the connections between faith and action, exploring the complex components of giving and organizing "here" to help women "there." Through intentional conversations and actions we hope to work to bridge the divide and create a world where all women are valued.

The word "story" is important for many reasons. Women have often been storytellers, preserving for their communities the important memories of where they come from and who they are. It is critical for each of us to learn that she has her own story to tell, and to learn how to hear one another's story and share our own with integrity and respect.[10]

Dialogue through the sharing of worship connects the stories of the individual to the stories of the faith community. The Fistula Stories initiative developed a study curriculum for communities of many different faith traditions including: indigenous, Muslim, Jewish, Buddhist, and Christian. The curriculum included prayers and sacred scripture of the faith tradition as well as stories of women from these faith communities. In these ways, worship can aid in creating a space where dialogue can occur.

Another form of interreligious dialogue is the observance and support of worship of a different tradition. The most common example of this is the visitation of one faith community to another's place of worship. Political and religious leaders have gained a lot of publicity in visiting different places of worship. In 2006, the Pope visited several mosques in Turkey[11] and in November 2010, President Barack Obama visited one of the largest mosques in Indonesia.[12] Local communities also often visit each other's places of worship. The purpose of these visits is not to convert or convince one another to another faith, but rather to give people from different faiths an opportunity to experience the worth of another's worship and work towards a more informed understanding of the context of another's faith story.

In addition to observing a service of regular worship, participants also can engage in interreligious dialogue when attending the ceremonies of different religious traditions. Acts of purification and initiation are two examples of rituals shared among many different faith communities. In the observance of another's ritual, individuals are challenged to articulate why and how his/her faith traditions are true. In this way, interreligious dialogue strengths the individual's faith and his/her relationship with another.

Purification/ Water Rites

Water is a primordial symbol in mythology. It is a symbol of purification and rebirth. Water can be a destructive and a constructive force. In Genesis 6, God used the floodwaters to destroy civilization, purify the world of corruption and rebirth creation on earth. In such purification, life can begin anew. Water is essential to all life on earth, and from water life emerged. Thus the universal primordial symbolism of water is appropriate. Mircea Eliade writes:

> There can be no question here of "influences" or of "borrowings," for such symbols are archetypal and universal; they show man's position in the universe, while at the same time evaluating his position in regard to his god (to absolute reality), and to history. This symbolism of water is the product of an intuition of the cosmos as a unity, and of man as a specific mode of being in the cosmos.[13]

Jung identified water as a primordial symbol or archetypal image that described the nature of the collective unconscious. Water represents the dissolution of form, the return to pre-existence and the beginning of new creation. The collective unconscious connects all of life and exists beyond form. It existed before creation and within in its depths new creation emerges. Therefore both water and the collective unconscious carry a sense of eternity and infinity.

William Taber, a Quaker theologian, also used water to represent a collective experience. Taber described the communion of Quaker worship as individuals entering into an eternal stream. As worshippers step into this stream, they are swept up in the current of the Holy Spirit. This is why messages that emerge from Quaker worship speak to the communal experience, not just the experience of the individual who is sharing.[14]

Many other religious traditions use the symbol of water in mythology and ritual. Rituals of washing re-enact myths of purification and rebirth. Most Christians use water in their rituals of Baptism. A Jewish bath, known as a *mikveh*, purifies the individual of defilement and connects the individual to Adam and Eve.[15] Muslims wash their hands ceremoniously before prayer. Hindus are famous for their bathing in the sacred river Ganges and often sprinkle holy water over each other during sacred rituals. Many Native American religious communities worship in a lodge; they host ceremonies that include the purification of the individual and community through steam and sweat.

Through the conversations that result in reflection of the collective experience, individuals are challenged to articulate how the observed ritual compares and contrasts with their own traditions. Questions can be asked about the observed rituals. Emotional responses can be processed. The commonality of the purification/cleansing experience allows for individuals of different faith traditions to engage in emotional and intellectual understanding of why a community practices in these ways.

Initiation Rites

Initiation rites are still very common among contemporary religious communities and represent mythology of life's transitions. The rituals created around initiation are often elaborate and extremely structured. For example, the Xhosa tribe in South Africa initiates its young boys into manhood through a ceremony of circumcision. Some Islamic groups also practice adolescent circumcisions. Jewish communities celebrate the beginning of adulthood through the ritual of bat/bar mitzvah. *Mitzvah* means "of the covenant" and the Jewish ceremony establishes the child as an adult member of the community.

In some cultures, men and women undergo different rituals of initiation. Women's rite of passage usually is connected with fertility and therefore with a woman's first menstruation cycle. Many of these female rituals of initiation have been lost over time because of cultural bigotry and the devaluing of the female experience. In the southwest of the United States, the Apache tribe secretly preserved the fertility ceremony during years of religious and political persecution. When young girls reach puberty, the family chooses a female medicine woman to guide the girl through the ceremony and through womanhood. Then, during a four-day ritual, the young girls, dusted with pollen—the symbol of fertility—travel symbolically through the stages of life and arrive transformed into womanhood.[16]

The classic rite of passage is divided into three parts: separation, transition, and reintegration. The youth is first separated from his/her community and then proceeds through the process of transition. When the youth enters into adulthood, the rite of passage concludes with a journey of reintegration into the community as a transformed individual. This process is similar to Joseph Campbell's model of the hero's journey.[17] The hero's journey outlines a rite of passage where the hero leaves his/her community and embarks on an adventure. During his/her adventure, the hero completes many challenges and in the process is transformed. The hero then returns to his/her community as a new person. Joseph Campbell has researched the presence of the hero's journey in mythology across the world and throughout history. His work supports Carl Jung's theory of universal mythology: archetypes and stories that are rooted into all human imagination.

c) Community support to enact new narratives in everyday/ritualized life

While people can talk, study and worship together unless these transformed narratives are integrated into everyday life, daily rituals and interactions, change is unlikely to happen. Ritual, the enactment of meaning, is not limited to the formal space of interreligious dialogue sessions or specific worship experiences. Rather, ritual can be everyday encounters and shared life moments. Thus, something as simple as sharing a meal can ritualize an interaction between two people, build a sense of trust, and foster authentic dialogue. Joseph Campbell explains this phenomenon further:

A cocktail party is a ritual...You are performing a social ritual. You are conducting it when you sit down to eat a meal; you are consuming a life. When you're eating something, this is something quite special to do. And you ought to have that thought when you eat a carrot as well as when you eat an animal, it seems to me. But you don't know what you're doing unless you think about it. That's what a ritual does. It give you an occasion to realize what you're doing so that you're participating in the inevitable energy of life in its exchanges. That's what rituals are for: you do things with intention, and not just in the animal way, ravenously, without knowing what you're doing.[18]

Community support for cultural change is instrumental. One group, the Hebron Rehabilitation Center is working hard at fixing houses and providing jobs for Palestinians in Hebron in order to transform Hebron from its state of despair into a place of economic and social prosperity.

On the other side of the partition wall, the Rabbis for Human Rights are working both in Jewish and Arab communities to transform views of the "other" into stories of mutual solidarity. In the story that began this piece, one of the Rabbis acted out his beliefs in justice and his actions changed a larger narrative for the young Palestinian boy. Often talking and writing are not enough to create change, but physical action is transformative.

Various groups are also looking at the role of ritualizing change in the process of cultural transformation. Janin is a city at the northern edge of the West Bank and home to most of the past suicide bombers. Janin has a large refugee camp that has experienced grave poverty and extreme oppression. Several years ago an organization, the

Freedom Theatre, was started in the Janin refugee camp by a Jewish family, with the purpose of providing a creative outlook for the anger and frustration that was breeding among the refugee youth. The Theatre has been a huge success and now serves as an outlet for emotional expression, self-critique and the re-framing of political issues.

The production of 2011 was a spinoff of "Alice in Wonderland" where Alice taught the creatures of Wonderland that they held the power to liberate themselves from the oppression of the Red Queen. Alice, during the process of teaching others about their power, discovers her own power to liberate herself from an arranged marriage. Transformational ritual such as theatre offers communities a change to engage new narratives symbolically which then allows them to reenact these new narratives in their everyday life.

Palestine and Israel have the unique circumstance to have assistance in the creation of new ritualized narratives. The Ecumenical Accompaniment Program of Palestine and Israel (EAPPI) and the Christian Peacemaker Teams (CPT) offer international accompaniment, documentation and publicity to victims of injustice. More often than not it is the Palestinians seeking nonviolent help, but the two organizations go to great length to treat all of the people involved in situations with respect and dignity.

Conclusion

In 1998 John Stephens defined the term meta-narrative as a "global or totalizing cultural narrative schema, which orders and explains knowledge and experience."[19] Meta-narratives are stories about stories[20] and their totalizing affect can manipulate intercultural interactions. The process of narrative transformation a three part process of a) dispelling bigotry formed by mythology though interactions with the "other" b) intra/

interreligious study to reform ideas about mythology, and c) community support to enact new narratives in everyday/ ritualized life paving the way for intercultural change. As we learn about each other we also learn about ourselves and thus the process of narrative transformation is beneficial to all.

One last caveat: After the Second World War, the Religious Society of Friends set up relief projects throughout Europe. Young adults from around the United States, United Kingdom and other parts of the world traveled to Europe to work on these projects. They lived in meager tents and shared responsibilities of cleaning and cooking. The young adults came from various religious traditions and during the course of their time together, they engaged in interreligious dialogue. Many of these young adults ended up in their respective religious leadership and ran into each other decades later. Living together transformed each of them into more faithful people. The small insignificant rituals of life that transformed established narratives challenged and changed an entire generation of leaders.[21]

Footnotes

[1] Asherman, Rabbi Arik. Rabbis for Human Rights. Interview by Author. Personal Interview. Jerusalem, Israel, January 3, 2011.

[2] "About Seeds of Peace." www.seedsofpeace.org/about (accessed February 6, 2011).

[3] Swidler, Leonard. "Understanding Dialogue" *Interfaith Dialogue at the Grass Roots*. Philadelphia, PA: Ecumenical Press, 2008. 121

[4] Gordon, Thomas. *Leader Effectiveness Training*. New York: Wyden books, 1977.

[5] "The Center for Nonviolent Communication" www.cnvc.org/ (accessed December 5, 2010).

[6] The Compassionate Listening Project.

www.compassionatelistening.org (accessed December 5, 2010).

[7] Sabbah, Michel. *A Moment of Truth: a Word of Faith, Hope, and Love from the Heart of Palestinian Suffering.* Palestine: Kairos Palestine, 2009.

[8] Hornung, Maria "Making Dialogue Real" *Interfaith Dialogue at the Grass Roots.* Philadelphia, PA: Ecumenical Press, 2008, p. 100.

[9] Manas, Meagan. Fistula Stories. fistulastories.org/curriculum/about/ (accessed December 7, 2010).

[10] Ibid.

[11] BBC News. "Pope makes Turkish mosque visit." BBC News Home. www.news.bbc.co.uk/2/hi/europe/6158811.stm (accessed December 7, 2010.

[12] Banks, Adelle. "Obama to visit largest mosque in Indonesia." www.christiancentury.org/article/2010-10/obama-visit-largest-mosque-indonesia (accessed December 7, 2010).

[13] Eliade, Mircea *Patterns in Comparative Religion* (New York, 1958), p. 164.

[14] Taber, William P. *Four Doors to Meeting for Worship.* Wallingford, PA: Pendle Hill Publications, 1992.

[15] Heilman, Samuel C. *Defenders of the faith: inside ultra-Orthodox Jewry.* New York: Schocken Books, 1992.

[16] "Rites of Initation." *Taboo - The Complete First Season (National Geographic).* DVD. Directed by Morris Abraham. U.S. and Canada: National Geographic Video, 2002.

[17] *Joseph Campbell - The Hero's Journey.* DVD. Directed by David Kennard. Unknown: Acacia, 2000.

[18] Collins, Tom. "Joseph Campbell - Mythic Reflections." Context Institute. www.context.org/ICLIB/IC12/Campbell.htm (accessed December 1, 2010).

[19] Stephens, John. *Retelling Stories, Framing Culture: Traditional Story and Metanarratives in Children's Literature* (Garland Reference Library of the Humanities). 1st ed. New York: Routledge, 1998.

[20] Lyotard, Jean-Francois. *The Postmodern Condition:*

A Report on Knowledge (Theory and History of Literature, Volume 10). Minneapolis: University of Minnesota Press, 1984.

[21] A story told to me as a young girl by a member of my Quaker meeting.

PART 4: INTERFAITH
ORGANIZATIONS

In the United States, interfaith work is the primary focus of two Quaker organization: the Christian and Interfaith Committee (CIRC) of Friends General Conference (FGC) and the Quaker Universalist Fellowship (QUF). Close ties connect these two groups, with some Friends belonging to both. QUF recently started a blog called quakeruniversalist.org which also features posts by CIRC. This chapter describes the history and work of these organizations, and also of the World Parliament of Religions, the organization that launched the modern interfaith movement in 1893.

CIRC and QUF are not the only Quaker organizations involved in interfaith reconciliation work, however. The American Friends Service Committee (AFSC) was founded by Quakers but has become a multicultural organization that has done considerable interfaith work, especially with respect to the Middle East. An article about the AFSC's work in this region is included in the final section of this book.

The Friends Committee on National Legislation (FCNL) is a Quaker lobby in Washington, DC, which works closely with other progessive faith-based lobbyists and has called upon Friends to become more engaged with the Muslim community and its efforts to promote peace and justice. When conservatives tried to prevent the creation of an Islamic center in lower Manhattan, FCNL circulated a petition that garnered 8,000 signatures and presented it to Faisal Rauf and his wife Daisy Khan of the Cordoba Institute. This chapter opens with a moving account of how Quakers stood in solidarity with this remarkable Sufi Muslim couple and their efforts to promote peace and toleration during a time of increasing Islamophobia.

Delivering the "We Stand with American Muslims" Petition

by Jim Cason

NEW YORK CITY, OCTOBER 13, 2010. Daisy Khan, Aylin Karamehmetoglu and other leaders of the Cordoba Initiative this week expressed deep appreciation to everyone who signed FCNL's "We Stand With American Muslims" statement. "When I first saw all of those names, it almost had me in tears," said Aylin Karamehmetoglu, who is chief of staff for the Cordoba Initiative Project that is the lead organization behind plans for the Islamic Cultural Center in New York City.

FCNL's Director for Communications Alicia McBride had arranged for the names of the 8,000 people who signed the statement to be printed on four large posters. On Wednesday, October 13, I delivered the large posters to the offices of the Cordoba Initiative in New York City and spent about an hour talking with the leaders of that project about the petition, about Quakers, about our FCNL efforts to build bridges of understanding with American Muslims and the future plans for the cultural center.

Standing in front of the four posters, Daisy Khan, who is Executive Director of the American Society for Muslim Advancement, asked, "Who are all of these people?" I explained, "These are people from all over the country who wanted to offer a statement of support for your efforts." Here at FCNL, I said, we knew immediately that there would be many people across the country who would want to add their support for this effort and that's why

---

Jim Cason is a lobbyist for the Friends Committee for National Legislation. Source: www.fcnl.wordpress.com/2010/10/13/delivering-the-we-stand-with-american-muslims-petitions. Used with permission of author and FCNL.

we developed this petition. As we spoke in the bustling offices of the Cordoba Initiative, several other staff filtered in and out of the room. "So many names, so many names," said another person.

As I entered the offices of the Cordoba Initiative with a friend who came along to take some pictures, we saw volunteers sitting in chairs, perched on couches, and occupying almost every empty space and table. Some typed on computers while others answered phones or sorted through the stacks of mail and other correspondence that has flowed into their offices since the public controversy over plans for the center first erupted this summer.

"We see the center as a collaborative effort for all," explained Daisy Khan. "The center is about collaboration, about peace and tolerance." She expressed concern that the debate about the community center had come down to "which side are you on? Are you against the center or in favor of it?"

I explained that we at FNCL hope that the conversations, interactions and exchanges that are sparked by this proposal offer an opportunity to get beyond the discussion of "do you support the cultural center or oppose it?" I told my hosts that we at FCNL have heard that some of the 8,000 people who signed the petition have also been organizing forums or writing letters to the editors of their local newspapers, making the point that this moment could provide an opening for Christians, Muslims and people of other faiths to learn more about each other and find out what they have in common.

We spoke for some time about the Koran's teaching that the spark of God is in everyone, a perspective, I said, that sounded remarkably similar to the Friends perspective that the Light of God is in every person. Daisy Khan, who is a leader of the Women's Islamic Initiative in Spirituality and Equality (WISE), expressed a particular interest in learning about the spiritual grounding of the Friends who were active with the Suffragette movement in this country. I suggested that when she visited the FCNL offices here in DC, we might also go across the street to the building that was the headquarters of the National Women's Political Party.

Pointing to several of the names on one of the posters, Daisy Khan asked if I could say a little more about the individuals who had added their names to the statement. Fortunately, I recognized the name of one Friend who I knew of. "Oh, he's a war tax resister," I said. "A war tax resister, what is that?" said Daisy Khan. I explained that many Friends objected to paying taxes that would go to pay for war. As a matter of principle, some of our constituents refuse to voluntarily pay the proportion of their taxes that pay for the Pentagon and other war fighting. "I think some Muslims could support that as well," she said with a smile.

While we were talking, Imam Feisal Abdul Rauf called in to add his appreciation to the 8,000 signers of the petition. "We know the Quakers. You have been with us," he told me. "Thank you." In was in his role as Imam of Masjid al-Farah, a mosque 12 blocks from the site where the World Trade Center had once stood, that Imam Feisal first proposed the building of the cultural center. We spoke for several minutes more before I returned to the conversation with his colleagues in the office.

The Cordoba Initiative and the American Society for Muslim Advancement have been overwhelmed by the reaction to their proposal. No one could have anticipated the hate speech and the stereotyping. Sitting in their offices, I was amazed at the humanity I saw from my hosts who have endured in the last month more insults and slanders than most people have to confront in a lifetime. As we spoke, Aylin returned to the challenges of how to get out their message in a media environment that seems sometimes to focus only on the controversy and the protests.

Yet Daisy Khan added that the awareness that 8,000 people could come together to stand with American Muslims was also a part of the untold story of this moment.

"We feel the interfaith community standing behind us," she explained. "This is the untold story. We would not have been able to survive the full-fledged onslaught without the aid of the interfaith community." She added that when the attacks first started coming in through the media they wondered how to respond. "But when we turned around, we realized that we had all of these interfaith people behind us, supporting us."

"Thank you," she added. "And please express our thanks to all of the people who have added their names to this statement."

Quaker Univeralist Fellowship: Twenty-Five Years of Quaker Universalism

By Rhoda R. Gilman

In May, 2008, the Quaker Universalist Fellowship turned 25 years old. Many Friends would argue that what we usually call Quaker universalism is as old as the Society of Friends itself and has been alive and well for 360 years, not only 25. Yet around the year 1980 there was a strong impulse among Friends on both sides of the Atlantic to reaffirm the universality of Quakerism in a world vastly different from that known by George Fox. The result was two new organizations, formed within a period of five years: the Quaker Universalist Group in the United Kingdom and the Quaker Universalist Fellowship in the United States.

The Society of Friends had emerged from World War II with a new generation of pacifist leadership and a global reach. A sign of this was the Nobel Peace Prize, awarded jointly to the Friends Service Council of London and the American Friends Service Committee in 1947. During the 1950s and 1960s, as the United States and the Soviet Union remained frozen in a balance of nuclear terror, old patterns of colonialism dissolved elsewhere in the world. New voices called for human rights, spiritual renewal, and a struggle for justice through nonviolent protest. Across Asia, Eastern faiths were reawakened both by the challenge of Western science and the hope for

Rhoda Gilman is a long-time member of Quaker Universalist Fellowship and former editor of the Universalist Friends. © *Friends Publishing Corporation.* Friends Journal, *August 2008. Reprinted with permission. To subscribe:* www.friendsjournal.org

independence and social change.

Among Friends a few like Teresina Havens had already been attracted by Buddhism with its close parallels to Quaker practice, and many had listened to the words of Mohandas Gandhi. Although his voice was stilled in 1948, he was soon echoed by others like Thich Nhat Hanh in Viet Nam and the Dalai Lama from Tibet. By 1970 popular culture in the West had been stirred, and a powerful wave of Eastern spiritual practice was sweeping through Europe and America, accompanied by a renewed interest in mysticism and esoteric religion of all kinds.

There was also a counteraction. While unprogrammed Friends, like other liberal Christians, flocked to Zendos and practiced mindfulness meditation on meetinghouse benches, Friends Evangelical churches grew by leaps and bounds through missionary work in Africa and Latin America. At the same time more traditional Friends in England and the United States defended the Christian foundations of Quakerism.

In 1977 John Linton addressed the Seekers Association in London. He had worked and worshipped for many years in India, and he spoke from his experience at the New Delhi Friends Meeting when he challenged Quakers to cut their historic ties to Christianity and fulfill their destiny as "a faith that no longer divides but unites humanity." The time was ripe, and Friends who had silently felt the same need went public in 1979 to form the QUG. Three years later American Friends invited Linton to bring his message across the ocean, and in 1983, at a gathering held in London Grove Meeting House near Philadelphia, the QUF took shape.

Both groups were small and have remained so. Quakers are busy folk, and some questioned the need for yet another organization to support. In America the QUF also faced barriers of distance and diversity, and active membership was almost by necessity concentrated in the mid-Atlantic states. For a few years the QUF held semiannual lectures and workshops. Papers given at them were printed as pamphlets and mailed to a wider membership around the country, accompanied by a short newsletter. Governance was informal, since IRS codes did not then require incorporation for religious nonprofits, and the active members were a small, well-acquainted group. In time lectures were dropped or were occasionally co-sponsored with other Quaker organizations, but publishing continued.

The *de facto* headquarters and distribution center of the QUF became the 1850 stone farmhouse of Sally Rickerman, who served as treasurer, membership clerk, printer, and sometimes editor. She also maintained outreach by mounting displays and selling pamphlets at the annual gatherings of Friends General Conference. Although the subscriber list was not over 300, pamphlets and the newsletter were mailed on their twice yearly schedule, and in 1986 the QUF produced a 100-page collection of six pamphlets originally published by the QUG in Britain. Its ambitious title was *The Quaker Universalist Reader Number 1.*

A rather sleepy appearance, however, belied the group's lively intellectual presence. Differing interpretations of universalism evoked searching discussions about whether identification with the Christian history and cultural heritage of Quakerism were essential to a spiritual understanding of Quaker practice, even if not needed for "salvation." In short, are universalists of differing religious faiths truly Friends? Can Christocentric Friends be considered universalist?

Boundaries were pushed even further as Friends in various meetings became concerned about embracing Wicca or paganism and accepting nontheists. Some who felt under suspicion by their own meetings maintained that the QUF provided them shelter and a spiritual home; others argued that Quaker universalism by its very nature should be a unifying force, embracing all, and not standing at the opposite pole from any beliefs. Two QUF pamphlets, including one by Dan Seeger, its most frequent and bestselling author, became staples of the "Quakerism 101" curriculum produced by Philadelphia Yearly Meeting.

Less controversial over the years were essays and meditations on Buddhist, Hindu, and Islamic thought and ongoing reflections on the theme of mysticism. Universalists argue for the relationship of early Quakerism to the mystical movements of late medieval Europe, and their interest in the history of that period has led to the reprinting of two 17th-century pamphlets never before made available to modern readers. [*The Light Upon the Candlestick*, 1663/1992; *Fifty nine Particulars — To the Parliament of the Comon-Wealth of England*, 1659/2002]. Also reprinted have been two studies on the militant forerunners of Quakerism in 17th-century England, written by David Boulton.

As it entered the 1990s, the QUF described itself as:

> . . . *an informal gathering of persons who cherish the spirit of universality that has always been intrinsic to the Quaker faith. We acknowledge and respect the diverse spiritual experience of those within our own meetings as well as of the human family worldwide; we are enriched by our dialogue with all who search sincerely. We affirm the unity of God's creation.*

During its second decade the communications revolution brought by computers and the internet had a transforming effect. The first step, taken in 1995, was to start a conversation among widely scattered QUF subscribers. Until then they had been largely silent, but an e-mail list allowed them to exchange views, life stories, and experiences. Within a few months there was correspondence from Canada, Australia, Japan, England, and all corners of the United States. Some pieces were suitable for short articles, and the newsletter soon took on the character of a small journal.

A year or so later a Web site was created. It went through several incarnations until in 2003 it became the main publishing arm of the QUF and revitalized the e-mail discussion list with new technology. By then the physical labor of printing, folding, stuffing, and mailing the newsletter and pamphlets, plus the hours required to keep an accurate roster of paid-up members, had outgrown the energy of a handful of aging volunteers. Meanwhile, the freedom and worldwide reach of electronic publishing promised a powerful way to spread ideas and sustain discussion. So the decision was taken to make all publications except books available without charge on the internet and to rely for income on contributions from sympathetic and like-minded readers. The task of mounting on the Web the library of pamphlets is still going forward hand-in-hand with the production of new materials. [See www.universalistfriends.org.]

The growing visibility of the QUF on computer screens across the world accompanied more activity at annual FGC gatherings. In 1996 an overflow crowd attended the QUF interest group session, and since then a week-long series of programs has been sponsored nearly every year. A further step was taken when members decided to devote a modest legacy received in 2003 to bringing distinguished plenary speakers to the gathering — a service that had been performed for some years by *Friends Journal*. Named in honor of Elizabeth Watson, an author and long-time spokesperson for Quaker universalism, the QUF lectureship sponsored John Shelby Spong in 2005 and Marcus Borg in 2007.

Those speakers, along with a lecture by Elaine Pagels, which QUF cosponsored with Philadelphia Yearly Meeting in 2006, reflect a new current within the wider world of mainstream Christianity. It has been stimulated during the past century by scholarly study of the Bible and by the rediscovery of ancient texts long excluded from the Christian canon. One spokesperson for this current, Patricia Williams, is the present editor of QUF's newsletter/journal *Universalist Friends*. She has recently been invited to membership in the Westar Institute, best known as the organization that sponsors the "Jesus Seminar," and she is the author of *Quakerism: A Theology for our Time*, published last year in England. "All Quaker libraries might wish to have at least one copy" of this book, according to a reviewer in the March, 2008, issue of the British magazine, the *Friend*.*

To Pat's work the QUF owes a milestone that marks the rounding out of its first 25 years. Sifting through articles published in both *Universalist Friends* and its British counterpart, the *Universalist*, Pat selected material for two additional Quaker universalist "Readers." Entitled *Universalism and Religions* and *Universalism and Spirituality*, the volumes bring together a wide range of Quaker voices from both sides of the Atlantic. Although differing greatly in the words and images they use, the authors, each in his or her own way, address the agonizing problems of 21st-century global civilization and the religious conflict that threatens to destroy it. All call for Quakerism to fulfill John Linton's vision of "a faith that no longer divides but unites humanity."

*Patricia Williams no longer serves on the board of QUF, and the newsletter has been replaced by a blog: quakeruniversalist.org, which is managed by Rhoda Gilman and Anthony Manousos. QUF continues to seek new ways to make its Universalist message relevant and available in the 21st century.

Christian Interfaith Relations Committee (CIRC)

Addressing "that of God" in every person, the Christian Interfaith Relations Committee (CIRC) attempts to promote mutual understanding and to engender closer ties among those of differing religious persuasions. CIRC is a committee of Friends General Conference (FGC), a national Quaker education and service organization for its member yearly and independently affiliated monthly meetings. FGC's activities include sponsoring gatherings, publishing books and pamphlets, and encouraging various forms of ministry among Friends.

Whether it is within the family of Friends or within the wider ecumenical and interfaith community, CIRC participates in and creates opportunities for cooperation and understanding, thus giving expression to the leadings of the Spirit and faith we profess.

CIRC was founded by Hicksite* Friends just prior to the first World Parliament of Religions so that there could be a Quaker presence at this historic gathering, which took place in Chicago in 1893. Ironically, there were two delegations of Quakers—Hicksite and Orthodox—who took part in this event designed to promote interreligious understanding. They were not on speaking terms.

---

*Hicksite refers to the branch of American Friends named after 19th century American Quaker Elias Hicks. Because of theological and other differences, Hicksite and Orthodox Friends separated into two groups in 1827. They reunited in the early 1950s.

This article was compiled by Anthony Manousos in collaboration with Tom Paxson (whose help was invaluable) and the Christian and Interfaith Relations Committee of FGC, which gave permission for its use.

Regarded by many as the beginning of the modern interfaith movement, the World Parliament of Religions provided a venue where Eastern religious leaders first had the opportunity to address Western people of faith. This experience helped to make Friends along with other Christians realize how important it is to listen to and dialogue with those from religious traditions other than one's own. In 1902 CIRC joined with three other Hicksite Committees to form Friends General Conference.

During its long history, CIRC has encouraged Friends to become involved in interfaith and ecumenical dialogue at both the individual and corporate level. In 1970 Ferner Nuhn, a member of CIRC, wrote an FGC pamphlet about "Friends and the Ecumenical Movement," focusing mainly on one-on-one encounters.

CIRC has also made it possible for the Quaker community to engage in dialogue with other religious communities through appointed representatives. In this way, Friends have been part of the ongoing religious dialogue that is transforming the Christian world. CIRC has also shown interest in the growing interfaith peace movement and has provided support for Friends interested in learning more about grassroots efforts to build interfaith understanding and trust in the wake of 9/11/2001. CIRC also supports ecumenical dialogue among Friends of different theological perspectives.

World Council of Churches

CIRC recommends appointments of representatives to the World Council of Churches (WCC) and the several commissions of the National Council of Churches (NCC). These appointees become invited members of CIRC and regularly report on their work to CIRC.

The WCC is an international Christian ecumenical organization. Based in Geneva, Switzerland, it has a membership of over 340 churches and denominations, and those churches and denominations claim about 550 million Christian members throughout more than 120 countries. The first Assembly of the WCC took place in Amsterdam in 1948. The Assembly continues to be the fundamental policy-setting body of the WCC, which is indeed a "council of churches." CIRC recommends appointments of FGC delegates to the WCC Assemblies. Sometimes these delegates are named by the WCC to commissions and other working groups of the WCC that meet between Assemblies, but sometimes the member churches are invited to nominate others, as was the case when FGC nominated Christina van Regensmorter to Faith and Order. These commissions and working groups do much of the work of WCC (as do the staff) between Assemblies, but only within the policies and guidelines laid down by the Assemblies or preparatory to the Assemblies. FGC, FUM, and Canada Yearly Meeting are the Quaker member "churches" of the WCC. For example, FGC's representatives to the Harare Assembly (1998) were Rebecca Kratz Mays (PYM) and Tom Paxson (ILYM); FUM's representatives were Eden Grace (NEYM) and Joe Vlaskamp (NYYM); and Canada Yearly Meeting's representative was Ellen Pye. Representations were reduced for the next Assembly held in Porto Alegre (2006). FGC's representative was Alex Kern; FUM's, Jane Mutoro and Ben Richmond; and Canada Yearly Meeting, Katie Aven, but each member church could also send an advisor to the delegation to Porto Alegre. Tom Paxson and Eden Grace served in that capacity for FGC and FUM respectively.

Quaker educator and theologian Howard Brinton attended the first gatherings of the WCC in 1948, along with other Friends who served as "observers." (Anna Brinton attended the first assembly of the NCC.) One of Brinton's goals was to make sure that the pacifist element in Christianity be acknowledged. After considerable discussion, the WCC agreed that "war is contrary to the will of God. War as a method of settling disputes is incompatible with the teaching and example of our Lord Jesus Christ. The part which war plays in our present international life is a sin against God and a degradation of man." Brinton proposed an additional "prophetic" statement: "The Church has always demanded freedom to obey God rather than man." This statement in support of civil disobedience was approved after a period of silent reflection.*

The WCC is the broadest and most inclusive among the many organized expressions of the modern ecumenical movement, a movement whose goal is Christian unity. While the bulk of the WCC's founding churches were European and North American, today most are in Africa, Asia, the Caribbean, Latin America, the Middle East and the Pacific. During the Cold War era the WCC encouraged dialogue between Christians in the West and those in Eastern Europe and the Soviet Union. One of the important roles played by the WCC today is to encourage dialogue between the global North and South.

Besides sharing its testimony as a peace church, Friends have influenced the decision-making process of the WCC. After being strongly urged to do so by both the Orthodox churches and the African churches, the WCC recently began a shift from parliamentary procedure to consensus decision-making. Eden Grace, a Friend from New England Yearly Meeting, who served on a Special Commission charged with restructuring the WCC, including its decision making procedures, played an influential role in this process.

WCC's peace efforts included promoting the Decade to Overcome Violence (DOV), 2001-2010. As a worldwide ecumenical organization, the WCC aims to facilitate the emergence of a global movement of churches for peace by lifting up both new and ongoing responses of churches

---

*See "Howard Brinton and the World Council of Churches" by Anthony Manousos. *Quaker Theolgy.* Summer, 2010. Issue 17. http://quaker.org/quest/Manousos-QT-17.html

and people around the world to various manifestations of violence. The WCC is also committed to analyzing and interpreting these responses with a view to further challenge and encourage creative responses. In addition, WCC, by commissioning studies and theological reflections on related issues, attempts to stimulate the churches to consider the interconnectedness of different forms of violence, as well as to broaden the scope of responses to violence in its totality.

Identity and Message of FGC Friends

Along with expressing Quaker concerns on peace and justice issues, CIRC helps to express the identity and message of FGC Friends in various ecumenical and interfaith contexts. CIRC undertakes theological work on the identity and message of FGC Friends, particularly on topics which arise in the context of our ecumenical and interfaith relationships. CIRC issues statements in its own name except where empowered by the Central Committee to speak on behalf of FGC. CIRC participates as way opens in meetings, conferences, consultations, workshops or study processes related to the identity and message of Friends.

The National Council of Churches USA (NCC)

The National Council of Churches USA is a community of 35 Christian communions in the United States. For more than 50 years it has been the primary national expression of the movement for Christian unity. Some 45 million congregants in more than 100,000 congregations belong to the faith groups that hold membership in the Council—a diverse ecumenical family including mainline Protestant and evangelical denominations, "living peace churches" such as Quakers, members of the Orthodox family of churches and most of the historic Black denominations.

FGC was involved in the NCC's predecessor, the Federal Council of Churches, which began in 1908. The NCC was formed in 1950. One of its first accomplishments was publishing the Revised Standard Version (RSV) of the Bible (1951). Notable Quaker New Testament scholar Henry Cadbury (1884-1973) played a leading role in this project. (The more recent New RSV with inclusive language is also a project of the NCC.)

The NCC shares many peace and justice concerns in common with Friends' organizations like the AFSC and FCNL. It has long voiced support for minimum wage laws, environmentalist policies, and affirmative action. NCC also played an important role in the civil rights movement in the 1960s. It partners with other groups, such as Bread for the World, Habitat for Humanity, and Children's Defense Fund, to press for broad policy initiatives that address poverty issues. The Council helped launch the Let Justice Roll grassroots anti-poverty campaign that has been successful in raising the minimum wage in a number of states since 2005.

FGC appoints representatives to NCC commissions such as Interfaith, Justice and Advocacy, and Education and Leadership Ministries. CIRC supports Friends' participation in the Faith and Order Commission of NCC. Such participation is sometimes undertaken in cooperation with Friends United Meeting (FUM) and Philadelphia Yearly Meeting (PYM) (both of which are members).

In the 1990s the NCC sponsored a series of consultations with the Historic Peace Churches (HPC) to explore the role of peace witness to Christianity. A number of Friends were involved in these three consultations, and two books were published, each containing a chapter by a Friend: "Jesus and Peace" by Paul N. Anderson in The Church's Peace Witness (1994) and "The Peace Testimony of the Religious Society of Friends" in *The Fragmentation of the Church and Its Unity in Peacemaking* (2001) by Thomas D. Paxson, Jr. The Faith and Order Commission of NCC came to conclude that the peace witness was central to being Christian.

NCC has played an active role in Middle East and other international peace efforts, as has the WCC. It has organized meetings and consultations over many years to create language and perspectives that helped to shape the Camp David Accords. NCC has gathered statements about Christian yearnings for peace and published them on a well-regarded Arab language website. NCC has sponsored trips and delegations to Israel/Palestine, Iraq, Iran, Lebanon and places in the Middle East to promote understanding and peace. The NCC has also been a major voice opposing the violence in Darfur.

NCC also sponsors local and national concerns, such as the Katrina Commission. (Thomas Swain, clerk of Philadelphia Yearly Meeting, serves on this Commission.) The Church World Service, a program of NCC, sponsors the CROP walk.

Many noteworthy Friends have been involved with the NCC. Ann Riggs served for many years as Associate General Secretary for Faith and Order. Dorothy Day has served on NCC's Justice and Advocacy Commission; Michael Birkel served on Interfaith Relations; and Michael Gibson on Education and Leadership Ministries.

To find out more, see www.ncccusa.org, FaithfulAmerica.org (a spinoff from NCC), and www.fgcquaker.org/circ/index.html

Historic Peace Churches (HPC)/ Fellowship of Reconciliation (FOR)

CIRC appoints a representative to the Historic Peace Churches/Fellowship of Reconciliation Consultative Committee, and carries a concern for the work of that Committee. CIRC is attentive to opportunities for ecumenical and interfaith cooperation in work for peace and justice, and supports the leadings of Friends to participate in particular initiatives which may arise. CIRC carries a particular concern for collegial relations with the "peace fellowship" organizations within our ecumenical and interfaith partner institutions.

Friends United Meeting (FUM) and Other Friends' Groups

CIRC engages with emerging networks of Friends peace organizations (for example, the Quaker Peaceful Prevention of Violent Conflict Network) with a concern for bringing an interfaith/ecumenical perspective to these networks. The NCC and WCC are places where different branches of Friends meet and work together on various theological and social concerns.

Interfaith Peacemaking After 9/11/2001

CIRC is also seeking ways to reach out to Friends who are involved with the growing interfaith reconciliation and peacemaking movement that has developed since 9/11/2001.

Anthony Manousos, who joined CIRC in 2005, carries this concern and is active in interfaith organizations locally, nationally and globally. In 2006 he led a workshop on "Islam from a Quaker Perspective" at the FGC Gathering. In 2007, he led a workshop on "Compassionate Listening and Interfaith Peacemaking." In 2008 he received CIRC support to travel to Melbourne, Australia, to attend the Parliament of the World's Relgiions. He has a blog at laquaker.blogspot.com and can be reached at interfaithquaker@aol.com.

"Are We At the Dawn of a New Age of Global Sprituality? Reflections on the Parliament of the World's Religions"

by Anthony Manousos

In December 2009, I attended the gathering of the Parliament of the World's Religions (PWR) in Melbourne, Australia. This gathering has taken place in a major world city approximately every five years since 1993. Despite the global economic downturn, 5,500 people from all over the world attended this extraordinary occasion. There were religious leaders and seekers present from every imaginable religion, including many I had never heard of, such as the Mandaeans, a pacifist gnostic sect that was driven out of Iraq after the United States invasion. (Many of them have settled in Sydney, where they have close ties with Friends.) This was a unique opportunity to get to know sects I had read about but never experienced, such as the Zoroastrians, Jains, and Rastafarians. It was also an opportunity to hear and meet with some major religious leaders including the Dalai Lama, outspoken Catholic nun Joan Chittister, progressive Evangelical activist Jim Wallis (editor of *Sojourners* and many bestselling books), Jewish peace activist Rabbi Michael Lerner (editor of *Tikkun* magazine), Catholic theologian Hans Kung, Muslim intellectual/activist Tariq Ramadan, and others. The PWR is sort of the "Olympics" of the interfaith movement.

With the theme of this year's gathering, "Hearing Each Other, Healing the Earth," there was a major focus on the environment, with religious leaders from around the world affirming the need to take action against global warming. The timing of the Parliament gathering—just prior to the Copenhagen Climate Conference—helped to amplify these voices. It was significant that Muslims, Christians, Jews, and those of other faiths joined together on this historic occasion. There were not only panel discussions and plenary speeches, but also a Hindu "Declaration on Climate Change," which was read out and ratified by an august assembly of Hindu saints from India and around the world. The Parliament is not a legislative body, so it did not pass any resolutions, but petitions relating to the environment were circulated among attendees and sent to Copenhagen.

During the opening plenary on Thursday night, an aboriginal elder danced and played the didgeridoo while the Melbourne symphony orchestra played and performers from various traditions sang. There were benedictions by Jews, Sikhs, Muslims, and Buddhists, as well as speeches by various religious leaders and dignitaries. Other plenaries that focused on the concerns of indigenous peoples and youth were just as extraordinary.

The first Parliament of World Religions took place at the Chicago World's Fair in 1893, which is considered the beginning of the modern interfaith movement. Thousands of people took part in this historic occasion—the first time that Christian and non-Christian religious leaders met and had religious dialogues on a more or less equal footing. (To learn more about this remarkable gathering, I recommend *The Dawn of Religious Pluralism: Voices from the World's Parliament of Religions, 1893*, ed. Richard Seager, 1993.)

A significant number of Quakers took part in the first Parliament, and many reports about it appeared in *Friends Intelligencer*. There were, in fact, two Quaker delegations: one Hicksite and one Orthodox! The Hicksite group went on to form the Christian Interfaith Relations Committee (CIRC), which became part of Friends General Conference (FGC) when it was founded in 1900.

There are similarities between the PWR and FGC Gatherings. Like the FGC Gathering, the Parliament is an educational forum, not a deliberative body, with workshops, notable speakers, and opportunities for networking. There are also parallels between the Parliament and the World Council of Churches (WCC). However, unlike the WCC, the Parliament is bottom-up, not top-down, in structure.

The goal of the PWR is to create a worldwide grassroots movement—to raise awareness and to transform the religious cultures of the world. That is an ambitious goal, but one being accomplished not only by its five-year gatherings, but by creating a network of "partner cities" that organize local events with a global perspective on interfaith work.

It is exciting to be part of a movement that seeks to transform the religious culture of the world, and thereby promote peace and justice.

For me, the interfaith movement and the Parliament have been deeply spiritual experiences, comparable to my becoming a Friend. When I joined Princeton Meeting in 1984, it was the beginning of a new life—a life based on spirituality and friendship such as I had never known before. Attending my first FGC Gathering in 1986 was a peak experience in this new life. Being surrounded by nearly 2,000 warm and enthusiastic Friends was like being in heaven! Since then, I have gone to the Gathering as often as I could—at least a dozen times—and have always felt uplifted.

Becoming involved with the interfaith faith movement after 9/11 was the next big step in my spiritual development. While Quakerism (thanks to FGC and FWCC) opened me up to a worldwide community of Friends, the interfaith movement opened me up to a much bigger world of people from diverse religious traditions— Buddhists, Muslims, Jews, Baha'is, Sikhs, et al. Despite our differences in religious practices and beliefs, we all share a common purpose and vision—the hope of building a pluralistic world where people of different faiths cooperate for the common good. When I went to the Parliament for the first time, it was like going to the FGC Gathering, only on a much grander and more universal scale. It was as if everyone I met—no matter how strangely garbed—was a Friend!

Since returning from the Parliament, I have been working full-time as a volunteer interfaith peace activist, organizing events, workshops, vigils, and other activities. In the summer of 2010, I plan to give presentations about the interfaith movement and the Parliament at various yearly meetings and also at the Gathering, where I will give an interest group talk sponsored by Quaker Universalist Fellowship (QUF).

The interfaith movement is comparable to the ecumenical movement, which began in the 19th century and came to fruition with the formation of the WCC in 1948. The WCC, which was supported by many (but not all) Friends—including FGC—dramatically transformed Christianity, especially after Vatican II, and helped to foster a spirit of cooperation and trust among Christians. The interfaith movement and the Parliament, I am confident, will bring about an even more historic transformation of religious cultures throughout the world in the 21st century. Hans Kung, who attended the first modern PWR in 1993, summed up the program of the interfaith movement with these memorable words: "There can be no peace among nations without peace among the religions. There can be no peace among religions without dialogue. And there can be no dialogue without a common ethic."

During the Parliament gathering, I gave a workshop on "Listening with a Heart of Mercy," which I felt was well received. The room was packed with over 60 people. I showed the documentary video *Compassionate Listening*, talked about my trip to Israel/Palestine with the Compassionate Listening project, and led the group in a compassionate listening exercise. My co-leaders were Noor

Malika, a Sufi Muslim, and Ruth Broyde-Sharone, a Jewish filmmaker. Both work with me on the local chapter of the Parliament. We discussed how to overcome obstacles to deep listening through a process very similar to our Quaker clearness committee.

There were so many outstanding workshops (a total of 650, with over one thousand presenters) that it was difficult to choose which to attend. I took a workshop with Michael Lerner and had a chance to talk with him later about compassionate listening. I attended a session in which Jim Wallis, Joan Chittister, Rabbi David Saperstein and others discussed what the religious communities needed to do to help end poverty. I attended a session on spiritual healing led by aboriginal people, which I found fascinating.

Over the course of a week, I was impressed by the surprising diversity of programs and how they met the needs of a wide range of people of different ethnic, racial, and religious backgrounds.

This Parliament will no doubt have a far-reaching effect on future religious leaders in the United States, and perhaps the world. Over a hundred seminarians from the U.S.—future ministers, imams, and rabbis—attended, thanks to a generous grant from the Henry Luce Foundation for a program entitled "Prepare Religious Leaders for a Multi-Religious World." Each of 15 seminaries and schools of theology sent four to ten students and one or two faculty members.

We had the opportunity not only to hear panel discussions with major scholars like Hans Kung, Tariq Ramadan, and Evelyn Tucker, Professor and co-director of the Forum on Religion and Ecology at Yale University, but also to take part in workshops by charismatic religious figures who are not well known but had much to teach, like the Rastafarian musician and author Yasus Afari , with whom I felt an unexpectedly deep heart connection. There was singing, dancing, and meditation, as well as art from all over the world.

On the last day of the Parliament I felt a leading to go to a session in which Tariq Ramadan was speaking. I have read one of his books and was deeply impressed. During the George W. Bush administration he was denied a visa and not allowed to enter the U.S. and teach at Notre Dame University because of alleged ties to terrorists; he currently teaches at Oxford University. He was giving a reflection on Islam and justice, and during the question period, I felt led to speak about his not being allowed to come to the U.S.; I apologized "on behalf of Americans who care about justice."

I was also impressed with a session given by Australian Quakers, which was attended by more than 60 people. The four presenters—Catherine Heywood, Susan Ennis, Beverly Polzin, and Sieneke Martin—each discussed a different aspect of Quakerism: history, worship, decision-making, and service, followed by small-group discussions, questions, and finally, a short (20-minute) meeting for worship. Brochures, pamphlets, and books were available for people to take home with them.

The closing plenary included not only blessings by various religious leaders, but also a statement by Indigenous leaders from around the world who met to discuss their common issues. They provided a seven-point program for addressing the concerns of indigenous peoples, including taking care of the Earth, respecting Indigenous peoples and their traditions, adopting the United Nations Declaration on the Rights of Indigenous Peoples, and returning the bones and relics of their ancestors.

The other highlight of the closing plenary was an address by the Dalai Lama. His appearance generated excitement as hundreds of people rose, applauded, and took pictures with their cameras and videos. As one of the best known, beloved, and respected religious leaders of the world, he offered encouragement—but also some "eldering." He concurred with our concern for the environment and for the rights of indigenous people, but he also warned us that we need action, not simply words. "You need to put our faith and principles into action and make a difference in the world. Otherwise you will become sleepy," he said, smiling. I hope we take his admonition to heart. I know that I feel very awake and energized after this gathering, and I look forward to sharing this energy with my religious community.

After the gathering, I traveled for a month to visit Australian Friends in Canberra, Sydney, Melbourne and Adelaide, where I found Australian Friends keenly interested and involved in interfaith work. This is not surprising since Australia, like the U.S., is a pluralistic society. Many are immigrants, and some have experienced mistrust and discrimination because of their religious beliefs. Quakers are needed to help create understanding and trust among these diverse groups, who sometimes feel alienated and need support.

Friends are also drawn to interfaith work because, as I see it, we are a universalist religion. We honor "that of God" in everyone and are open to learning from others, as well as sharing our own experiences of the Inward Light. This attitude is indispensable to those engaged in interfaith work.

A Canberran Friend gave me a booklet containing AYM advices and queries, which were adapted from those of Britain YM. I was favorably impressed by how the booklet's Advice No. 6 characterizes interfaith outreach:

Do your work gladly with other religious groups in the pursuit of common goals. While remaining faithful to Quaker insights, try to enter imaginatively into the life and witness of other communities of faith, creating together bonds of friendship.

The words that speak to my condition are "gladly," "imaginatively," and "friendship." These words beautifully describe how I experience and understand interfaith work.

It is my hope and prayer that Friends everywhere will open their minds and hearts to the interfaith movement and discover what it means to be part of what early Friends called "the kingdom of God," and what Martin Luther King Jr. felicitously called "the blessed community." This, I believe, is where the Spirit is leading us in the 21st century.

PART 5: FRIENDS AND ISLAM

One of the major spiritual and moral challenges for Friends and other people of faith after 9/11 was how to reach out in friendship and understanding to the Muslim community during a time of religious conflict and growing Islamophobia.

Many Friends responded to this challenge by visiting local mosques to express solidarity with and support for their Muslim neighbors. Some became involved with local intefaith councils, or invited Muslims to speak at their Meetings. Some began studying the Qur'an or fasting during Ramadan, or reading books by and about Muslims, in order to dispel stereotypes and become better acquainted with this much maligned religion.

In keeping with Quaker practice, Friends also engaged in self-examination through questions, or queries, like the ones by Linda Lotz published here.

QUF published two pamphlets about Islam—one by Michael Sells, a noted Arabic scholar who has translated the early parts of the Qur'an, and one I wrote called "Islam from a Quaker Perspective." Both pamphlets are included in this chapter.

CIRC responded through its involvement with the World Council of Churches, which sponsored Christian-Muslim dialogues. One of the most important of these initiatives was "A Common Word," a statement issued by over 300 Muslim scholars, inviting a response from Christian theologians. The CIRC response, included here, addresses the Muslim community with these words of affirmation:

We hope to be your partners in promoting understanding between our communities of faith. Both your Scriptures and ours call us to peacemaking. "Blessed are the peacemakers" (Matthew 5:9a). As the Qur'an states (49:13), "People, we created you from one man and one woman, and made you into nations and tribes, so that you may get to know one another. In the light of God, the most honored of you are the most mindful. God is all-knowing, all-aware."

We shall urge members of the Religious Society of Friends to create opportunities for deep listening and dialogue with Muslims in their communities in order to improve our mutual understanding and to work together with Muslims (and others) to make a more just and peaceful world.

As part of this effort to help Friends deepen their understanding of Islam, I led the first workshop on Islam at the FGC Gathering in 2004. The high point of this workshop was a field trip to the mosque in nearby Springfield, Massachusetts. For most of the 30 or so Friends who participated, it was their first time inside a mosque as well as their first experience of Muslim hospitality. Our hosts provided tea, fruit drinks, sodas, and cookies. We were warmly greeted by the imam (spiritual leader/minister) and by the president of the mosque. The imam chanted passages from the Qur'an and helped us to appreciate the beauty as well as the spiritual meaning of this sacred text. We had the opportunity to ask questions and to talk with Muslim women as well as men. We also had the chance to observe and to participate in the evening prayers. For some Friends, praying with Muslims was the spiritual high point of our workshop and of their time at the Gathering.

Efforts such as these to reach out to the Muslim community are an important first step in building relationships that can help to dispel stereotypes and build the foundation for a world of religious harmony instead of strife.

Queries for considering
the intersection of Islam and violence

by Linda Lotz

Linda Lotz, long-time activist and staff at the American Friends Service Committee, is married to a Muslim and deeply committed to interfaith peace and justice work. She provided these queries for a workshop about Islam that took place in the Philadelphia area in October, 2006. Her queries address some of the hard questions that need to be considered by those undertaking serious interfaith work.

♦ What do I know about the beliefs, customs, and history of Muslims worldwide? What sources do I rely on for information about Islam and the actions of modern day Muslims?

♦ What topics related to Islam and the experience of modern day Muslims would be helpful for me to explore through personal readings, travel, discussions at Meeting, and local interfaith discussions or projects?

♦ What core beliefs and values do Muslims and Quakers share?

♦ How have core Christian beliefs and traditions been used to support the use of violence? If individual followers engage in acts of violence and terrorism, does this make Christianity an inherently violent religion?

These queries used with the author's permssion.

♦ How do I feel about the attacks of 9/11? What have I learned about the motivations of the attackers, and the issues which formed the base of their grievances?

♦ What do I know about the political goals of Al Qaeda?

♦ What do I know and how do I feel about the role of the US in the Middle East prior to 9/11? How do I feel about the US response to the attacks on 9/11?

♦ What do I know and how do I feel about the goals and motivations of the policymakers who have promoted the "War on Terrorism"?

♦ How should Quakers view the "War on Terrorism" in light of the Peace Testimony?

♦ How could Quakers and Muslims work together to build world peace?

♦ If the US were to be suddenly occupied by people of another culture and language (or Martians?), how would I react? How would I respond if those occupiers were responsible for widespread oppression and deaths? Would I join a resistance movement? What kinds of actions would I take to end the occupation?

♦ What would have to happen in my life that I – or someone I know – would consider becoming a suicide bomber?

Islam from a Quaker Perspective

by Anthony Manousos

INTRODUCTION

Islam from a Quaker Perspective was written not long after 9/11/2001 when I felt led to fast during Ramadan as a way to reach out to and support the Muslim community. This was a time when over 1,200 Muslim immigrants were being detained without due process by the Bush administration, and many thousands more were being questioned, intimidated, and/or deported. During this period of fear mongering and Islamophobia, I felt it imperative to help dispel stereotypes about Muslims and to encourage constructive dialogue. Many Friends shared this concern. This pamphlet was first published by *Friends Bulletin* and by the Quaker Universalist Fellowship in the fall of 2002. In the spring of 2003 Wider Quaker Fellowship circulated over 4,000 copies to its readers in 105 countries. In 2007 German Friends published a German version, *Der Islam Aus Sicht Eines Quäkers.*

One of the most hopeful developments since 9/11 has been the growing interfaith movement. As I began visiting mosques and attending interfaith events after 9/11, I found myself drawn into this amazing movement. I came to know many wonderful Jews, Christians, Muslims, and other people of faith (as well as professed agnostics) who are working together to build bridges of understanding and to promote justice and peace. As I suggest in my article "Friends and the Interfaith Movement," the interfaith movement is transforming our society (and the world) in much the same way that citizen diplomacy helped to end the Cold War in the 1980s and the ecumenical movement transformed religious life in America during the

1950s and 1960s.

Over the past five years I have given numerous workshops and talks about Islam and interfaith peacemaking, mainly at Quaker gatherings, such as Friends General Conference and the three Western yearly meetings. As I prepared for these workshops, I came to appreciate the truth of Catholic theologian Hans Kung's prophetic words:

* No peace among the nations without peace among the religions.
* No peace among the religions without dialogue between the religions.
* No dialogue between the religions without common ethical standards.
* No survival of our planet in peace and justice without a global ethic.

I have been tempted to rewrite this pamphlet in light of the new experiences and knowledge I have gained since it was published in 2002. But to do so would detract from the value of this pamphlet as a personal response to an historical crisis.

To help bring this pamphlet up to date, I have added some footnotes and a list of resources. I have also included an article about interfaith peacemaking that was published in *Friends Journal* in 2007 (see Part 1: "Why the Interfaith Movement Matters").

Some have criticized this pamphlet for ignoring or sugarcoating the real problems in the Muslim world, such as suicide bombing, the horrendous treatment of women in many Muslim countries, etc. This is a huge topic that I hope to write about in the future. Suffice to say for now that Friends are deeply concerned about these problems and are seeking solutions consistent with our Quaker values. The most effective way I know to address these concerns is by working in solidarity with moderate and progressive Muslims who share our concerns. Whenever acts of terrorism take place, or there are violations of women's rights in Muslim countries, Muslim organizations in the USA such as the Council on American-Islamic Relations (CAIR) or the Muslim Public Affairs Council (MPAC) denounce violence and speak out strongly for peace, justice, and human rights. These Muslim voices of moderation carry more weight in the Muslim world than those of non-Muslims full of self-righteous outrage. Unfortunately, what moderate Muslims say often goes unreported in the media. What we usually hear instead are inflammatory statements by Islamic militants or by Islamophobes who believe in the myth of redemptive violence. As I make clear in this pamphlet, our task as peace makers is to support those who advocate the way of nonviolence.

Those who would like to know more are welcome to contact me at interfaithquaker@aol.com or to go to laquaker.blogspot.com or universalistfriends.org/weblog.

PART I: OBSERVING RAMADAN

After the tragic events of September 11th, 2001, I felt led to undertake a spiritual discipline that would help me to deal with feelings of grief, anger, and confusion and also to discern where the Spirit was leading me during this troubled time. I decided to fast one day a week until war, or the threat of war, ended.

I chose the Muslim form of fasting—abstaining from food and drink from sunrise to sunset—because I felt it would help me to feel more solidarity with those who belong to what the Quaker writer James Michener called the "world's most misunderstood religion."

On the first day of my fast (Friday, September 14), I read a moving story about Ramadan in a pamphlet by Gene Hoffman, a peace activist who pioneered in "compassionate listening" work in the Middle East. During Ramadan Gene paid a visit on a poor Palestinian family who made her lunch but didn't eat a bite of food. "Why are you doing this for me?" she asked. Their reply touched her heart and mine: *"Ramadan kareem.* 'Ramadan is generous.'"

This and other stories piqued my interest in Ramadan and those who observe it. What are Muslims really like? What can we learn from Islam that can help us in our spiritual work and in our work for peace and justice?

In 1991, during the Gulf War, I made my first serious effort to understand Islam and what is really happening in the Middle East. I incorporated Islamic texts into a world literature course I was teaching at a university. With my wife, who is a Methodist pastor, I co-taught a class on Islam using material recommended for interfaith work, such as R. Marston Speright's excellent introduction to Islam, *God is One: the Way of Islam* (Friendship Press: NY, 1989). We also studied the work of Father Elias Chacour, the Palestinian priest/peace activist who wrote *Blood Brothers* and *We Belong to the Land.* His works opened our eyes to what was happening in Israel from a Palestinian Christian perspective. I became friends with Sis Levin, who came to work for the American Friends Service Committee's Middle East program in Pasadena, California, during this period. Sis' husband Jerry (a CNN Cable News bureau chief) was held hostage in Beirut in 1984. Sis wrote *Beirut Diary*, a compelling account of her efforts to free her husband and to learn the truth about the Middle East situation. As a result of her experiences, Sis became an ardent peace activist and worked tirelessly to build bridges of understanding among Christians, Jews, and Muslims. These writers helped to dispel many stereotypes and provided valuable insight.

In this age of religious conflict that threatens to engulf the world in war, I have taken to heart Gandhi's words, which seem more important now than ever: "It is the sacred duty of every individual to have an appreciative understanding of other religions."

From past experience studying Buddhism, I realized that it isn't enough just to read books and study a religion. The best way to understand and appreciate a religion is to practice it, just as the best way to appreciate music is to play it—preferably in the company of other practitioners. Such practice does not require conversion, but immersion. I decided that the best way for me to understand Islam would be to observe Ramadan and to spend time with practicing Muslims.

Ramadan, I learned, is one of Islam's most important holy days—indeed, one of its "Five Pillars," or essential practices. During this month of observances, the Qur'an was first revealed to the Prophet Mohammed through the angel Gabriel. This event is to Muslims what the birth of Christ is to Christians—a revelation and incarnation of God's Word (the Eternal Logos) in human history. It is a solemn as well as joyous occasion. By day, Muslims dedicate themselves to God through the discipline of fasting. By night, they celebrate the benevolence and compassion of God through special prayers and meals. Muslims are also supposed to read the entire Qur'an during this holy month and give liberally to charities.

I began my Ramadan fast on November 17, 2001. In addition to fasting, I also made a commitment to read the entirety of Abdullah Yusuf Ali's monumental work, *The Meaning of the Holy Qur'an*, which was highly rec- ommended by Muslims.

During the weeks that followed, I visited both Shi'ite and Sunni mosques and joined in communal prayers. I also incorporated some Muslim prayers into my daily re- ligious practice. Using Michael Sell's translation, I learned to say the opening prayer of the Qur'an in Arabic:

> In the name of God, the compassionate, the caring,
> *bi smi llahi r-rahmani r-rahim,*
> praise be to God, lord sustainer of the worlds
> *al-hamdu   lillahi rabbi l-'alamin*
> master of the day of reckoning,
> *maliki yawmi d-din*
> to you we turn to worship
> *iyaka na'budu*
> and to you we turn in time of need
> *wa iyaka nasta'in*
> lead us on the straight road
> *ihdina s-sirata l-mustaqim*
> the road of those you have given to whom
> *sirata l-ladina an'amta 'alayhim*
> not those with anger upon them
> *ghayri maghdubi 'alayhim*
> not those who have gone astray.
> *wa la d-dalin.*

This prayer sums up the essence of Islam and is to Muslims what the Lord's prayer is to Christians. Each day I rose before dawn, prayed this and other prayers, ate breakfast, and studied the Qur'an. I prayed at least five times each day, facing north (the direction of Mecca for those in California) and bowing with forehead to the ground in the manner of Muslims.

When I told Muslims that I was observing Ramadan, they were extremely pleased and impressed. They were not only eager to discuss Islam with me, they also wanted to know more about my Quaker faith. Observing Ramadan thus became an opening for what the Quaker scholar and ecumenist Douglas Steere called "mutual irradiation"— the sharing of the "Light that enlightens all men and women" (John 1:9).

The most common reason that Muslims gave for fasting during Ramadan was that it helps us to empathize with those who are poor and don't have enough food and water. Others spoke of self-discipline, or of religious obligation. A Muslim physician and religious leader from Orange County, California, named Maher Hathout pointed out that the ability to fast—to delay gratification—is what distinguishes human beings from animals. It is also a test of faithfulness and integrity since only God knows if we are truly fasting, or sneaking food when no one is looking!

Many Muslims seemed surprised that a non-Muslim American had the self-discipline to fast. Sad to say, we Americans are seen as an extremely self-indulgent people, given to compulsive overeating and to equally compulsive dieting. When we diet, we generally do it for selfish reasons—to improve our health or our appearance. Fasting, on the other hand, is a discipline that helps us to become *unselfish* and spiritually healthy. As the Greek Orthodox saint John Chrysostom observed: "Fasting is medicine" (*Homilies*, III. ca. 388 C.E.) Practiced with humility, fasting helps to free us of our addictive behaviors, and can deepen our connection with God and with our fellow human beings—especially with those who are poor and hungry.

I learned this lesson very keenly one afternoon when the hunger pangs became so intense, and my energy level so low, that I had to quit work at four o'clock. I walked to a nearby park to watch the sun set (which seemed to take forever). My throat parched, and my belly rumbling, I realized that I could break my fast and end my discomfort at any time, whereas hundreds of millions of people (most of them children and mothers) don't have this option. That night, after my meal, I sat down and wrote checks to charitable organizations with more joy than I have ever before experienced. Fasting, I discovered, can do wonders to stimulate compassion and the urge to be charitable.

Fasting can also be a humbling experience. I was surprised to learn that most young Muslims are eager to start fasting since it is a mark of adulthood. (Children don't have to fast, nor do the sick, pregnant or nursing women, the frail elderly, and travelers.) A charming story called *Magid Fasts For Ramadan* by Mary Matthews describes how an eight-year-old Muslim boy decides to fast for Ramadan because his big sister has turned twelve and has begun fasting, and he wants to be grown up like her. Because Magid's parents say that he is too young to fast, he secretly feeds his lunch to the ducks. When his parents find out, they take their son aside and tell him that it is admirable for him to want to fast, but it's not healthy for one so young. Besides, the father explains, Muslims must always tell the truth! The fact that many Muslim teenagers feel like Magid and take pride in fasting gave me pause. Whenever I was tempted to give up my fast, I recalled their example and said to myself, "If teens can do it, so can I!"

Muslims who were spiritually mature reminded me that fasting means abstaining not only from food and drink, but also from other habits that intrude upon our relationship with God and our fellow human beings. During Ramadan, I was told, one should abstain from backbiting, judgmentalism, and anger. This proved at times far more challenging than simply skipping lunch.

I was also told that during this holy season one's spiritual life is supposed to be heightened. Prayers uttered during this period "count" more than prayers at any other time, and acts of kindness are supposed to carry more weight with God.

But I liked best what one Muslim mother said: "Ramadan is a time when I try to become a better person." The practice of fasting and prayer certainly made me *want* to become a better person. It also made me more acutely aware of my human foibles, and of my deep need to feel connected with God and with other human beings.

RAMADAN AND THE QUR'AN

Ramadan is celebrated because it is the month in which the Angel Gabriel first began to reveal the Qur'an to Mohammed. Qur'an literally means "recitation." Muslims believe that the Qur'an is literally the Word of God, transcribed exactly as it was revealed to the Prophet. Muslim scholar Yusuf Ali observes: "It is the duty of every Muslim—man, woman, or child—to read the Qur'an and understand it according to his own capacity" (xi).

Since reading the entire Qur'an is recommended for all Muslims during Ramadan, I made this a part of my daily practice. It is not an easy work to read or to understand, however. It is written in Arabic which native speakers insist is indescribably beautiful, but which doesn't translate easily. It is also full of subtle cultural allusions that require extensive explication.

One of the works that helped me to appreciate both the poetry and meaning of the Qur'an was Haverford College Professor Michael Sells' *Approaching the Qur'an* (White Cloud Press: Ashland, Oregon, 1999). His recent work on the Qur'an and Islamic culture has attracted considerable attention in the Quaker community as well as in the popular media. *Approaching the Qur'an* deals with the short, mostly early Suras (or chapters), which are lyrical and highly allusive (and at times elusive). Selections from this book were published in pamphlet form by the Quaker Universalist Fellowship. I recommend purchasing the book because it contains a CD with excellent recitations from the Qur'an along with commentaries explaining the cultural background, religious meaning, and poetic effects of the text.

The Qur'an is meant to be recited aloud. In the Muslim world, those who are skilled in reciting the Qur'an are regarded with the respect and admiration that Westerners accord to master musicians and singers. Listening to the Qur'an recited well is an unforgettable experience, even if you don't know the words. Sells' book makes the music and meaning of the Qur'an come alive for Western readers.

As I read the Qur'an as part of my daily devotions, I came to think of it as similar in many ways to a Beethoven symphony. To appreciate the majestic scope of such a work, we must experience it in its entirety. Themes and motifs appear and reappear in subtle variations, and are rephrased in different contexts, with different nuances of meaning and emotional tone. We must not only read, but listen to the Qur'an being recited—and we must listen with our hearts as well as minds, as one would to a work of literature or to music. Only then does the beauty and meaning of the Qur'an begin to unfold.

Muslims feel that the Qur'an cannot truly be "translated" at all since it can only be fully understood in Arabic. Therefore, Yusuf Ali's work is not called the Qur'an but rather *The Meaning of the Qur'an.* Ali's version of the Qur'an is a 20th century classic of spirituality and scholarship. Deeply spiritual as well as learned, Ali's commentary contains allusions to British poetry, the Bible, and also the latest discoveries in science.

This work is one that beginners or non-scholars may find a bit overwhelming (it consists of 1,700 pages, in very small print). When I finished reading Ali's *The Meaning of the Qu'ran,* I was reminded of what the 18th century English critic Samuel Johnson said of Milton's *Paradise*

Lost: "It is one of the great productions of the human mind, but no man would wish it longer than it is."

The essential message of the Qur'an is clear and simple: there is one God, who is infinitely compassionate, but also infinitely just. We were created to serve and honor God and to render an account of our lives on the Day of Judgment. Those who believe in God and live moral lives will be rewarded (whether they happen to call themselves Muslims, Christians, Jews, or whatever). Those who are disobedient and immoral, or worship many Gods or none, will be punished. The Qur'an also gives detailed instruction relating to the entire gamut of human conduct—worship, war, marriage, divorce, inheritance, punishment for crimes, etc. These rules comprise the Sharia, or Laws, and are the basis of Islamic jurisprudence.

The Qur'an was written for people at all stages of spiritual development. Commentators note that the Arabs were at a very low moral level when Mohammed appeared as their Prophet. They were addicted to polytheism, infanticide, feuding and vice of the grossest sort. The purpose of the Qur'an is to raise people from the lowest to the highest possible level of spiritual development. For that reason, you find in the Qur'an passages about heaven and hell that are intended primarily for those who need strong incentives to be good and "God-fearing." Other passages are written for those who have internalized their moral imperatives and are seeking a deeper connection with God and their fellow human beings based upon the ethic of love. In the Qur'an one finds teachings that range from the most elementary etiquette ("be sure to knock on the door before entering") to the most sublime ethics.

EID MUBARAK: THE "BLESSED CELEBRATION"

No discussion of Ramadan would be complete without describing the celebrations that take place each day at sunset, and also at the conclusion of the 30-day fasting period. Ramadan is not a time of repentance like Lent (which commemorates Jesus' 40 days of struggle against temptation in the desert); it is a time of celebration, like the birth of Christ for Christians. When the sun sets, a Muslim is supposed to go to the mosque or to his home and break fast with prayers and special food. Traditionally, Muslims break fast by eating dates and drinking water or milk (as the Prophet is said to have done). There is then a time of prayer, followed by a sumptuous feast called *iftar.*

It was my privilege to celebrate *iftar* at various mosques and also at the home of a Muslim family. I came to know this family through some peace activities I was involved with. When I showed up at a special meeting called by our city's mayor, I met a woman from Kashmir who had just joined the Cultural Affairs Commission. I invited her to speak at one of our Quaker events, and we began meeting to discuss ways of raising awareness about Muslim culture. Soon a friendship developed.

When my wife and I were first invited to her house, I realized that it was the first time I had ever been in the home of a Muslim and experienced Muslim hospitality. Soon after the sun set, we broke fast by eating various fruits and drinking sugared tea (sugar helps to restore one's energy). After some prayers, we ate a feast consisting of various curry dishes and some special foods from Kashmir. The evening was spent in a wide-ranging conversation about everything from religion and politics to family life and customs.

On the final day of Ramadan, I went with this family to celebrate *Eid-ul-Fitr* (one of Islam's two major holidays). When I arrived at their home, I was greeted with *Eid Mubarak* ("Blessed Celebration"). For morning prayers, we drove to a sports arena at the Fair Grounds in Costa Mesa, California. An estimated 14,000 Muslims gathered for this event—of all nationalities and colors, including many Anglo converts. The men and women went their separate ways. We men entered a large hall and lined up facing the north east (the direction of Mecca). There were large screen TVs so that we could see the speaker. The usual upbeat talks were replaced by more somber, reflective sermons. Prayers were said for the victims of the Sept. 11 terrorist attacks and the loved ones they left behind. More prayers were uttered for the loss of innocent life in Afghanistan, Palestine, Kashmir and other hot spots around the world. Preachers spoke of their concerns for the erosion of civil liberties in the post-9-11 era, which have hit the American Muslim and Arab-American communities especially hard. This Eid was also different in a few positive ways. American Muslims expressed deep gratitude to Christians who offered support, particularly those who broke bread with their Muslim neighbors by hosting them for the evening fast-breaking meal of Iftar.

One speaker observed, "Now we can only pray together that the rest of the world stumbles upon this simple but powerful formula for peace."

I went home with my host family, had breakfast (my first meal during daylight hours in a month), and watched with delight as the children were given their Ramadan gifts. It felt a lot like Christmas, only there was no tree or special decorations. The presents were not even wrapped (which the kids didn't seem to mind). This simplicity seemed very Quakerly. I felt very much at home, and very thankful to God. In these dark days, the light of Ramadan—and my new Muslim friends—has been a precious gift!

PART II: ARE MUSLIMS FRIENDLY?
A THEOLOGICAL OVERVIEW

The question, "Are Muslims Friendly?" holds a double meaning for Quakers (who are also known as "Friends"). It means not only "Are Muslims sociable and hospitable?" but also, "Do Muslims have anything in common with

Friends, theologically speaking"?

Even though there are an estimated three to six million Muslims in the US, I couldn't have answered the first question based on personal experience prior to September 11th because I had never actually socialized with Muslims. During my observation of Ramadan, I met with numerous Muslims and found them to be very friendly. They were keenly interested in sharing their faith and also in learning about what Quakers believe. We discovered much common ground, and also some intriguing differences. This interfaith sharing was an extremely rewarding exploration—one that I hope that many others will seek for themselves.

Trying to explain "what Quakers believe" proved challenging because Friends display such diversity of views and because most Friends (the author included) have not taken sufficient pains to learn how to articulate our faith and practice. Indeed, many Friends (especially in the Western USA) have an aversion to theology and see it as potentially divisive, prideful, and "notional."

Nonetheless, I found myself with no option but to express what I knew about Quakerism and to try to see it from a Muslim perspective. Many of the topics I address in this essay were ones that came up for discussion when I went to mosques or visited Muslims in their homes.

As has been noted before, the basic faith and practices of Islam are relatively easy to describe. Friends' faith and practices are much harder to pin down, however. Because we believe in "continuing revelation," and have no formal creed, our religious views and practices have evolved over time. Contemporary Friends range theologically from evangelical Christian to non-theistic universalist. There are at least two main Quaker branches—those who have paid pastors and ascribe to a Christian belief system (so-called pastoral Friends), and those who do not have paid pastors and tend to be universalist/liberal Christian in outlook (unprogrammed Friends). Unprogrammed Friends meet in silence, without any set order of worship, and "wait upon God" to inspire them with uplifting messages or guidance for action. This second group will be the focus of this discussion.

Islam began during a period sometimes described as the "Dark Ages," among a people addicted to polytheism and tribal warfare. The Qur'an's main purpose is to stress the "basics" of monotheism and to instill ethical values leading to unity and peace.

Quakerism emerged in the 17th century during a time of religious war and turmoil, much like what is happening today in certain parts of the world. One of the major missions of Quakerism has been to take a nonviolent approach to conflict, especially religious conflict.

Quakers differed from the vast majority of Christians of that time who believed that only the "elect" (i.e. those chosen by God) would be "saved." Quakers believed that *all* people, even those who have never heard of Christ or the Bible, have a divine spark within them.

Quakers and Muslims both agree that *every* human being—whether Christian, Jewish, Muslim, or "pagan"—is a child of one universal, loving God and therefore worthy of respect. Muslims believe that God has provided all people with prophets and a "Book" to guide them on the path of Truth. Quakers feel that within every person there is an "Inner Light" that enables us to experience Truth directly and to have a personal relationship with God.

Muslims I spoke with sometimes asked how Quakers felt about the Trinity, the Atonement, and other Christian doctrines. I replied that most unprogrammed Friends (of which I am one) are not interested in such matters. They tend to be practical and to "let their lives speak" rather than speculate about religion.

Unprogrammed Friends often describe their religion as consisting of five *testimonies*: simplicity, peace, equality, integrity and community. *Testimonies* are not dogmas but rather evidences or manifestations of how we put our faith into practice. *Simplicity* means putting aside anything that stands between us and God—whether it be religious images, wealth, "notions," or excessive busyness. *Peace* means harmony with the will of God, and includes the concept of social justice. *Equality* is based on the idea that there is "that of God" in every one and therefore every human being deserves to be treated with equal respect and dignity. *Integrity* means that our deeds must match our words. *Community* is the basis for our spiritual practice—it is the place where we test our insights, commune with God and each other, and seek to follow the leadings of the Spirit.

Keeping these beliefs and testimonies in mind, let's look at some of the similarities and differences between Quakers and Muslims.

Simplicity. Muslims, like Quakers, seek to simplify religion and to integrate it with everyday life. Yusuf Ali, translator and author of *The Meaning of the Qur'an*, saw parallels between Islam and the Protestant movement from which Quakerism emerged: "The Protestantism of the 16th century gave a fresh stimulus to the main ideas for which Islam stands, *viz.* the abolition of priestcraft, the right of private judgement, the simplification of ritual, and the insistence upon the simple, practical, everyday duties of life" (p. 998).

Simplicity is reflected in the Quaker style of worship and worship place. A Quaker meetinghouse, like a mosque, is extremely plain. There are no crosses, no religious symbols or representations of any kind. There are also no set prayers or order of worship, and no priest or paid minister. The Quaker practice is to free the mind from any distractions so that it can focus on Truth and be led by God's Holy Spirit.

Peace. Muslims insist that Islam is a peaceful religion, and that its very name suggests "peace." *Islam* (which means "Surrender") is derived from the Arabic word *Salaam*, which is used today as a greeting among Muslims (*Salaamu alaikum*, which means "Peace be with you"). To become a Muslim one must "make peace with" or "surrender to" God.

Islam is not a pacifist religion, however. Most Muslims I met point out that the Qur'an permits the use of violence for self-defense if one's religion, home or family is attacked. Muslims are enjoined by the Qur'an to struggle against oppression and injustice. "You may kill those who kill you, and you may evict them whence they evicted you. Oppression is worse than murder" (2:154).

It is important to note, however, that the Qur'an imposes strict limitations on the use of violence. In *Reading the Muslim Mind*, Hassan Hathout (a well-respected Muslim leader in the Los Angeles area) observes that the Qur'anic rules of war forbid Muslims from harming houses of worship (non-Muslim as well as Muslim), or even the trees or animals of one's enemy. Under such stringent rules, it would be morally wrong for a Muslim to crash land into the World Trade Center, or for the US to drop a bomb on Hiroshima or on Afghanistan. Hathout concludes: "Since modern war is so devastating, war itself should cease to be an option in conflict resolutions. War should be obsolete just like slavery!" (p. 102).

The word *jihad*, as used by some Muslim groups and by the Western media, is sometimes translated as "holy war." Moderate Muslims are disturbed by this usage and point out that the word in Arabic means "struggle," not "holy war." When Mohammed returned from a battle, he is said to have told his followers: "We have left the minor *jihad*, now we must begin the major *jihad*"—meaning the moral struggle within one's soul is far more important than the struggle on the battlefield. For most Muslims, this moral struggle is the true meaning of *jihad*.

Although the Qur'an condones violence in self-defense, it holds up reconciliation as the highest goal: "Repel evil with what is better, then will the one with whom there is enmity become an intimate friend" (41:34). This recalls Jesus' words: "Do not resist an evildoer, but if anyone strikes you on the right cheek, turn the other one also" (Matt 5:39).

Quakers and Muslims would both agree that when we turn our enemies into friends through "what is better," i.e. nonviolent means, we are acting in accordance with the highest teachings of our religion.

Integrity. Quakers originally called themselves the Religious Society of Friends of Truth. Truth-telling, or veracity, has always been an essential part of Quaker witness. This is one reason that Quakers refuse to swear an oath to tell the truth: we are supposed to tell the truth *at all times*, and not simply under oath.

Islam also places great emphasis on truthfulness and integrity. In the *Hadith* (a collection of Mohammed's sayings), the Prophet was asked: "Could a believer ever be a coward?" and he answered, "Maybe." "Could a believer ever be miserly?" the Prophet was asked, and he answered, "Maybe." But when asked, "Could a believer be a liar," the Prophet answered, "No. Never!" (quoted by Hathout, p. 83).

Community. Although Quakers believe that each individual must find his or her direct encounter with the Divine, they feel just as strongly that we must ground ourselves in a spiritual community committed to the discovery of Truth. For this reason, Quakerism has sometimes been described as a form of "group mysticism."

While Muslims believe that each individual is directly responsible for his or her relationship with God, they also feel a deep commitment to the community, or *umma*. Indeed, one of the primary missions of Islam is to lead all believers into a unified community that transcends tribe, nation, and race.

Equality: A core belief of both Muslims and Quakers is that each person is equal in the sight of God. As a result of this conviction, Quakers have been on the forefront of movements to end slavery and to insure equal rights for women, people of color, and the oppressed.

Most contemporary Muslims, especially in the United States, believe that it was the original intent of the Qur'an and the Prophet Muhammed to promote equality and dis-

164

courage discrimination based upon sex, race, or national origin. Many current practices associated with Muslims, such as the wearing of veils by women, are regarded as culturally based customs rather than religious obligations. They note that Islam originally granted women the right to hold property and to file for divorce—rights that women in Christian lands did not possess for many centuries.

Christ as Messenger/Savior. Muslims believe that Jesus, like Abraham and Moses, was a great prophet (or Divine Messenger), but not God or the biological offspring of God. While Muslims revere Mary and Jesus, and regard Jesus' teachings as divinely inspired, they feel that it is blasphemous to worship Jesus rather than God or to consider Jesus as equivalent to God.

Many liberal Friends would agree with these Muslim views. They do not believe that Jesus was literally the "Son of God" or that he died on the cross as a propitiatory offering for humanity's sins. Instead, they are apt to regard Jesus as an inspired teacher or as an incarnation of Divine Love and Truth. While they do not worship Jesus, they take very seriously his teachings, particularly his injunction to "love our enemies" and "turn the other cheek." In this respect, unprogrammed Quakers have more in common with Muslims than with traditional Christians and Christ-centered Friends.

Aversion to Theological Controversy. The Qur'an makes it very clear that theological hairsplitting and disputation are to be avoided: "And dispute ye not with the People of the Book, except with means better (than mere disputation)...." As noted previously, modern Quakers also seek to avoid theological disputes. Rather than try to convert others through argument, the Quaker motto is "let your life speak."

Even though Quakers and Muslims differ on many points of theology as well as on some social issues, we agree on many essentials. As we become better acquainted with each other and with our faith traditions, we may find that apparent differences are not as important as

165

they first appear. As George Fox once said: "The Lord has many ways to lead His people...." Commenting on the fact that not all prophets and messengers are mentioned in the Qur'an (40:78), Yusuf Ali writes: "We must recognize the Truth wherever we find it" (p. 1225).

PART III: QUAKER/MUSLIM RELATIONS: SOME HISTORICAL BACKGROUND

During this time of conflict between the Islamic and non-Islamic world, many thoughtful persons are studying history to understand the root causes of our current problems. The history of Muslim/Christian relations has been extremely problematic, but there have been some bright spots—particularly as far as Quakers are concerned—that bode well for the future.

During the 17th century, Quaker missionaries went out over the whole world, including Muslim nations, to share their vision of the Inward Light and Universal Truth. Some of the these valiant missionaries were women like Mary Fisher. She voyaged to Turkey to tell the Sultan and his Court about "the Truth." When asked what she thought of Mohammed, she replied "that she knew him not, but Christ enlightened every man who came into the world. Him she knew..." Concerning Mohammed, she said, "They might judge him false or true according to the words and prophecies he spoke.'" The Turks acknowledged this to be a reasonable response, and she was well treated. In fact, she was treated far better in Turkey than she would have been treated in New England during this same period, where being a Quaker was punishable by imprisonment, flogging, or death.

Throughout the 17th century, Muslims and Christians engaged in what today would be called "low intensity warfare." They sometimes captured each other's ships and made slaves of their captives, subjecting them to cruel treatment. It therefore seems remarkable, indeed almost miraculous, that a Quaker named Thomas Lurting successfully used non-violent means to avoid being sold into slavery when he and his crew were captured by Turks in the year 1663.

Instead of resisting his Turkish captors, Lurting responded with friendliness and cooperation. He was so courteous, and so fearless, that the Turks were lulled into a false sense of security. On the second night, after the Turkish captain had retired, it began to rain. Lurting persuaded each of the Turkish guards to go to sleep. When they were all asleep, he took their weapons.

At this point, the Christian crew again wanted to butcher the Turks, but Lurting insisted that no blood be spilled.

When the Turks realized that these peculiar English Christians would not hurt or enslave them, they became willing to help. Lurting gave them free run of the ship, which caused some of the English sailors to grumble. The Quaker replied, "They are strangers. I must treat them well."

When the ship reached a place near a Muslim town about fifty miles from Algiers, Lurting let the Turks loose on shore and even provided them with bread and other necessities. On shore, Lurting wrote, "the Turks all embraced me very kindly."

This story was published and became widely known in England. Perhaps this is what William Penn (Quaker leader and son of a well-known English admiral) had in mind when he wrote: "Let us try what love can do, for if people see that we do love, they would not harm us." This nonviolent approach is one that Quakers have used—and have tried to teach—for the past three hundred fifty years in various situations of conflict.

Friends' outreach in the Middle East began in 1889 when a Quaker school for Palestinian girls was started in the village of Ramallah, ten miles north of Jerusalem. This school was expanded to include boys in 1901, and eventually included a baby clinic and Friends Meeting. The Ramallah Friends School now has over 950 students who receive an education in English and Arabic.

The American Friends Service Committee (which was started to provide alternative service for conscientious objectors during World War I) undertook relief work in Syria in 1922 and has continued to work for relief, reconciliation and justice in this region ever since. In 1948, under the auspices of the United Nations, the AFSC established the Gaza Strip program to provide food, clothing, tents and medical care to the 250,000 Palestinian Arab refugees. The AFSC later worked under the auspices of the Israeli government to establish a similar program to help Palestinian Arabs in Western Galilee.

Because the American Friends Service Committee aided both Jewish and Palestinian refugees, and because Quakers were awarded the Nobel Peace Prize in 1948, they came to be widely trusted by all parties in this highly volatile region. Just before the British withdrew from Palestine, Harold Evans, an AFSC staff person, nearly became mayor of Jerusalem!

Since 1949 the AFSC has been involved in numerous development and peacemaking activities in the Middle East. From 1990 to 1993, the AFSC provided funds and material assistance to the Gulf region following the Gulf War. It has actively campaigned to end the Iraqi sanctions and has engaged in numerous efforts to bring together Israelis and Palestinians interested in promoting an "enduring peace" based on justice.

Not only the AFSC, but individual Friends have also traveled to the Middle East and worked for peace and justice. Among them is a veteran Quaker peace activist from Santa Barbara, California, named Gene Hoffman. Using techniques she had learned in counseling, Hoffman listened deeply to the Israeli and Palestinian points of view. She found that the practice of listening nonjudgmentally helped to create a climate of understanding (if not agreement). She called it "compassionate listening." Listening deeply to all sides in a conflict situation may be one of Quakerism's most important contributions to peacemaking.

VISIONING A FUTURE WITHOUT "HOLY WAR"

As the shadow of terrorism looms large in the American consciousness, it is easy to fall prey to fears of unending war and impending environmental catastrophe. Such fears may paralyze us, or lead us to take actions that are counterproductive. That is why it is important to take time for prayer (and perhaps fasting as well) to discern where the Spirit is leading us during these difficult times.

What observing Ramadan has taught me is that by reaching out to those in a different faith tradition, we can begin to take those small but necessary first steps that can bring us closer to peace. As a Friend, I believe, and try to practice, what Fatma Reda once observed: "Peace is achieved one person at a time, through a series of friendships" (quoted in *The Little Book of Peace*, Patricia J. Chui, editor, p. 28).

Ending the longstanding conflicts that have divided Christians, Muslims, and Jews will not be easy, but it was not easy to end the Cold War, either. The Berlin Wall fell, and the Cold War ended, in part because "ordinary" people of the East and West took risks, reached out in friendship to one another, and were unwilling to let the politics of fear divide us.

Reconciliation between Christians, Muslims, and Jews will require an even greater effort by people of faith willing to reach out beyond their comfort zones to build bridges of understanding and friendship. It will require the work of scholars and religious leaders willing to listen to each other and to find common ground. Finally, it will require the work of enlightened political leaders willing to take risks to create a compassionate and just peace in the

Middle East.

This work will probably not be completed in our lifetime. The forces promoting fear and militarism, and profiting from terrorism, are powerful and determined. But it behooves us to seek Divine Guidance, to begin where we are, and to do whatever we can to make this world a place where people of all faiths can live together in peace. Observing Ramadan, and seeking to understand the Spirit that inspired it, can be a small, Friendly step in this direction.

Becoming a Friend of God:
The Path of Sufism and Quakerism

by Anthony Manousos

Outwardly, Quakerism (the mystical branch of Christianity) and Sufism (the mystical branch of Islam) may seem worlds apart. Sufism is associated with dervish dancing, exotic Middle Eastern music, and the ecstatic poetry of Rumi. Quakerism is associated with peace activists, plain-dressed people sitting silently in old meetinghouses, and William Penn, the founder of Pennsylvania, and the icon of oatmeal. But there are deep affinities between these two spiritual paths, and it is no accident that Quakerism and Sufism refer to its practitioners as "Friends."

Sufism is the mystical heart of Islam. It emerged in the 8th century CE as an Islamic ascetic movement. Some scholars see connections between Sufism, Buddhism and Christianity and no doubt such connections exist, but most Sufis see their practice as deeply rooted in Islam. Early practitioners of Sufism include Hasan al-Basri (642-728) and Rabiah al-Adawiay (d. 801), the first great female Sufi teacher and poet. Perhaps the most famous Sufi is Jalal a-din Rumi, who founded the Mevlevi order (known as whirling dervishes) and has become the most popular poet in America, thanks to Coleman Barks' imaginative translations. Sufis played a political role in Islamic history, often standing up for the rights of the poor and oppressed. Sufism has also encouraged women to be spiritual teachers and leaders.

Quakerism began in the 17th century in England as part of the Puritan movement to reform Christianity by restoring it to its primitive roots. Quakers believe that each person can have direct access to God or Christ through the Inward Light and the practice of silent worship. Quakers are perhaps best known for opposing war and for championing the rights of women, African-Americans, homosexuals and other oppressed groups. Like Sufism, Quakerism is a mystical faith that emphasizes the direct experience of the Divine Within rather than outward rituals or the words of scripture.

In 2002, I published a pamphlet called *Islam from a Quaker Perspective* which attempted to explain Islam to Quakers, and Quakerism to Muslims, in the most succinct possible way. In this pamphlet, I focused on mainstream Islam and showed that there are many parallels between mainstream Islam and Quakerism. I deliberately omitted any reference to Sufism in part because I wanted to explain what the majority of Muslims believe and practice, and thereby help readers appreciate what James Michener called "the world's most misunderstood religion."

I'm currently working on a book that will go deeper and explore the inner world of Islam and Christianity as I have experienced it through my study and practice of Quakerism and Sufism.

My hope is that what I have to share abut Sufism and Quakerism will inspire readers to go deeper in their spiritual life and to become more intimate with the source of truth within us and within every living being we encounter. The following are two sections from this work-in-progress.

Practicing Simplicity

Sufis and Quakers would both agree with Henry David Thoreau: "As you simplify your life, the laws of the universe will be simpler; solitude will not be solitude, poverty will not be poverty, nor weakness weakness." To draw closer to one's true self, and to God, one must simplify one's life both outwardly and inwardly.

Sufis take pride in their simple lifestyle. The name "Sufi" is said to derive from the Arabic word "wool," a reference to the coarse woolen cloak worn by Muslim ascetics, who came to known as "woolen ones" or Sufis.

The simplicity of their lives was in stark contrast to the affluence enjoyed by religious and secular leaders of the Muslim community. Indeed, Sufi poverty was a rebuke to worldly and prideful elites. Sufis justify their poverty by the example of the Prophet Mohammad, who lived a simple, austere life. The Prophet is quoted as saying, "Poverty is my pride." This saying became the watchword for authentic Sufis.

Poverty *per se* is not a Sufi virtue, however. What Sufis seek is spiritual poverty (*faqr*), which means emptying oneself of vain desires so that one can be filled with the Divine. According to the *Sufi Book of Spiritual Ascent*, "Whoever wants poverty because of the nobility of poverty dies a poor man, but whoever wants poverty so that he may occupy himself with God Most High dies rich" (p. 273). By means of such poverty, one draws closer to the "Beloved," as God is called in this poem attributed to Abu Ali al-Rudhbari:

> Poverty and patience—these are my two garments...
> The most fitting garment is that given by the Beloved
> On the day of visitations, in garments that are robes of honour!
> If You are not there, my hope, all life is just mourning...
> (p. 276).

Quakers also practice simplicity as an outward testimony of an inward experience of the Divine. For Friends, the goal of simplicity is to de-clutter one's inner and outward life so that we can find space for communing with what Thomas Kelly calls "the holy Center."

> Simplification comes when we "center down," when life is lived with singleness of eye, from a holy Center, where the breath and stillness of Eternity are heavy upon us and we are wholly yielded to God. Some of you know this holy, recreating Center of eternal peace and joy and live in it day and night. Some of you may

see it over the margin and wistfully long to slip into that amazing Center where the soul is at home with God. Be very faithful to that wistful longing. It is the Eternal Goodness calling you to return Home (*Plain Living*, p. 21).

Kelly used impersonal terms like "Eternal Goodness" rather than "The Beloved" to characterize the Divine, but the warmth which he speaks of his relationship to "that amazing Center" is reminiscent of Sufi poetry. Sufis and Quakers both agree that to reach this inner sanctuary, the source of one's true life and power, one must practice not only outward simplicity, but deep, inward silence.

Silence in Sufism and Quakerism

God is silence and is most easily reached in silence. – Baha Ad-din Naqshband (1318-1389), founder of the Naqshband Sufi order

All this talk and turmoil and noise and movement is outside the veil; inside the veil is silence and calm and peace.—*Bayezid Bistami*

Be still in thy own mind and spirit from thy own thoughts, and then thou wilt feel the principle of God to turn to the Lord God, whereby thou wilt receive his strength and power from whence life comes, to allay all tempests, against blusterings and storms. This is it which molds into patience, into stillness, into stayedness, into quietness, up to God, with his power. –*George Fox, 1658*

Silent worship, or contemplation, is the heart of Quakerism and also an essential feature of Sufism. While silent worship is central to Quakerism, Quakers do not simply sit in silence but engage in a variety of inward practices, some of which are similar to those practiced by Sufis. In his classic work, *Guide to Quaker Practice*, the 20th century Quaker educator Howard Brinton describes these practices.

He notes that during worship Friends may engage in "self-examination"—looking at our thoughts and desires and discerning what is preventing us from having a deeper communion with God. This is similar to what Sufis call "watching one's thoughts."

Another technique mentioned by Brinton is "repeating to oneself a passage from the Bible or some devotional poem or some words and reflection on their meaning." This is similar to what Sufis call *zikhr.*

Friends may also recall prayers learned by heart, or engage in prayers of thanksgiving or petition, what is sometimes called "holding others in the Light."

"Such prayers are not merely petitions," observes Brinton. Then he adds a phrase that recalls the Sufi practice of invoking the Beloved. "[These prayers] are more like communion with a friend or lover when inmost desire is exposed in the light of another presence."

Finally, there is wordless prayer, what Brinton calls "an upsurge of feeling and will towards God."

The goal of these worship practices is to align one's will with the Divine Will—which is also the goal of Sufism, and indeed of all authentic worship.

Sufism uses a variety of techniques to open the mind and heart to the Divine: music, dance (e.g. whirling dervishes), watching one's thoughts, *dhikr* (chanting or repeating one of the names of God), and meditation. According to Llewellyn Vaughan-Lee in his book *Sufism: the Transformation of the Heart*, one particular order of Sufis—the Naqshbandis—come closest to Quakers in their emphasis on silent worship:

While some Sufis profess [God's] name vocally, others prefer silent invocation. This is the particularity of the Naqshbandi Order, whose founder, Baha ad-din

Naqshband, said, "God is silence, and is most easily reached in silence." The silent *dhikr* can be inwardly repeated at all moments, and thus becomes a continual prayer of remembrance. But whether repeated vocally or silently, the *dhikr* ultimately takes us beyond words, beyond forms, to the heart of hearts, where He whom we call upon is always present (p. 54-55).

The practice of silence can be wonderfully liberating, but it can also terrifying when we are attached to our ego and its agendas. For this reason, silence is used as a form of punishment for school children and prison inmates who break the rules. But for those who are willing to let go of the ego and its incessant chatter, and open up the heart to the Divine, stillness can be a god-send. Buddhists call this holy stillness Nirvana (extinction), Christians call it "dying to self," and the Sufis call it *fanaa*, self-annihilation. Frightening as this may sound to the ego-centric, dying to self can be the beginning of a true life—a life of genuine, selfless love.

A Quaker Perspective on the Qur'an and the Bible

By Anthony Manousos

George Bernard Shaw once observed that England and America are two countries separated by a common language. It could also be said that Christianity, Islam and Judaism are three religions separated by a common religious heritage. The three great monotheistic faiths all claim Abraham as their common spiritual ancestor. They ascribe to many of the same religious narratives and honor many of the same prophets. They worship one God who is the ruler of the universe. Nonetheless, acrimonious and sometimes bloody disputes have arisen among these self-styled "children of Abraham."

During our current age of religious conflict, scriptures are cited to justify everything from war and terrorism to peace making and social justice. It is important for people of faith, as well as for skeptics, to have a basic understanding of what the Bible and the Qur'an actually say and how they are being interpreted from a variety of theological/philosophical perspectives.

In this essay I will explore some of some areas of controversy regarding the Bible and the Qur'an, including the nature of God ("Do Muslims, Jews and Christians worship the same God?"), how these scriptures were composed, and how the ambivalence towards war and peace found in these texts reflects the different levels of spiritual development. I am not trained as a biblical or qur'anic scholar, but I have had scholarly training in English literature and have read the Bible and the Qur'an for many years on a daily basis as part of my spiritual

---

Reprinted from Quaker Theology #14. *Used with permission. To subscribe, go to: www.quaker.org/quest.*

practice. I have also written a pamphlet about *Islam from a Quaker Perspective* and pondered what scholars have written about both these scriptures.

In this essay I will sum up some of what I have learned and offer some reasons why Friends and others who care about peacemaking in the modern (or postmodern) world would do well to increase their scriptural literacy by reading both the Bible and the Qur'an.

I realize that many unprogrammed Friends, like many Americans, are "biblically illiterate." Hence the Quaker joke:

What do Quakers from Friends United Meeting [the branch of Quakers known for being mainstream Christians] bring to their bible study class? Answer: A Bible and a cup of coffee.

What do liberal, unprogrammed Friends bring to their Bible studies? Answer: a cup of coffee.

Joking aside, there are signs of growing interest in the Bible even among liberal Friends. Friends General Conference, the national gathering of liberal Friends, has Bible studies in each of its Gatherings and publishes some of the talks given by speakers at these events. Another hopeful indication has been the recent publication of the *The Quaker Bible Reader,* a collection of essays by Friends from different branches of Quakerism. I was also encouraged to learn that some Meetings (such as Orange County Meeting here in California) are making an effort to study the Qur'an.

As a Quaker interested in peacemaking and spirituality, I see three primary reasons to study the Judaeo-Christian-Islamic scriptures:

1) Knowledge of scripture helps us to be more clear and effective when we dialogue with "people of the book," i.e. Christians, Muslims, and Jews. Such knowledge is essential if you believe (as I do) that interfaith dialogue plays an important role in post 9/11 peace and reconciliation work.

2) Scriptural literacy helps us to discern when people are misusing their scriptural tradition either out of ignorance or because of a political agenda. Americans have been described as "Christ-haunted" and "biblically illiterate," which is sad but true, and a source of many problems in today's world. Many Muslims and Jews also lack direct knowledge of scriptures, either their own or those of other faiths; they rely instead on second hand opinions that sometimes create misunderstanding and mistrust. To counteract ignorance and religious prejudice, we need to study and to share what we know to be accurate and true about the scriptures. Early Friends knew their scripture intimately and did not hesitate to argue against what they saw as "errors." George Fox was knowledgeable enough about the Qur'an to quote it authoritatively when writing a letter to the Sultan of Turkey calling for humane treatment of sailors captured by the Turks.

3) The Bible and Qur'an are sources of genuine spiritual wisdom which, if read with discernment, sensitivity, and intelligence, can help transform our lives. Friends were among the first Christians to recognize divine wisdom not only in the Bible but also in the Qur'an.

It is no easy task to become scripturally literate or to "read the scriptures in the spirit in which they were written" (to use the Quaker phrase). It takes many years of study, and a willingness to keep an open mind as well as a critical spirit.

Let's begin by briefly describing how Friends view the Bible, their primary scriptural heritage. Like most 17th century Protestants, early Friends read the Bible incessantly and were steeped in its language and imagery practically from birth. It has been said that if all the Bibles in England were destroyed, George Fox would have been able to reconstruct the Bible from memory. If this story were literally true, Fox would be a Christian version of what Muslims call a *hafiz* (someone who has memorized the entire Qur'an and can recite it by heart).

Even though Friends read and quoted the Bible as much as any Protestant sect, they differed from most Protestants because they did not see the Bible as the primary source of authority. Instead, Quakers believed that they could have direct access to the Divine through prayer and meditation. In Fox's view, the Bible was not the "Word of God"—the ultimate authority—but simply the words of God. The Word of God was the living, inward Christ who could be experienced directly without the intermediary of priest or book. Once someone received a genuine religious insight from this Source, he or she usually found it confirmed in the Bible. George Fox described this process of coming to experience and verify the Truth in his *Journal:*

Now the Lord God opened to me by his invisible power how that every man was enlightened by the divine light of Christ. I saw that the grace of God, which brings salvation, had appeared to all men, and that the manifestation of the spirit of God was given to every man, with which to profit. These things I did not see by the help of man, nor by the letter, though they are written in the letter; but I saw them in the light of the Lord Jesus Christ, and by his immediate spirit and power, as did the holy men of God by whom the holy scriptures were written.Yet I had no slight esteem of the holy scriptures, they were very precious to me; for I was in that spirit by which they were issued; and what the Lord opened in me, I afterwards found was in agreement with them.

Given this emphasis on direct experience of the Divine rather than on scripture, it is not surprising that Quakerism has produced few eminent Bible scholars. In the 20th century, serious biblical exegesis has been attempted by only a relatively small numbers Quaker academics, such as Henry Cadbury, Rufus Jones, Douglas Steere, Howard Brinton, and Elizabeth Watson. Of these, only Henry Cadbury played a significant role in modern biblical scholarship.

Today the Bible is read by liberal Friends as a source of spiritual inspiration and moral instruction, but it is not seen as an inerrant or infallible source of authority. Friends tend to be drawn to the Jesus Seminar and to theologians like Marcus Borg, who combine an historical reading of scripture with a progressive social agenda.

The evangelical vs. liberal perspective on other religions

Before going any further with this discussion, it is important to clarify differences between the liberal and evangelical Quaker approach to other religions. Let's begin with a brief summary of a complex historical narrative. When Quakers moved westward in the 19th century, many were influenced by the evangelical revival that was sweeping the country. During this tumultuous period, western Quakers split into two opposing branches: the evangelicals and the liberals.

Evangelical Quakers were bible- as well as Christ-centered and accepted most of the doctrines of traditional Christianity, most particularly the notion that you had to accept Jesus Christ as your personal savior or you would go to hell. Evangelical Quakers identified themselves primarily as Christian, and only secondarily as Quakers.

Liberal Quakers took a very different path. They turned towards a more mystical, universalist approach to their faith and welcomed into their fold Jews, Buddhists and "refugees" from doctrinaire Christian faiths who were looking for a non-dogmatic approach to religion. Today most liberal Friends are universalist rather than Christian in outlook.

This profound difference is illustrated by two books

about Islam that were published by Friends in the West after 9/11/2001. As a liberal Friend, I wrote a pamphlet called *Islam from a Quaker Perspective* to explain Islam to Quakers, and to explain Quakerism to Muslims. It was a deeply personal essay, the result of my decision to fast during Ramadan as a way to understand the Muslim faith and practice from a spiritual perspective. This pamphlet was co-published in 2003 by *Friends Bulletin* (the magazine that I edit for Western Friends) and the Quaker Universalist Fellowship. It was reprinted the following spring by the Wider Quaker Fellowship and sent out to around 4,000 subscribers in 103 countries. This pamphlet makes no effort to convert Muslims to Quakerism; that would be unthinkable for liberal Friends.

During this same period, Barclay Press, an evangelical Quaker publishing house located in Newberg, Oregon, published a book called *My Muslim People* by Dr. Abraham Sarker, a Muslim convert to Christianity who (as far as I know) is not a Quaker. The purpose of this book is to equip evangelical Christians with the knowledge and tools they need to "save" Muslims from their "false" religion. Sarker was born a Muslim in Bangladesh and trained to become a Muslim missionary with hopes of converting Americans to the "true faith." But while in America, he dreamed that he was "burning in a lake of fire" and was told by God in an "audible voice" that he should "Go, and get a Bible." When he did so, he found Christ (thanks to some help from a friendly American evangelist named Peter) and became a Christian.

Sarker describes how his conversion led to his being rejected by his family and persecuted by the Muslim community. With a convert's zeal, he discusses the shortcomings of Islam and explains why Christianity is the "only hope" for Muslims.

In spite of his proselytizing zeal, Sarker tries to be as accurate as possible in presenting the Islamic faith. He makes it clear that in order to convert a Muslim from his "errors," you need to know the facts about his religion.

Despite its biases, Sarker's book is a "must read" for anyone who wants to understand an evangelical Christian perspective on Islam. This book is also indicative of how many (but not all) evangelical Quakers feel about Islam.

One more point needs to be clarified: not all Christ-centered Friends are exclusivist in their outlook and believe that you must accept Christ to please God and avoid going to hell. It is possible to be a devout Christian Quaker and at the same time respectful and open to Islam, Judaism and other faiths.

To cite an example, Michael Birkel, a professor of religion at Earlham College, approaches Quakerism from a deeply Christian perspective and is also very open to interfaith dialogue with Muslims. In his recent Plenary Address at Ohio Valley Yearly Meeting, he writes with great sensitivity and insight about the importance of interfaith dialogue with Muslims. He concludes:

> We should not expect agreement, nor victory after all, it's not a contest. Instead we might find the common ground that comes of listening. We might experience growing respect, despite conflict and challenge. Maybe you and your conversation partners will come to agree on how to disagree. Articulating that "how" can be wonderfully liberating, even exhilarating. Misunderstanding can be an opportunity to learn rather than a reason to be offended. That requires a kind of generosity based in trust.
>
> You might discover a new dimension of what it means to love your neighbor. Like John Woolman's experience, we can find that our first motion, our motivation, is love, and from there we can be genuinely open to others while being faithful to what is truest in our own tradition.

Birkel's words would no doubt resonate with Marshall G.S. Hodgson (1922 - 1968), a professor at the University of Chicago who was one of this century's major Islamic scholars. A practicing Quaker, Hodgson had a deep respect for other cultures and civilizations and challenged the Eurocentric view of history prevalent in his time. In his preface to his magisterial study, *The Venture of Islam,* Hodgson offers a quotation from John Woolman that epitomizes the perspective of liberal Friends:

> To consider mankind other than brethren, to think favours are peculiar to one nation and exclude others, plainly supposes a darkness of understanding.

Do Christians and Muslims worship the same God?

Before discussing scriptures, I would like to focus our attention on God since God is considered the revealer of scriptures, as well as their main subject, by all three Abrahamic faiths. A question that has often been posed lately is: do Jews, Muslims and Christians worship the same God? As we shall see, this question has arisen for reasons that have more to do with politics than theology.

Ever since President George Bush stated after 9/11/2001 that Muslims, Christians and Jews worship the same God, many right-wing Christians have taken exception with the President's effort to be pluralistic and conciliatory. Some have gone so far as to describe the "Muslim god" as the antithesis of the "Christian God," or even an "idol." Ted Haggard, former President of the National Association of Evangelicals (and now under a cloud because of his secret homosexual liaisons), stated:

> The Christian God encourages freedom, love, forgiveness, prosperity and health. The Muslim god appears to value the opposite. The personalities of each god are evident in the cultures, civilizations and dispositions of the peoples that serve them. Muhammad's central message was submission; Jesus' central message was love. They seem to be very different personalities.

Richard Land, a top official of the Southern Baptist Convention, cited the Bible to justify this claim: "The Bible is very clear about this. There is only one true God and His name is Jehovah, not Allah."

Haggard and Land were articulating a common view among evangelicals. In a poll of evangelical leaders at the community level, 79 percent disagreed with the statement that Muslims and Christians "pray to the same god."

More ominously, General William G. Boykin, a born-again Christian who sees U.S. military exploits in apocalyptic terms, stated: "I knew that my God was bigger than his [i.e. Osman Otto, a Muslim warlord]. I knew that my God was a real God and his was an idol."

The view that God and Allah are different entities is the result of linguistic as well as theological misunderstanding. English-speaking Muslims often use the Arabic word "Allah" ("the God") when referring to the supreme deity. The same word is used by Arab-speaking Christians and Jews when referring to God. Furthermore, calling "Allah" an idol invented by Muslims makes no theological sense. Muslims consider idol worship, including portraying God by any sort of image, to be *shirk* (i.e. idolatry), which an unpardonable sin by Islamic standards.

A deeper question involves discerning whether the Muslims, Christians and Jews share the same basic understanding of God. In 2004 *The Christian Century,* a magazine for liberal Christians, ran a series of five articles in which leading Christian theologians addressed this question, and then a Muslim scholar named Umar F. Abd-Allah was given a chance to express an Islamic perspective.

In addressing the question of Islam's understanding of God, Prof.. Abd-Allah (whose name means "Servant of God) explored its social and political context. Why are Muslims being singled out and asked whether they worship the same God as do Christians and Jews? From a Muslim viewpoint, the answer is obvious, and indeed, self-evident. There is only one God. According to the

Qur'an, Muslims are required to believe that they worship the same God as did Abraham, Moses and Jesus.

But the Muslim scholar then raised a deeper question: do all Christians or Jews or Muslims share a common understanding of God? He writes:

When focusing on the diversity of religious predicates, we might ask: "Does anyone worship the same God?" Can any faith or its followers sport an essentialist label? Which religion can claim to have held a monolithic theological view even within its creedal schools? Hillel and Shammai, the sagely Pharisaic "pair," sat together at the head of the Great Sanhedrin but posited sharply divergent visions of God's character and actions. The Alexandrian Fathers and their counterparts in Antioch were not always affectionately immersed in Christian fellowship. For that matter, earlier Jews and Christians not only differed from their Hellenistic brethren on how they viewed God and Christ but held jarringly different notions of the basic structure of reality.

Re-framing this question in this way opens up an entirely different perspective. It becomes clear that each believer has a different view of God, depending on his or her stage of spiritual/psychological development and/or theological perspective.

In today's world, the theological boundary is not between Muslims and Christians, or even Muslims and Jews. Rather it is between competing understandings of God. This becomes clear if we consider Prof Abd-Allah's question in contemporary terms: Do Christians such as Jim Wallis, Marcus Borg, Pat Robertson and Ted Haggard all worship the same God?

My own Quaker-influenced understanding of God is closer to that of Muslims and Jews in the peace movement than it is to fundamentalist Christians who support war. (Both positions have scriptural warrant, as I will explain later.) Furthermore, many fundamentalist Christians and extremist Muslims share a similarly exclusivist and possessive view of God (i.e. "my God is better, bigger, stronger than your God"). This view of God is one that progressive Muslims, Christians and Jews find repellent, or at least immature.

To conclude this brief overview of how different faith traditions view God, it is worth noting that many Muslims would strongly object to the claim that Islam portrays God/Allah as a stern and cruel being who demands to be obeyed unquestioningly. With the exception of one, all 114 chapters of the Qur'an begin with the phrase: "In the name of God, the Merciful, the Compassionate." Mercy, compassion and forgiveness are among the most commonly mentioned attributes of God in the Qur'an. In one of the sayings (hadith) of the Prophet Muhammad we are told that "God is more loving and kinder than a mother to her dear child." Most Muslims as well as most Christians and Jews believe in a God that is compassionate and forgiving as well as peaceful and just.

Composition of the Bible and Qur'an

The Bible and the Qur'an derive from a common religious tradition and express similar spiritual verities, but they were composed under strikingly different circumstances.

The Bible (the Greek word meaning "The Book") consists of two parts, the "Old" (Hebrew) and the "New" (Christian) Testament (or Gospels). The Hebrew Bible (known to Jews as Tanakh) is actually a series of 39 (or 46, depending on the version) books or writings compiled from 1000-660 BCE [Before the Common Era]. The New Testament was composed by a variety of writers between 60—110 CE. The contents of the New Testament were formalized by Athanasius of Alexandria in 367 CE, and finally "canonized" (officially authorized) in 382 CE.

Some Christians and Jews believe that everything in

the Bible is literally true. Some Christians believe that the Bible has one unifying message, pointing to Christ. Other Christians and Jews see the Bible as a source of Divine wisdom composed by a variety of human authors and reflecting a diversity of meanings and religious perspectives. Efforts to view the Bible, or even the New Testament, as a unified whole have proven problematic at best.

In considering the composition of scripture, the following issues need to be considered:

◆ How were the scriptures composed?
◆ Who composed them, when, and for what reason?
◆ Is the text we have what the original author(s) wrote or said, or has it been altered over time?

Determining the answers to these questions is extremely difficult. Traditionalists believe that the scriptures were written by the authors whose names are given in the scriptures, e.g. the first five books of the Bible were composed by Moses, the gospel of Matthew was written by the apostle Matthew, etc. Traditionalists also believe that the scriptures have been preserved verbatim and therefore can be seen as "inerrant."

Beginning in the 18th century, many scholars have come to question these traditional accounts for textual and historical reasons. Close readings of scriptures revealed many stylistic discrepancies showing that these works were written by numerous individuals over a period of many years, and for complex theological reasons.

How did certain scriptures become "canonized"

In the first two centuries after the death of Jesus dozens of "gospels" and epistles attributed to the apostles were written, including the gospels of Mary Magdalene, Thomas, and Peter; the Epistle of Barnabas; the Acts of

Andrew and John; the Revelation of Peter, etc. All of these works were rejected by the Church for various reasons. How did certain gospels come to be considered "canonical" (i.e. fit for use by the church) and others rejected as inauthentic or heretical?

These questions have preoccupied Christian scholars for the last couple of centuries.

So far, however, most Muslim scholars have not grappled with questions such as these because the Qur'an is assumed to have always been a unified work directly inspired by God. The Qur'an (meaning "Recital") consists of 144 suras, or chapters, that were revealed to one man, Mohammad, over a 22-year period, from 610 CE until shortly before his death in 632 CE. As a result, the Qur'an is a much more unified work than the Bible, although some apparent contradictions and inconsistencies have been noted and will be discussed later.

Twenty years after the Prophet's death, in 653 CE, the first "authorized" version of the Qur'an was compiled under Caliph Uthman. The earliest manuscripts of the Qur'an date back to around 100 years after the Prophet's death. Most Muslims believe that every word in the Qur'an is an exact transcript of what God revealed to Mohammed, with absolutely no changes in wording since it was first transmitted and written down. Today only fundamentalist Jews or Christians would make such a claim about their Scripture.

Controversies Regarding "Canonization" of the Qur'an

Some modern non-Muslim scholars have questioned whether the Qur'an was preserved perfectly, word-for-word, as Mohammad received and recited it. Since we do not have an "authorized" version of the Qur'an dating back to the Prophet's lifetime, we will never know for sure, just as we will never know for certain what happened after the crucifixion of Jesus. We are told that the Prophet's revelations came in fragmentary inspired utterances that were copied down and memorized by believers. After his death, these fragments were gathered together into a unified work through a process that has never fully been explained or understood. Caliph Uthman is supposed to have authorized Muslim religious leaders to gather these different versions and produce a standardized text. However, some modern scholars, such as the archeologist Arthur Jeffrey, believe that there were "wide divergences" among these early Qur'anic texts:

> When we come to the accounts of 'Uthman's recension, it quickly becomes clear that his work is no mere matter of removing dialectical peculiarities in reading, but was a necessary stroke of policy to establish a standard text for the whole empire – there were wide divergences between the collections that had been digested into Codices in the great Metropolitan centres of Medina, Mecca, Basra, Kufa and Demascus. Uthman's solution was to canonize the Medinan Codex and order all others to be destroyed. There can be little doubt that the text canonized by Uthman was only one among several types of text in existence at the time.

This passage is quoted by the ex-Muslim Christian convert Sarker with great satisfaction, since any suggestion that the text of today's Qur'an is not exactly as Mohammmad received it would undermine the Muslim claim that the Qur'an is a "perfected" scripture while the scriptures of the Jews and Christians were added to and corrupted over time.

However, there is no scholarly consensus about the significance and extent of variations in Qur'anic texts prior to Uthman. Most secular scholars tend to agree with the traditional view of Islamic scholars that the Qur'an was revealed to Mohammad in its entirety and redacted into its present form during the reign of Uthman.

Some "iconoclastic" scholars, such as John Wansbrough and his students Michael Cook and Patricia Crone, have questioned whether the Qur'an as we know it was revealed in its entirety to Muhammad, since the earliest surviving copies of the complete Qur'an date back to around a hundred years after the Prophet's death. These iconoclasts argue that the original Qur'an was expanded and altered as the Islamic empire evolved.

It should be noted, however, that some Muslims question the motives of these secular scholars. As we have seen, those who are seeking to discredit Islam (such as Sarker) use this scholarship to undermine faith in the Qur'an as an inspired text. For centuries Christian scholars have argued that the Qur'an is a forgery, a plagiarism of Christian and Jewish sources, etc. In an article entitled "The Great Koran con trick," Martin Bright examines the pros and cons of this new scholarship. Bright makes it clear that Patricia Crone has a dark view of Islam as religion. According to Bright:

In *Meccan Trade and the Rise of Islam*, Crone argued that the early Muslim converts turned to Islam because it promised an Arab state based on conquest, rape and pillage. "God could scarcely have been more explicit. He told the Arabs that they had a right to despoil others of their women, children and land, or indeed that they had a duty to do so: holy war consisted in obeying."

Bright notes that Ziauddin Sardar is one of the few Muslim intellectuals to have responded to these new iconoclastic scholars:

[Sardar] has called their work: "Eurocentrism of the most extreme, purblind kind, which assumes that not a single word written by Muslims can be accepted as evidence." Writing in the aftermath of the Rushdie affair, Sardar placed the western revisionists firmly in the post-colonial orientalist camp, from where colonial "experts" have consistently told Muslims that they know best about the origins of their primitive, barbarian religion. "The triumphant conclusion of Crone and Cook," he says, "was that Islam is an amalgam of Jewish texts, theology and ritual tradition."

Whatever the merits of the new scholarship, it is clear that politics played a role in the canonization of Islamic scriptures as well as of the Christian gospels. Politics may play a role even in "objective" scholarship.

It is also clear that the divergences between versions of the Qur'an were not as wide as those between versions of the Christian gospel. In his recent book *Constantine's Bible,* David L. Dungan points out that dozens of Gospels were composed in the first couple of centuries after the death of Jesus. One of the tasks of Eusebius (and the Catholic Church) was to winnow this plethora of gospels down to four. This process took place immediately prior to and during the time of Constantine for political as well as theological reasons so that the Church (and the Roman empire) would have a unified scripture and so that theological dissent could be suppressed. Uthman may have had a similar intention, but his job was much simpler since there was only one Qur'an and the discrepancies, if any, were probably minor.

Another controversy regarding the Qur'an involves the Satanic Verses (which Salman Rushdie used as a theme in his book of the same name). According to one of Mohammad's biographers, Ibn Ishaq, the Prophet wanted so much to please his opponents in Mecca that God supposedly sent him verses implying it was acceptable to seek intercession from certain popular idols such as al-Hat, al-Uzza and Manat. Mohammad allegedly confessed later that it was Satan, not God, who had inspired him to promulgate these verses and they were retracted. Almost all modern Islamic scholars reject this story as historically improbable and lacking the kind of corroboration required to be considered an authentic haddith (or saying) of the Prophet. Others have said that it doesn't really matter if Mohammad was tricked by Satan since he was human, and therefore fallible; what matters is that God corrected his mistake and it doesn't appear in the Qur'an today.

Because scriptures play such an important role in the faith development of "people of the book," such disputes are inevitable. The wisest approach is to be aware of these controversies but not to let them blind us to the insights and wisdom that we can acquire from a careful and sensitive reading of scripture. Augustine affirmed that the goal of the religious life is to practice "faith, hope, and love." A person who "keeps a firm hold upon these [virtues] does not need the Scriptures except for the purpose of instructing others" (Dungan, p. 135). Most liberal Quakers, as well as many Muslims, Christians, and Jews, would probably agree with Augustine on this point.

Translation and Politicization of the Scriptures

Muslims believe that the Qur'an cannot be translated because the Arabic of the Qur'an is divinely inspired and too beautiful to be rendered into another language. Therefore, any rendering of the text into another language is considered an interpretation, not a translation.

The same might be said about translations of the Bible: each one is an interpretation, not simply a word-for-word rendering of the text. Each of the many Bibles that I own has a different interpretive perspective. My Catholic Bible contains commentary that accepts textual-historical criticism and promotes a Catholic take on the Gospels (complete with pictures of the stations of the cross). The language of this Catholic version is modern and very readable. My conservative Protestant Bible rejects textual-historical criticism and sees the Bible as the inerrant word of God. It uses the King James translation which conservative Christians seem to favor as if it were authorized not by a self-serving King but by God Himself. My Jubilee African-American Bible offers an African-American perspective on faith and social justice. This version uses plain, modern English that can be read aloud with great effect.

A similar diversity of perspectives can be found among different translations/interpretations of the Qur'an. But unlike Christians, Muslims in America today can be penalized for having the "wrong" interpretation of their scripture.

Let me give an example. In my pamphlet *Islam from a Quaker Perspective,* I recommended a translation/ version of the Qur'an by the eminent Muslim scholar Abdullah Yusuf Ali. Recently I was shocked, but not surprised, to learn that this version has been banned from school libraries in Los Angeles because of its alleged anti-Semitism

I learned about this through CAIR Watch (www.CAIRwatch.org), a website devoted to exposing the alleged terrorist tendencies of a moderate Islamic organization called the Council on American Islamic Relations (CAIR). Headquartered in Washington, D.C., with 32 regional offices and chapters in the U.S. and Canada, CAIR was founded in 1994 as a Muslim civil liberties and advocacy group.

CAIR has successfully formed a partnership with the National Council of Churches and held dialogue with representatives of the National Association of Evangelicals. But it is viewed with suspicion by groups that accuse it of supporting Palestinian terrorism. The motto of CAIR Watch is "Keeping an Eye on Hate."

Because CAIR Watch uses techniques employed by Steven Emerson and others who see Islam as the embodiment of evil and part of a vast conspiracy to dominate the world, it is worth examining how this group exposes CAIR's alleged anti-Semitism: According to this website,

In February of 2002, Los Angeles city school officials pulled more than 300 copies of *The Meaning of THE HOLY QURAN* from area school libraries. The Quran —an English translation published by Maryland-based Amana Publications—was found to have had numerous anti-Jewish commentaries contained within it. One of the cited commentaries read, "The Jews in their arrogance claimed that all wisdom and all knowledge of Allah was enclosed in their hearts. Their claim was not only arrogance but blasphemy." (Doug Smith, Henry Weinstein and Teresa Watanabe, *Los Angeles Times,* 'Schools Remove Donated Books,' February 7, 2002)

This commentary by Yusuf Ali is quoted accurately and paraphrases what the Qur'an actually says. It should be noted that the Qur'an's attitude towards Jews is a complex one. The Qur'an pays tribute to the Jews for being monotheistic and "people of the Book." It celebrates Jewish prophets like Abraham, Moses, Joseph, etc. But it also criticizes Jews for imagining that they are a "Chosen People" who have a monopoly on God or scriptures. Whether this criticism is anti-Semitic depends on your definition of the term and your attitude towards Muslims.

Given the large Jewish population in Los Angeles and the tensions that arise because of perceived anti-Semitism, it is not hard to see why the L.A. school officials would remove this Qur'an from its shelves. School boards have banned books for all sorts of reasons that seem strange to those of us who cherish the First Amendment. An illustrated edition of "Little Red Riding Hood" was banned in two California school districts in 1989 because the book shows the heroine taking food and wine to her grandmother. The school districts cited concerns about the use of alcohol in the story.

Shakespeare's *The Merchant of Venice* was banned from classrooms in Midland, Michigan, in 1980 because of its portrayal of the Jewish character Shylock. If alleged anti-Semitism is a criterion for banning books in public schools, the Gospel of John should also be banned. It accuses Jews not of blasphemy and arrogance but of killing Christ—an allegation that has caused far more suffering to Jews than any disparaging words in the Qur'an.

However, the CAIR Watch website uses classic McCarthyite techniques to discredit CAIR through guilt by association and unproven accusations. It notes that this edition of the Qur'an was published by an organization that was under investigation for financing terrorism.

In March of 2002, the editor of this Qur'an, the International Institute of Islamic Thought (IIIT), had its Virginia offices raided by the FBI, in a probe that targeted 14 businesses accused of financing terrorism. One of the groups IIIT was said to have financed was the World and Islam Studies Enterprise (WISE), the Palestinian Islamic Jihad front run by Sami Al-Arian. (Paul Sperry, World Net Daily, "Editor of Koran raided by feds,'" April 12, 2002)

CAIR Watch correctly stated that the offices of IITT were raided, but it doesn't mention that no arrests were made and no charges proven against it. Raids against Muslim businesses occur fairly frequently and are often a sign of anti-Muslim bias. CAIR Watch mentions Sami Al-Arian, a pro-Palestinian professor who was arrested but has not been convicted by a jury of any crime, even after ten years of intense government scrutiny and persecution. The anti-CAIR website goes on:

> Only months after the L.A. ban and IIIT raid, in September of 2002, CAIR began providing American libraries with "The Meaning of THE HOLY QURAN"through its "Explore Islamic Culture & Civilization" project. And in May of 2005, CAIR began a new program whereby the group gave a free copy of the Amana-produced Qur'an to anyone who asked. (Americans Against Hate, "CAIR DISTRIBUTING BANNED QUR'AN," May 26, 2005)

CAIR Watch implies that CAIR distributed the Qur'ans for the express purpose of promoting anti-Semitism, but from what I know about CAIR, I am confident that its purpose was conciliatory, not inflammatory. After the news media revealed that soldiers in Guantanamo had treated the Qur'an in ways considered disrespectful by Muslims, the Muslim community was outraged and some Muslims in other countries resorted to violent protests. Instead of denouncing the US government (and thereby running the risk of inciting a violent reaction here in the USA), CAIR chose instead to give out free Qur'ans.

When Pope Benedict made insensitive remarks about Islam that led some Muslims to react with violence, CAIR denounced the violence and called for American Muslims to donate to Catholic charities responsible for rebuilding Christian churches burned down by irate Muslims. (Destroying any house of God, whether it be a synagogue, church, or mosque, is expressly forbidden by the Qur'an.)

Despite allegations of its anti-Jewish bias, I would still recommend Yusuf Ali's version of the Qur'an since its commentary is excellent. My recommendation would include a caveat regarding its comments about Jews.

I must also point out that for generations, Christian commentaries on the Gospels celebrated its overt and highly inflammatory anti-Semitic passages. Probably the most glaring example is Mathew 27:25 in which the Jewish crowd is alleged to have shouted to Pilate: "Let [Christ's] blood be upon us and upon our children."

This savage and utterly unbelievable self-indictment has been used to justify the murder of countless Jews. Take these comments from no less an eminence than John Wesley, in his *Explanatory Notes on the Whole Bible,* published in the 1750s and still featured today on the very popular crosswalk.com website:

His blood be on us and on our children. As this

imprecation was dreadfully answered in the ruin so quickly brought on the Jewish nation, and the calamities which have ever since pursued that wretched people . . . .
(Crosswalk: bible.crosswalk.com/Commentaries/ WesleysExplanatoryNotes/wes.cgi?book=mt&chapter=027)

More concise but of the same sort is the *Peoples New Testament* commentary of 1891, on the same site:

His blood be on us. That is, let us have the responsibility and suffer the punishment. A fearful legacy, and awfully inherited. The history of the Jews from that day on has been the darkest recorded in human annals. (bible.crosswalk.com/Commentaries/ PeoplesNewTestament/pnt.cgi?book=mt&chapter=027)

Even many recent commentaries still let this outrage pass: one Catholic commentary merely reports that this is "the evangelist's commentary on the responsibility for Jesus' death." Lutheran and Oxford Bible commentaries I consulted simply ignored this passage. [*The New American Bible*, Thomas Nelson: NY, 1970. *The New Oxford Annotated Bible, Revised Standard Version:* Oxford Press, 1963. *Concordia Self-Study* Bible, New International Version, St Louis, MO: 1984.]

One modern translator of the Gospels who challenges this anti-Semitism is Willis Barnstone. In *The New Covenant* (Penguin, NY: 2002), Barnstone wisely observes:

"This line, 'Let his blood be upon us and upon our children!' has given rise to much dispute and skepticism. The Jews in the street are shouting, 'Let the guilt of his murder be upon us, the Jews, forever.' On Passover evenings the Jews would be in their houses, celebrating the Passover meal. They would not be in the street asking the Romans to crucify a rabbi, and, had they been, they would not be shouting for crucifixion and at once declaring their guilt forever by shouting for crucifixion" (p. 194-195).

For those interested in reading a translation of the Gospels that is sensitive to the "Jewishness" of Jesus and his followers, I highly recommend William Barnstone's thoughtful translation.

In the interest of full disclosure, I should point out that I have been given two free Qur'ans by CAIR: one by Mohammad Marmaduke Pickthall and one by Mohammad Asad. I was never given one by Abdullah Yusuf Ali. I hope this means that CAIR has stopped distributing Yusuf Ali's version of Qur'an, perhaps in response to adverse criticism.

The Ambivalence of Scripture towards War and Peace

As a Quaker, I am loath to admit that the scriptures of Judaism, Christianity and Islam can be used to justify war, even genocide, as well as pacifism. Yet it is undeniable that one of the names of God in the Hebrew Bible is YHVH Tzva'ot, which means "Lord of Hosts," i.e. of Armies. The significance of this dark side to divinity came home to me most graphically in 1992 when I made my first trip to Israel with a group of clergy. Standing before Jericho, not far from the Mount of Temptation where Jesus spent forty days in the desert, a pastor read the following chilling passage:

> When the trumpets sounded, the people shouted, and at the sound of the trumpet, when the people gave a loud shout, the wall collapsed; so every man charged straight in, and they took the city. They devoted the city to the LORD and destroyed with the sword every living thing in it: men and women, young and old, cattle, sheep and donkeys (Joshua 6:20-21).

Nothing in any scripture I know equals the blood-curdling horror of this passage. Not only women and children, but even animals were eradicated in the name of the Lord!

The cult of the warrior god has unfortunately not disappeared. Recently former Sephardi chief rabbi Mordechai Eliyahu wrote a letter to Prime Minister Ehud Olmert citing scripture to justify the eradication of Palestinians. He said that if some Palestinians continue to fire Kassam rockets into Israel, Israelis are justified in doing whatever it takes to stop them. "If they don't stop after we kill 100, then we must kill a thousand," he said. "And if they do not stop after 1,000 then we must kill 10,000. If they still don't stop we must kill 100,000, even a million. Whatever it takes to make them stop."

In the letter, Eliyahu quoted from Psalms 18:32. "I will pursue my enemies and apprehend them and I will not desist until I have eradicated them." Eliyahu wrote: "This is a message to all leaders of the Jewish people not to be compassionate with those who shoot [rockets] at civilians in their houses."

Some Muslim clerics use similar passages in the Qur'an to justify the killing of civilians on the grounds that Israel is an armed camp occupying Muslim territory and Palestinians have the right to do whatever it takes to oust their oppressors ("Must Innocents Die? The Islamic Debate over Suicide Attacks" by Haim Malka, *Middle East Quarterly* Spring 2003).

One of the most notorious verses of the Qur'an is 9:5:

"When the sacred months are over, slay the idolaters wherever you find them. Arrest them, besiege them, and lie in ambush everywhere for them. If they repent and take to prayer and render the alms levy, allow them to go their way. God is forgiving and merciful." Another one is 47:4-5: "When you meet the unbelievers in the battlefield strike off their heads and, when you have laid them low, bind your captives firmly. Then grant them their freedom or take a ransom from them, until War shall lay down her burdens.

These are warlike, certainly, but it is worth noting that both passages also include provisions for mercy to captives; there was no such luck for the people or animals in Jericho, or several similar cases in the Bible!

Such bloody interpretations of scriptures are vigorously challenged by Jewish and Muslim moderates as well as by many Christians. Religious moderates condemn terrorism (whether by individuals or by states) and point to other passages in scriptures that call for nonviolence.

In my pamphlet *Islam from a Quaker Perspective* I note that the "Qur'an imposes strict limitations on the use of violence," which can be interpreted to require an abstention from all forms of modern warfare.

In *Reading the Muslim Mind*, Hassan Hathout (a well-respected Muslim leader in the Los Angeles area) observes that the Qur'anic rules of war forbid Muslims from harming houses of worship (non-Muslim as well as Muslim), or even the trees or animals of one's enemy. Under such stringent rules, it would be morally wrong for a Muslim to crash land into the World Trade Center, or for the US to drop a bomb on Hiroshima or on Afghanistan. Hathout concludes: "Since modern war is so devastating, war itself should cease to be an option in conflict resolutions. War should be obsolete just like slavery!" (p. 102).

Many rabbis active in the peace movement have taken a similar position and have condemned the violence in the Middle East as contrary to the spirit of the Jewish prophets.

What are we to make of these divergences of opinion regarding scriptures? First, we must admit that scriptures do not present a unified, logically consistent viewpoint on war or peace. Scriptures can be used to justify almost any atrocity, including suicide bombing and genocide. They can also inspire us to strive "with all our hearts, strength and mind" for peace and justice.

Which passages we choose to follow, and how we interpret the scriptures, depends a great deal more on our level of spiritual development than on logic.

For this reason, it is difficult, if not impossible, to convince anyone to forsake an ethic of violence and embrace an ethic of peace simply by quoting scriptures (although it is helpful to know the scriptures if you are having a discussion with someone who sees them as authoritative).

Scriptures and Stages of Faith

To understand how people can have totally different understandings of what the scriptures have to say about war and peace, the work of James Fowler has been extremely helpful to me. In training to become a Methodist minister, Fowler studied psychology as well as theology. He was a Professor of Theology and Human Development at Emory University and director of both the Center for Research on Faith and Moral Development and the Center for Ethics until he retired in 2005.

Fowler's great achievement was to apply the concepts of developmental psychology such as Jean Piaget, Erik Erikson, et al. to faith development. According to Fowler, adults generally progress through the following stages in their faith journey:

Stage 4: "Synthetic-Conventional" faith (arising in adolescence) characterized by conformity.

Stage 5: "Individuative-Reflective" faith (usually mid-twenties to late thirties), a stage of angst and struggle. Individuals take personal responsibility for their beliefs and feelings.

Stage 6: "Conjunctive" faith (mid-life crisis) acknowledges paradox and transcendence relating to reality behind the symbols of inherited systems.

Stage 7: "Universalizing" faith, or what some might call "enlightenment."

This is a somewhat crude simplification of Fowler's subtle and complex analysis, but it suggests a useful framework for understanding how our reading of scripture changes during our lives. The notion that our spiritual understanding evolves over a lifetime is of course nothing new. The Apostle Paul wrote in a famous passage from his letter to the Corinthians: "When I was a child, I spake as a child, I understood as a child, I thought as a child, but when I became a man, I put away childish things."

As adults, most of us no longer read the Bible literally, as we did as children. We no longer accept uncritically what our teachers told us about God and the Bible. We have gone through a period of questioning. We have taken personal responsibility for our beliefs as well as for our actions. We have come to recognize that God, Truth, Reality, etc. is too complex, too subtle, to be reduced to any verbal formulation or to any dogma. As we have encountered a variety of people and life experiences, our understanding of life and the Bible grows more complex. We realize that the Bible uses the language of poetry and paradox to suggest the complexities of the human condition and divine reality.

This maturation process does not happen automatically, however. The stages of faith described by Fowler are associated with periods of life, but do not automatically occur at a certain age. We can get "stuck" at a certain stage and never evolve any further. Stress and crises may cause us to regress to an earlier stage. When we feel threatened and fearful, we often return to conventional, tribalistic modes of thinking and feeling. We then interpret scriptures in ways that reinforce the world view of our particular religious or national group.

As we mature and grow in our faith, we not only come to embrace the paradoxical and complex nature of religion (and life), we grew less fearful and more accepting. When passages of scriptures that seem strange to us are explained by an enlightened interpreter—whether Jewish, Christian, or Muslim—we are less apt to be feel defensive. We "feel where the words come from," to use John Woolman's phrase, and sense the wisdom underlying the unfamiliar words.

If we keep an open heart and mind, we may reach the stage that James Fowler describes as "enlightenment" and become "universalizers":

> The rare persons who may be described by this stage have a special grace that makes them seem more lucid, more simple, and yet somehow more fully human than the rest of us. Their community is universal in extent. Particularities are cherished because they are vessels of the universal, and thereby valuable apart from any utilitarian considerations. Life is both loved and held to loosely. Such persons are ready for fellowship with persons at any of the other stages and from any other faith tradition.

This is the spiritual state to which early Friends aspired, and to which we still aspire today. William Penn beautifully described these "universalizers": "The Humble, Meek, Merciful, Just, Pious and Devout Souls, are everywhere of one Religion; and when Death has taken off the Mask, they will know one another, tho' the diverse Liveries they wear here make them Strangers."

"The diverse Liveries" we wear are our religious and cultural traditions as well as our unique personalities. We need to respect these differences. We also need to acknowledge the controversial, the discordant elements in scripture—the "ocean of darkness," to use George Fox's term—but we also need to see beyond them to what George Fox called "the ocean of Light." Thanks to the interfaith movement, my understanding of scripture has broadened as well as deepened and I can see a little more clearly the Light in each religious tradition as well as in each human soul.

"A Common Word"

By Anthony Manousos

I was recently asked to recommend a question to ask participants at an interfaith event in which lay people were supposed to engage in dialogue. What came to mind was the simple commandment, found in both the Old and New Testament, and also in the Qur'an: "'Love God and love your neighbor." What does this commandment mean to you, from your faith perspective?"

This commandment has been used by Muslim scholars to initiate an interfaith dialogue among Islamic and Christian theologians. The fruits of this pioneering dialogue can be found in *A Common Word: Muslims and Christians on Loving God and Neighbor* (Eerdman: Grand Rapids, MI, 2010). This book, consisting of essays by leading Muslim and Christian scholars, offers hope that the two largest monotheistic religions (comprising over half the world's population) can overcome their historic antagonisms and build a culture of peace based on the Two Commandments shared by all three Abrahamic faiths: "Love God and love your neighbor."

Sound too good to be true? No one in this book says it will be easy to convince the extremists (and the ignorant) on both sides to embrace love rather than hatred, but "A Common Word" is certainly an important step towards building a worldwide consensus among believers that Islam and Christianity can get along peaceably.

This unprecedented Muslim outreach to the Christian community began on October 13, 2007, when 138 Muslim scholars sent out a letter (entitled "A Common Word Between Us and You") to leaders of the Christian faith, calling for peace and understanding. (Since then, there have been more Muslim signatories, bringing the total to over 300.) These noteworthy signatories represent a broad range of nationalities and theological perspectives.

According to its author, Prince Ghazi bin Muhammud of Jordan, this letter represents a "normative Ijma [consensus] by the Ummah's [Muslim community's] scholars," that must be taken seriously by Muslims everywhere.

"A Common Word" was written a year after Pope Benedict XVI gave a controversial talk at the University of Regensberg in which he criticized Islam and quoted derogatory remarks about Mohammad made by a Byzantine emperor. Although the Pope disavowed these incendiary sentiments, they nonetheless provoked a strong backlash in the Muslim community.

Prince Ghazi (an extraordinary scholar who received a BA *summa cum laude* from Princeton and a Ph.D from Cambridge University) wrote a conciliatory response that was endorsed by major Muslim scholars around the world. As a result of this letter, Pope Benedict went to Jordan where he visited a mosque (an historic moment) and was warmly welcome by the Prince and other Muslim dignitaries.

Christian theologians responded to "A Common Word" with a thoughtful and encouraging rejoinder. This so-called "Yale Response" appeared in *The New York Times* (November 2007) and is republished in this book with a commentary by leading Yale scholars Miroslav Volf, Joseph Cumming, and Melissa Yarrington.

Thus began a series of dialogues and colloquia among the world's top Muslim and Christian religious scholars that is ongoing. (Jewish scholars were also invited to take part as observers so they wouldn't feel excluded. Muslim-Jewish dialogue is also taking place in the same conciliatory spirit.) Some of the best papers from these "Common Word" conferences are published in this book.

Unless one is theologically trained, these essays don't make easy reading. But it is nonetheless fascinating to read how finely trained theological minds work, and how they explore the intricacies and complexities of such a seemingly simple statement as: "Love God and love your neighbor." What is meant by "love"? What is meant by "God"? Or "neighbor"? Do Muslims and Christians mean the same thing by these words? Scholars engage the text and commentaries in a myriad of provocative ways to provide intriguing answers to deep theological questions. For example, many Christian scholars argue that Christianity sees God in terms of Love, while Islam sees God in terms of justice. Rez Shah-Kazemi counters that while the word "Love" as understood by Christians is problematic for many Muslim scholars, Islam sees God as "lovingly compassionate and merciful" and he gives examples from both mainstream Muslims and Sufis to make his point. Miroslav Volf deals with the question of the Trinity from the standpoint of Love. If God is Love, how could God love before the creation of man and of the universe, unless God were somehow both unitary and triune in nature. These simplifications don't do justice to the subtle ways that these arguments were woven, but I found these discussions heartening. When scholars come together to explore theological ideas in a respectful manner, they are promoting love and understanding— which, as John Kerry points out, is surely "God's work."

There is of course a political subtext to these theological discussions, as Tony Blair and John Kerry explain in their foreword and epilogue to this book. These scholars do not address many sensitive political issues, such as the occupation of Muslim lands by Western armies, and the lack of religious freedom in many Muslim countries. One hopes that as trust builds and understanding grows, it may become possible for scholars to deal with these thorny issues in constructive ways.

To find out more, I recommend that you not only read this book but also go to the website: acommonword.com. There you will find a wealth of statements, news items and endorsements by notable scholars from around the world, all calling for peaceful coexistence between Christians and Muslims. (You will also find bigoted responses from close-minded believers, but that only shows why this theological heavy lifting needs to take place.) This is an ongoing project that has already borne much good fruit. For example, you can see a video of Prince Ghazi welcoming Pope Benedict to a mosque in Jordan, an historic moment since he is only the second Pope to visit a mosque. The news item page notes that an historical conference of Muslim scholars met to repudiate a reading of the Qur'an that has be used by violent extremists like Osama bin Laden to justify their personal calls for jihad. It was also encouraging to read that a leading Pakistani scholar issued a 600-page fatwa against terrorism in London in March 2010. Such reports refute the idea that Islamic scholars support terrorism and jihad. Some of course do (just as some Christian leaders promote war against Islam), but the vast majority of Muslim scholars oppose terrorism and are calling for peaceful dialogue.

It is heartening to see so many leading Christians and Muslims as signatories and participants in this important dialogue. I was pleased to see a response by British Friends, but I was disappointed that the one by American Friends was not included, even though one was sent out two years ago. Here is the text of the American response, published here for the first time:

The Christian and Interfaith Relations Committee (CIRC) of Friends General Conference of the Religious Society of Friends (Quakers) welcomes and celebrates A Common Word between Us and You. The truly diverse group of Muslims who gathered and signed this history-making document should inspire Christians to work among themselves to find how they can, despite their many differences, come together and agree on a statement affirming the need for peace among the religions of the world, and particularly between Muslims and Christians, who together account for such a significant portion of the world's population. CIRC therefore wants to affirm A Common Word between Us and You and the spirit of reconciliation that informs it.

Relationships between Quakers and Muslims go back many years. Friends have a long heritage of educating for peace. In the Friends School at Ramallah, which has been in existence for over 100 years, Christians and Muslims have studied together and cooperated to better their lives. In response to a plea from the United Nations, the American Friends Service Committee initiated a relief program to serve refugees in Gaza in 1949. Quaker service has continued there since that time. In addition to emergency relief work, a current focus is the Quaker Palestine Youth Program, which has worked closely with local non-governmental organizations, Palestinian Ministries, educational institutions, and international organizations to enhance opportunities for marginalized Palestinian youth. Quakers in Ramallah have also founded a Peace Center that works to promote peace and understanding. The Quaker presence in the Middle East is also felt in Christian Peacemaker Teams, such as those in Hebron and Iraq. Tom Fox was a Quaker martyr for peace.

For us, our labors to promote understanding between faiths is an expression of our peace testimony. Early Quakers expressed their convictions on peace in a statement to the king of England, Charles II, in 1660:

"We utterly deny all outward wars and strife and fightings with outward weapons, for any end or under any pretence whatsoever. And this is our testimony to the whole world. The spirit of Christ, by which we are guided, will never move us to fight and war against any man with outward weapons, either for the kingdom of Christ, or for the kingdoms of this world."

George Fox, commonly regarded as the founder of Quakerism, spoke of living "in the virtue of that life and power that took away the occasion of all wars." We strive to live in that same life and power. We perceive that same desire in your outreach to the Christian world in A Common Word Between Us and You.

In conclusion, we hope to be your partners in promoting understanding between our communities of faith. Both your Scriptures and ours call us to peacemaking. "Blessed are the peacemakers" (Matthew 5:9a). As the Qur'an states (49:13), "People, we created you from one man and one woman, and made you into nations and tribes, so that you may get to know one another. In the light of God, the most honored of you are the most mindful. God is all-knowing, all-aware."

We shall urge members of the Religious Society of Friends to create opportunities for deep listening and dialogue with Muslims in their communities in order to improve our mutual understanding and to work together with Muslims (and others) to make a more just and peaceful world. CIRC commits itself to spreading knowledge of A Common Word Between Us and You as widely as possible among Friends. Additionally, in CIRC's ecumenical work, from the local to the national and international level, it will be an advocate to call Christians to share the concern for peace between Christians and Muslims that is so powerfully expressed in your document.

APPROACHING THE QU'RAN

by Michael A. Sells

INTRODUCTION BY RHODA GILMAN*

In this section (which was originally published by QUF as a pamphlet in 2001), we offer to Friends ten short chapters, or "suras," from the Qur'an, translated with accompanying commentary by Michael Sells. The selections are from 36 suras included in Sells' book, *Approaching The Qur'an: The Early Revelations*, published by White Cloud Press (Ashland, OR, 1999). We hope that readers who are touched by the beauty of the verses and intrigued by the explanations will go on to read further in the book itself — and not only to read, but to listen, for the book as published is accompanied by a compact disc (CD) on which six of the shorter suras are recited in Arabic. As one listens, one may follow them in the text, which gives a full transliteration and a word-for-word English gloss.

As Sells explains in his introduction to the book, the Qur'an is for speakers of Arabic primarily an auditory experience. Its poetry and its power, often resting in associations of sound as well as meaning, are almost incapable of translation. For this reason among others, the Qur'an has been little understood or appreciated in the West. It tends to remain an enigma, even for seekers like universalist Friends, who are generally open to the spiritual truths of other religions and cultures.

©1999 by Michael A. Sells.Printed with permission from White Cloud Press. Extracted from Approaching the Qur'an. Rhoda Gilman is a long-time member of QUF and former editor of Universalist Friends.

In this rendering, which has been honed by years of use in the classroom, Sells seeks to bring readers an appreciation for the subtle feeling and spiritual resonance of these brief "Early Revelations" given to the prophet Mohammed. They are, as he points out, only a small part of the Qur'an, but, perhaps, the part most often taught and committed to memory by followers of Islam. The words are regarded by those followers as a direct transmission from God via the Prophet.

From time to time QUF publications have carried discussions of traditions other than Christianity, but Islam has been neglected. Historically this seems strange, for Islam, along with Judaism and the varied beliefs of American Indians, was one of the first non-Christian bodies of thought that 17th century Friends encountered. Early Friends, including George Fox, approached Islam without hostility and with a conviction that its followers were potentially open to the Inward Light. Yet they made little effort to study or understand the truths that might be found in the Qur'an.

Several years ago at an FGC gathering the absence of material on Islam was brought to the attention of members of the QUF steering committee along with a request that we try to fill the gap. Now, thanks to Michael Sells, we are able to take a step in that direction. When we asked what led him to Quakerism and Islamic studies, he replied as follows, writing in the third person:

Michael Sells encountered Quaker meeting for worship for the first time while he was a graduate student at the University of Chicago. His roommate suggested he attend the 57th Street Meeting. He was immediately struck by the diversity of voices in the meeting. Compelling messages from a variety of religious and nonreligious perspectives sounded and were heard in the depth of the surrounding silence. He remembers hearing messages bristling with Old Testament prophecy, Christian-centered reflections, psychological self-reflections, personal concerns expressed in a manner more open than he had heard in public, Buddhist-centered messages, and messages of political engagement. He recalls that this was the first time he had encountered such a diversity of perspectives not only being accepted, but actually being embraced within a religious context. He ultimately found in the Quaker Universalist Fellowship a larger framework for the cultivation of such a diversity.

At the time he was encountering Quakerism for the first time, Michael Sells was working to finish his graduate studies toward a Ph.D. in comparative literature. During the next two years he completed a dissertation on comparative mystical language in Greek, Islamic, and Christian mysticism. At the same time his interest in Arabic and the Islamic world was growing. He has since made Arabic and the Islamic civilization a central part of his research.

Of all traditions, Islam is the one that encounters the fiercest prejudice in the United States at this time. Recently Sells returned from a three-week stay in Damascus. He recalls the deep hospitality, respect, and warmth with which he was accepted by people from every stratum of society. After returning home, he began seeing again the image of the Arab and the Muslim on the news media and in newspapers. At times he found himself wondering if the image seen in the U.S. had anything to do with the culture and life in a city like Damascus. Having lived for five years in North Africa and the Middle East, he had developed the conviction that Muslims have the exact same proportion of peaceful and violent personalities, successful and failed marriages, tenderness or neglect of parents toward children or children toward parents, and honest or deceitful discourses as do communities in the United States.

After 16 years of teaching the religions of the world at

Haverford College, Michael Sells is more convinced than ever of the infinite depth of wisdom within each religious tradition, from Islam to Hinduism, from the Igbo of Nigeria to the Ojibwe of Minnesota. He has also encountered and written about the way religious symbols can be manipulated to motivate and justify horrendous violence, as was the case in Bosnia. Because the Muslims have been dehumanized through stereotyping in Western media, Sells has focused his teaching, research, and writing on those aspects of Islamic culture that are "lost in translation." The rich worlds of nuance, humor, gentleness, wit, dissent, meditation, and love poetry, all of which are central to Middle Eastern and other Islamic societies, are commonly stripped from the image of Islam as it is presented, sometimes by outsiders, sometimes by those claiming to be its leaders in the West. The result of such loss is a monodimensional and wooden image of the people and the culture. In *Approaching the Qur'an*, Michael Sells attempts to bring across the combination of intimacy and majesty that is central to the Qur'an and which tends to be lost in many translations.

We are grateful to Michael Sells for these comments as well as for his generous permission in letting us reprint selections from his book.

Three calligraphy styles presenting the phrase *bi smi Allah ar-Rahman ar-Rahim* (In the name of God the Compassionate the Caring), which precedes each sura of the Qur'an.

1 THE OPENING

In the name of God
the Compassionate the Caring
Praise be to God
    lord sustainer of the worlds
    the Compassionate the Caring
master of the day of reckoning
5 To you we turn to worship
and to you we turn in time of need
Guide us along the road straight
the road of those to whom you are giving
not those with anger upon them
not those who have lost the way

Because of its eloquent statement of devotion and the manner in which it pervades religious life, *The Opening* has been called the Islamic equivalent of the Lord's Prayer in Christianity. The word translated "opening," *fätiha*, means the opening in the sense of the opening of a chapter or a story. Unlike the other early hymnic Suras, *The Opening* occurs not at the end of the Qur'anic written text, but at the very beginning. It is the most recited of all Qur'anic Suras, not only in prayers and liturgy, but also in everyday life. After business transactions, for example, *The Opening* is recited by both parties as a mark of good faith and a solemn affirmation of the responsibilities affirmed by each partner.

    The Opening is the only Sura in which the phrase "In the Name of God the Compassionate the Caring" does not occur before the Sura, but is actually considered part of the Sura itself. Just as that phrase is woven into the pattern of simple activities as a form of reminder so "Praise be to God" *(al-hamdu li lläh)* has become part of everyday speech. It is used after any good news or any praise, and as a response to the greeting "How are you?"

The two qualifications of God are "lord of the worlds" (the creator deity) and "master of the day of reckoning" (the deity who brings finality to all acts and all lives). The response for those hearing or reciting *The Opening* is to turn toward God in worship and for refuge.

The "the road straight" frequently is translated as "the straight path." The term rendered here as road, *sirät,* would have connoted something grand to the inhabitants of the Arabian peninsula. There are many words in Arabic for paths; the Arabs of Muhammad's time traveled through the desert on barely discernible paths. By contrast, the word *sirät* means a paved road, such as the roads of the Romans which the Arabian travelers might come across in their journeys.

53: 118 THE STAR

In the Name of God the Compassionate the Caring
By the star as it falls
Your companion has not lost his way nor is he deluded
He does not speak out of desire
This is a revelation
5 taught him by one of great power
and strength that stretched out over
while on the highest horizon —
then drew near and came down
two bows' lengths or nearer
10 He revealed to his servant what he revealed
The heart did not lie in what it saw
Will you then dispute with him his vision?

He saw it descending another time
at the lote tree of the furthest limit
15 There was the garden of sanctuary
when something came down over the lote tree, enfolding
His gaze did not turn aside nor go too far
He had seen the signs of his lord, great signs

The first eighteen verses of *The Star* are considered among the earliest revelations of the Qur'an and are the most explicit reference to Muhammad's prophetic vision. The Sura begins (1-12) with the divine voice swearing by the falling star that "your companion" has not gone mad or lost his way. "Your companion" is interpretated as Muhammad. His vision is also called a revelation *(wahy)* and is explicitly said to be rooted not in desire *(hawä),* which the Qur'an associates with the inspiration of the poets (Sura 26). The object of vision is never actually described. Instead, the text evokes the process of vision by tracing a movement along the highest horizon and then a descent and drawing near to the distance of "two bows' lengths." The passage ends with an affirmation of the validity of the vision: The heart of the prophet "did not lie in what he saw." This affirmation becomes a proof text for the claim among many mystics and philosophers that the locus of spiritual vision and mystical knowledge is the heart.

In a second passage (13-18), the divine voice, referring to Muhammad again in the third person, describes another vision ("He saw it descending another time"). Here, "the lote tree of the furthest limit" is placed in or near the enigmatic "garden of sanctuary." We are told almost nothing about the tree, except that something came upon it in an enveloping manner. Of key importance is the "gaze" of the prophet, which does not "turn aside" or "go too far." This one verse became the paradigm for Islamic reflection on the proper state in contemplation. As in many evocative passages in the Qur'an, what is left unsaid is as important as what is said. Here, the power of the vision is evoked through a depiction of the gaze of the viewer, but the vision itself is never described in detail or given fixed form in a way that limits thought or imagination.

When the Qur'an states "He saw it descending another time," the antecedent of the pronoun *(hu,* it/him) is unstated, and thus the referent of the "it" is not determinable from the passage. The identity of the referent became a matter of controversy, with the debate centering upon whether or not the deity can be seen in this world. Those for whom the vision of God can only occur in the afterlife tend to interpret the it/he as referring to the messenger-angel Gabriel.

The bismillah invocation in the form of an ostrich.

87 THE MOST HIGH

In the Name of God the Compassionate the Caring
Holy be the name of your lord most high
Who created then gave form
Who determined then gave guidance
Who made the meadow pasture grow
5 then turned it to a darkened flood-swept remnant

We will make you recite. You will not forget
except what the will of God allows
He knows what is declared
and what lies hidden
He will ease you to the life of ease
So remind them if reminder will succeed
10 Those who know awe will be brought to remember
He who is hard in wrong will turn away

He will be put to the fire
neither dying in it nor living
He who makes himself pure will flourish
15 who remembers the name of his lord and
performs the prayer

But no. They prefer the lower life
Better is the life ultimate, the life that endures
As is set down in the scrolls of the ancients
the scrolls of Ibrahím and Músa

The Most High centers on a repeated theme of the
early Meccan Suras: the Qur'anic text and its messenger
as a "reminder." The divine voice proclaims that
Muhammad can only remind but not compel his listeners
to heed the reminder. God is depicted here as the one who
knows what is in the open and what is hidden. This notion
of the deity will be developed throughout the Qur'an by
the use of divine names such as the all-seeing *(al-basïr)*,
the all-hearing *(as-sami`)*, the one who knows inside and
out *(al-khabïr)*, and the all-knowing *(al-`alim)*. The human
being hides things from others and from himself. The being
that knows these hidden, most intimate details, that
knows ourselves better than we know ourselves, is the
Qur'anic God, Allah.

Those who cannot be brought to remember their
essential role and responsibility as human beings are said
to prefer the lower life *(al-hayät ad-dunyä)*. The word for
"lower" here is also the word, when used as a noun, for
"world," a meaning that has led some translators to render
the phrase "the life of the world." Although there may be
a play on the two senses of *dunyä* here, grammatically
the term cannot mean "life of the world" and I have
adhered to the more immediate meaning of the term. The
other problem with terms like "life of the world" or
"worldly" is that the Qur'an generally does not view the
world in negative terms, seeing it instead as the gift of an
infinitely generous creator that, however transitory it may

be, is to be cherished rather than despised.

The final verse suggests that the central message of *The Most High* is the same one that was revealed to Abraham (Ibrähïm) and Moses (Müsä).

90 THE GROUND

In the Name of God the Compassionate the Caring
I swear by this ground
— you have come to dwell on this ground —
by the begetter and by the begotten,
we created the human being in hardship
5   Does he think there is no power over him
He says: look at the goods I devoured
Does he think no one sees him

Did we not endow him with eyes
lips and tongue
10 and guide him to the two high plains

And yet he did not climb the steep pass
What can tell you of the steep pass?

To free a slave
To feed the destitute on a day of hunger
15 a kinsman orphan
or a stranger out of luck in need

Be of those who keep the faith
who counsel one another to patience
who counsel to compassion
They are of the right

As for those who cast our signs away
they are of the left
20 Over them a vault of fire

The oath at the beginning of *The Ground* evokes as a

sign the ground, area, or region (presumably the district around Mecca, held as a sacred territory). In verse 2 it speaks directly to the prophet and indirectly to other Meccans, in stating, "you have come to dwell on this ground." The Arab term rendered here as ground, *balad*, can mean both town and countryside and there is a difference of opinion concerning the exact area designated by the term — whether it means the town of Mecca or the territory or land on which Mecca sits. I have chosen an English term, ground, that can be as open in usage as the original Arabic. After invoking as signs this special ground and the "the begetter and the begotten," the Sura turns to one of the fundamental messages of the early Meccan period: condemnation of indifference and callousness toward the orphaned and the poor.

The condemnation of indifference to the suffering of others is brought back to the sign of the land in a graphic manner. The emancipation of a slave or caring for the disinherited is portrayed as the climbing of a high pass, the steep, narrow, treacherous ledge that rises up along the face of desert mountains.

The Sura ends with a divine command to people to counsel one another to patience and compassion, and with a warning to those who deny the signs. The word for sign (*äya*) means both a physical sign (such as the land) and also a verse of the Qur'an. The verses of the Qur'an are both a remembrance of signs that are present throughout the world and themselves signs, which, like the signs of nature, point to a deeper reality forgotten or neglected in everyday human consciousness and endeavor.

91 THE SUN

In the Name of God the Compassionate the Caring
By the sun and her brightening
By the moon when it follows her
By the day when it displays her
By the night when it veils her
5 By the sky and what constructed her
By the earth and what shaped her
By the soul and what formed her
and revealed her debased
and revealed her faithful
Whoever honors her flourishes
10 Whoever defiles her fails

The people of Thamud called truth a lie
in their inhumanity
when they sent out their worst

The messenger of God said
God's camel mare
give her water!

They called him liar
and hamstrung her for the slaughter
15 Then their lord rumbled down upon them
for their crime and wiped them away
with no fear of what came after

The Sun begins with one of the most extended oaths
of the Qur'an. The sun is portrayed surrounded by a court,
in the most lyrical Qur'anic tone. The word for sun (*shams*)
is grammatically feminine in Arabic and takes the
grammatically feminine pronoun *hä*. By making *hä* the
key rhyme word throughout the first part of the Sura, the
Qur'anic voice creates a partial personification. In other
words, a "gender figure" is produced. The "her" is never
fully personified as a woman, but is always on the verge

222

of such a personification.

The second part of the Sura evokes the civilization of Thamūd. For the people of Arabia, there were few symbols more potent than the tribe of Thamūd and the ruins of their great city that may have been part of the Nabataean culture whose capital was Petra, the "red rose city as old as time."

In both early Islamic poetry and the Qur'an, the destruction of Thamūd became a parable for the passing of civilizations. The poets attributed the passing of the civilization to the incessant work of fate/time *(dahr)*, which wears down all things and thwarts human aspirations. The Qur'an attributed the destruction of Thamūd to the refusal of its people to heed the words of their prophet, a refusal that led to the destruction of other peoples before and after Thamūd as well.

In disobeying their prophet, Sālih, the people of Thamūd slaughtered God's camel mare. Nothing was more taboo in ancient Arabia than the unjustified killing of a camel mare. The central ritual of pre-Islamic poetry was the camel sacrifice and distribution of the meat throughout the tribe. The improper slaying of a camel mare was a sacrilege or abomination of such enormity that it led to tribal wars that lasted generations.

By slaughtering God's camel mare, the people of Thamūd committed what was by both ancient tribal standards and Qur'anic standards an abomination. The depictions of the destruction of Thamūd are also eerily similar to depictions of the events of the day of reckoning and may serve as a parable for them as well.

93 THE MORNING HOURS

In the Name of God the Compassionate the Caring

By the morning hours
By the night when it is still
Your lord has not abandoned you
and does not hate you

What is after will be better
than what came before
5 To you the lord will be giving
You will be content

Did he not find you orphaned
and give you shelter
Find you lost
and guide you
Find you in hunger
and provide for you

10 As for the orphan —
do not oppress him
And one who asks —
do not turn him away
And the grace of your lord —
proclaim

Muhammad was orphaned as a young boy and came under the protection of his grandfather. When his grandfather died, his uncle became his guardian. In a tribal society based on family and clan protection, the loss of his father and grandfather left Muhammad vulnerable to enemies in Mecca, particularly when he began reciting the Qur'anic messages that threatened the interests and beliefs of more powerful men.

In this short Sura, the Qur'anic emphasis on helping the orphaned and the disinherited is directly tied into a reminder (to Muhammad and to the listener in the more general sense) of the sufferings Muhammad experienced in his youth. Many commentators believe that this Sura was a consolation to Muhammad for the opposition and persecution he suffered as a prophet in the early Meccan years.

PART 6: FRIENDS, JEWS AND ISRAEL/PALESTINE

There is much truth in the old joke about a rabbi who observed: "Some of my best Jews are Friends." So many Jews have joined the Religious Society of Friends that they have formed their own affinity group, as Richard Bellin explains in his piece "A Brief History of Jewish Friends in FGC." Claire Gorfinkel, another Jewish Friend, has written a Pendle Hill pamphlet entitled I Have Always Wanted to be. Jewish and Now, Thanks to the Religious Society of Friends, I am (PHP #350, 2000).

Jews tend to feel comfortable in the Religious Society of Friends in part because of its emphasis on ethical living and social witness rather than on doctrine and creed. Since unprogrammed Quakerism is an experiential religion, Friends are not required to believe in the divinity of Jesus, or even in the divinity. Pablo Stanfield provides a thoughtful analysis of what Judaism and Quakerism have in common. It should be noted, however, that Pablo's theological views do not represent those of other Jewish Friends. Like unprogrammed Friends in general, Jewish Friends include the full theological spectrum: Buddhist, Wiccan, pagan, Universalist, nontheist and even polytheist.

One of the biggest challenges facing Jewish Friends, as well as Friends in general, is the question of Israel/Palestine. This issue is also a huge challenge for those involved in interfaith dialogue and reconciliation. How can we bring Muslims, Christians and Jews to the table and have a respectful dialogue around this contentious issue?

It is tempting simply to ignore this challenge, but it is impossible to do so for seveal reasons:

1) There cannot be peace in the world until there is peace in the Middle East. There can be no peace in the

Middle East until there is a just, compassionate peace in Israel/Palestine.

2) As American citizens, we have a moral responsibility for what happens in Israel/Palestine because our tax dollars pay for the support of the Israeli government. More American aid goes to Israel than to any other foreign government. Estimates vary, but we give at least three billion dollars in military and other aid to Israel each year. We are therefore morally responsible for how this money is spent and what it is used for.

3) Friends of Christian background feel a deep emotional and spiritual connection with the land where Jesus was born, and where Christians are increasingly at risk. Friends also feel connected to Israel/Palestine because of the Ramallah Friends School, where Quaker values have been taught to Palestinians for over 100 years.

For these and other reasons, many Friends feel led to become involved as peacemakers in this region. They stand in solidarity with Christians, Muslims and Jews who are seeking nonviolent solutions for the conflicts in Israel/ Palestine. When I visited Israel and the West Bank in 2004 as part of the Compassionate Listening Project, I was moved and impressed by these unsung heroes who were speaking out and risking their lives on behalf of peace and justice.

Included in this section are articles about Israel/ Palestine by Max Carter, Director of Quaker Studies at Guilford College, and Ralph Beebe, an Evangelical Friend who taught at George Fox University. This handbook fittingly ends with a talk given by David Rush, a Jewish Friend who took part in a recent Compassionate Listening Project; and also by articles describing work undertaken by the American Friends Service Committee.

David Rush believes that Compassionate Listening is an important key to peace and reconciliation in the Middle East. Israeli Jews and Palestinian Muslims are both deeply wounded people. Both have stories of pain and suffering and oppression that need to be heard. The tragedy is that it is difficult for Jews to hear the stories of Palestinians, and vice versa. Each side complains that the other side hasn't heard or presented the whole story. Compassionate listening is an important tool for building the trust necessary for peace.

In addition to compassionate listening, Friends have created opportunities for young Palestinians to develop leadership skills and for peace advocates on both sides to be heard, as is evident in the article by Tim Sallinger about the Interfaith Voices for Peace panel that the AFSC organized in Washington, DC, in March 2011.

As Quakers, we have a vital role to play in helping both sides to hear "that of God" in each other and to work for a compassionate, just peace.

I hope that these essays will give us a sense of the complexity of viewpoints and perspectives that need to be considered as we seek to be peacemakers in a region where peace has been so elusive.

A Brief History of Jewish Friends at FGC

by Richard A. (Dick) Bellin

Jewish Friends has existed as an informal, loosely organized activity within Friends General Conference since the early 1980s.

In January 1983 Joy Weaver published an article in *Friends Journal*, "I Never Lost It." This article resulted from a very unpleasant experience at the 1982 FGC Gathering at Slippery Rock State College (PA), which she summarized in the article as follows:

> The occasion was the Advancement Committee's threshing session on community outreach....Early in the session the statement was made, and later defended, that those people raised in the Jewish faith who could not "accept Christ" should be encouraged to seek fellowship among Friends, but should not be permitted to attain membership.

> Although there was some heated discussion on the issue, mainly from Friends who felt it to be a creedal statement, I came away feeling that I had attended not a *threshing* session, where ripe ideas were harvested, but a *thrashing* session where the whole, carefully nurtured crop of my religious belief was cut down and trampled into the fields.

The first meeting of Jewish Friends as a group occurred the following year at the 1983 Gathering at Slippery Rock. Since then the group has met every year at Gathering. However, the group has never arranged to become a formally organized activity within FGC. The annual

---

Richard A (Dick) Bellin is a member of Friends Meeting of Washington (DC). He serves on the Meeting's Finance and Stewardship Committee. He is also in his second term as a Trustee of Baltimore Yearly Meeting. Dick is Registrar and Website Coordinator for Friends Conference on Religion and Psychology fcrp.quaker.org

meeting is ad hoc, arranged and scheduled by someone who plans to be at Gathering. There is always at least one, and usually two, afternoon meetings. On Friday evening of Gathering week Jewish Friends conduct a simple Shabbat ceremony.

At the 1985 Gathering, also at Slippery Rock, there was a panel discussion entitled "Some Of My Best Jews Are Friends." The panel participants were Maxine Kaufman, Judy Kerman, Free Polazzo, and Joy Weaver as moderator. There have been other articles in *Friends Journal* and the *Quaker Universalist Journal* by Jewish Friends, including Joy, Judy Kerman, and Ruth Jacobs.

Soon after the 1987 Gathering Jewish Friends held a retreat hosted by Friends Meeting of Washington (DC). Since then there has been a retreat at Cambridge Meeting (MA), as well as two at Powell House. The Pittsburgh Meeting (PA) hosted a Seder attended by several participants from the Jewish Friends group.

At the 1988 Gathering at Appalachian State College in Boone (NC,) Joy Weaver facilitated a workshop about being both Jewish and Quaker.

After the 1983 meeting Joy started a printed newsletter, *Old Foundations*. This publication contained articles and news items submitted by many people. Joy continued as editor until she stopped its publication several years ago. It was replaced by an e-mail discussion list, which exists today. The list is hosted at Googlegroups maintained by three people— Joy Weaver, Bill Selzer, and Dick Bellin. It is private and unlisted, subscription by request only. As of January 2011 there were 75 subscribers. Most are Jewish Friends, some are Friends who are not Jewish, and a few are neither. All are welcome. The primary purpose of both the printed newsletter and the subsequent e-mail list has been to explore what it means to be both Jewish and Quaker. To subscribe, send a request to jewishfriends-subscribe@googlegroups.com.

Jesus the Jew, the Meshiach and the Inner Christ

by Pablo Stanfield

Over the last half-century a number of people have observed the parallels between Quaker practice and Judaism. It is no surprise to most in our more universalist tradition of Friends that many Jewish people have found a spiritual home in Quaker meetings, whether because of being Seekers, finding a common ground with a non-Jewish spouse, or following whatever other personal leading, often pacifism and nonviolence. As one Jew in my home meeting told me after over twenty years of active Quaker life: "I never had to give up one jot of my Judaism to become a Quaker."

What are some of those similarities? In both religions there is an absence of creed, meaning that each person is free to define his/her experience of the Sacred, his/her own theology. Second, there is respect for the individual with the the values that follow from that, whether we say it is because "there is that of God in every person," or say it follows from seeing that each person is created in the image of the Creator. All the testimonies and many of our distinctive practices grow out of this, just as do many of the *halakhic*[1] rulings of the Talmud. Both have a requirement that the individual make her/his own relationship with the Divine; to some degree both religions are do-it-yourself. Likewise both traditions emphasize acting on one's faith: if you are not applying your values

---

© *Friends Bulletin Publishing Corporation. Published in* Western Friend, *March 2011. Reprinted with permission of the author, who added some material. To subscribe: www.westernfriend.org. D. Pablo Stanfield is a member of University Friends Meeting in Seattle, WA.*

and the guidance of your spiritual experience to make the world better, to co-create with God and bring about *malkhut Adonai*, the "Kingdom of God," then you have misunderstood the teachings. Both are practical faiths: they require you to live your belief, here and now, in this world, not waiting for some possible future state of perfection.

Another similarity is that, nowadays at least, talking about the Divine is not common. Unlike our evangelical Friends or some of the most orthodox or Chassidic Jews, most Jews and non-Christocentric[2] Friends are uncomfortable with the connotations of the word "God." Our weak attempts to describe our concept of the Holy Oneness are frustrated by our limited language so we use multiple alternatives, "Spirit, Inner Guide, Inward Light," or "*Shekhinah, Adonai, haShem.*"[3] As a result, Jews who visit silent Quaker Meetings rarely have the off-putting experience, common when they visit other churches, of an anthropomorphic deity named Jesus whom they do not recognize and who often is portrayed as "supersessionist"[4] and wanting to "convert" or change them. Liberal Friends rarely have or talk about sudden conversions, or of being saved, although many will share profoundly life-directing mystical experiences and convictions in which they see Divine guidance. This conforms with Jewish norms, which also assume that daily practice and constant *teshuva* – repentance or return—are required to stay on track and to grow into who we are. This lack of God talk leads many to assume that a kind of agnostic humanism is our norm, and in both groups we find atheists who may assume that our spirituality is really a kind of metaphor or psychological atavism.

More common among unprogrammed Friends, however, is the experience of commonalities with Buddhism, especially Zen. Many who have taken tours through Eastern religions in the past decades practice a kind of syncretic Quakerism with aspects of Zen, Sufism, New Age, Native American or Wiccan symbolism or ritual added in. I must confess that this could easily describe my Quakerism: I call myself a Daoist Jewish Quaker, for the Judeo-Christian heritage is infused in our culture – even of those who are allergic to explicit mention of any doctrine from it. In the last five years I have reached clarity that I cannot use the word Christian to describe my beliefs at all – the essential elements of the Christian faith since at least 325, the year the Council of Nicæa established the Creed, are not my experience of God or my understanding of the teachings of Rev Yeshu'a bar Maryam of Nazareth. Even though most Christocentric Friends in the unprogrammed branch do not subscribe to the details of those creeds, I cannot accept identifying with even an "alternative Christianity," as I used to.

At the same time, I find in my studies, both of Quaker history and writings and of the Talmud and Jewish understandings of Torah, that I am very much in the mainstream of the Quaker movement, returning to the teachings of Jesus and rediscovering, as the first Quakers said, the life and power of the primitive church when it was filled with the Paraclete after Pentecost. The reason is that those early Christian Jews were very in tune with their Rabbi Jesus the Jew. In following Jesus, I left the Calvinism of my upbringing and later all the Christian sects I knew and found Quakerism; in following Jesus I explored my Jewish roots and discovered the Jewish-ness of Jesus and Quakerism. To some degree the failure of Christians to understand, ever since the Jesus Movement was taken over by non-Jews in the Second and Third centuries, the teachings of their Master – let alone live by them – is a result of the anti-Semitism that invaded the religion after the destruction of Judea in the year 135. To the degree that Christians either fail to comprehend the truly Jewish teachings of Rabbi Jesus or reject his Judaism, they block their own ability to understand those teachings. I would hope, having been astonished at Christians who deny it, that most Quakers at least recognize that Jesus was a Jew and understand the logic of this viewpoint.

What I am saying here is not news nor even novel among most scholars. There are many books, both scholarly and popular, coming out of the Quest for the Historical Jesus and linguistic analysis of newly found manuscripts or even the canonic scriptures. Archaeology has shed new light on the Israelite religion of the Second Temple period when Jesus lived. Altogether these developments have led to better insights into the sources of Christian doctrines and nuanced understanding of what Jesus probably taught and what the early Christians wrote and how Gentiles modified earlier writings.

We can state with a certain reliability several things about Jesus of Nazareth and the Jews who were his disciples until the Second Century. We can also speak about how teachings of the Sages of the Talmud enlighten us about what Jesus taught. I wish to do that by speaking about my understanding from my experience. When evangelical Friends have tried to tell me that I must have a relationship with Jesus, I have sometimes said that I have one; it is not that different from my relationship with Mohandas Gandhi, who died halfway around the world when I was not yet two years old, yet influences my life. But if Quakerism affirms anything, it insists that knowing about someone, even God, is not the same as truly knowing them. I know God, who has blessed me with direct contact and guidance, but never as Jesus, only as *Shekhinah*[3].

Nearness of God. There is One, who is very near, like a loving Father, who provides for us on all levels: wherever we are physically, emotionally or spiritually: the *Shekhinah*, The Presence, the holy Spirit (*ruach ha-Qodesh*), is accompanying us, available for help. We cannot think of Spirit and Creator as separate, not even as differing faces or persons of the Godhead: they are "the burning Oneness binding everything," in Kenneth Boulding's inspired words. They are different in that we perceive them by different means, but we are part of their one-ness and creation. I am in awe of this Power and of my ability to be in awe of It. I sense its sacredness and feel it pulsing through all Life, because life and love are its nature. Jesus and early Quakerism were unitarian and clear. This is the foundation of my worship and my spiritual growth—and has been since I was in the womb. There has never been a time when I was cut off from it, although I may have felt disconnected. There was never a time it was unavailable to me, to any Jew, or to any other person in creation, although we may not have detected its nearness; it is a question of consciousness, what John the Evangel (probably also a Hellenized Jewish Christian, but his writings have been much reworked and colored with anti-Semitism) calls the Logos (the Word, the knowledge, the awareness). As Sha'ul the Lesser (Paulos) of Tarsus put it: "For I am certain that nothing, neither death nor life, nor angels, nor principalities or powers, neither this world nor the world to come, neither height nor depth, nor anything in all creation, can separate us from the love of God which is ours [in the Light]..." (Romans 8: 38)

What is God's love? This is perhaps the thorniest query we can come to. Some Christian commentators have made much about Rev Yeshu'a's prioritization of Divine Love and compassion, the availability of Divine forgiveness for repentant sinners, a concept that was standard in Israelite religion from the time of the Babylonian captivity. I have no doubt that the Holy One is gracious and merciful; the Hebrew, Greek and Arabic scriptures all affirm it after all. The idea was not original with Jesus, having appeared in Genesis and Exodus. From early times Hebrews had referred to the Lord as Almighty Providence, *El Shaddai*. The Universe does provide everything for our needs as well as all the things that eventually kill us. It rains on the just and unjust persons' fields and the sun shines equally for the sinner and bully as for the pious and generous peacemakers. So the person who does not have spiritual sensors to detect the embraces and kisses of the Truth may not immediately notice what one is to be thankful for in all the Thanksgivings the faithful offer. Both Judaism and Quakerism then start with a command to listen: *Sh'ma'* [Listen!] is the central verb in the Jewish declaration of faith quoting from Moses, and Friends' distinctive worship requires deep listening, between words to where the words come from. Somehow the requirement to love the Lord with all one's heart, all one's soul and mind, and with all one's efforts leads the saints of both traditions to overflow with it and share it with the world: they become the fountains of Divine loving kindness and proof of the Holy Quality. They then are led to *tiqqun*, to let their lives speak, loving all those whom they touch, through repairing the world, through co-creating the Rule of Peace, the Kingship of God. They do not see this as a fight between Good and Evil, since the Creator made both, but as natural as a bird's morning song.

Human perfectibility in Judaism and Quakerism. The Quaker description of this state of "perfection" in which humans at their best show their divine attributes is that we can be guided by the Inward Light. Judaism points out that each person is created in the image of God. The closing of the canon has obscured the prophetic tradition of Israel, and yet the Torah emanates each day from Sinai and new revelations of Truth appear in every generation. The Talmud continues to evolve as new insights are published each year. Quakers speak of "that of God in every one" that can bring forth continuing revelation. In the evolution of both traditions, practices and positions are now accepted that early Friends and early Jews would have found incomprehensible, if not unacceptable. And yet many modern Jews and Quakers see this as the perfecting of their communities. Where does the Light of inspiration and insight come from?

Origin of the Inward Light. My belief is that Jesus taught that this Inward Light came from the Messiah. My understanding of the texts that are most assuredly

Jesus' own words, especially when considered in the ambiguity of his native language Aramaic, never finds him claiming to be the Anointed One prophesied to come and rescue the lost of Israel. Yet he speaks with the authority of the prophets, those who said, "Thus says YHWH the Lord:..." Who is this Meshiach? Today rabbinical Judaism teaches that every child must be treated as holy: he or she may be the Chosen One, a great *tzadik* who bears the world on their shoulders, or even the Redeemer who pays the cost to bring all the people back to the right way, *teshuvah*. Maybe Rev Yeshu'a suspected it and his disciples were right: maybe he was the Messiah, just as each one of us, imitating his contact with the Spirit, must play a role as the Messiah, too, so that together we save the world. After all, we are all Children of God, and Persons (the real meaning of *ben adam*, son of man), and thus all Christs. Quakers have usually asserted that all those who serve the Lord are one body, whatever their stated denomination. The role of sacrifice and Temple ritual has disappeared from Judaism, but hints of it are still referred to in Jewish worship and direct reference is made in Christian theology. Quakers don't talk about it, but the sacrifice of one's ego (said many ways in past times), the need to submit to the Right Way so that all of life is sacramental, is in line with Jesus's Jewish teachings. And it wasn't even original with him 2000 years ago.

Several Jewish teachers and philosophers have maintained that Jesus taught nothing that was not already part of Judaism in the First Century. Others contend that his was simply a question of emphasis, focus or calling the Jewish people back from the temptations of Hellenic culture and Roman imperialism. Perhaps Quakerism can help Judaism reclaim Jesus, for in rediscovering primitive Christianity, "the early church restored from the Apostasy," as George Fox said, the early Children of the Light rediscovered many of the Jewish aspects of that diverse Jesus movement and its Jewish founders – although they failed to identify them as such.

There are many teachings of Jesus that I find essential for my guidance and which are found in liberal Judaism. As I read the journals and teachings of the admirable first Quakers, I hear them saying the same things. I have no trouble celebrating in the joy and Chassidic singing of Jewish Renewal; it complements wonderfully the focus, seriousness and mysticism of my Quaker Meeting. (*Synagog* is merely Greek for meeting, after all.) Both are practices that bring me closer to my Creator and open the way for my service or ministry to the rest of humanity and the Divine. I am thankful for my Rebbe's leading me into this place.

Notes

[1] *Halakha* is the Jewish law, literally meaning "correct walking," reminding us that Quakers scrutinized "disorderly walking."

[2] The belief that the New Testament trumps the Old and that Jesus and Christianity supersede and replace Moses and Judaism, implying that Jews must "convert" to claim their covenant.

[3] *Shekhinah*, the (in-dwelling) Presence or Holy Spirit, *Adonai*, my Lord, or *haShem*, the (holy) Name, are common Jewish ways of referring to G-d, either because direct reference feels too sacrilegious, or because the word God doesn't describe the amorphous, mystical Ground of Being, the I-Am-that-I-Am.

Reflections for a Peace Sabbath

By Ralph Beebe

Ralph Beebe, Professor Emeritus of History at George Fox University (Oregon), often speaks in person, on the radio, and occasionally on television, trying to explain the situation in the Middle East. Ralph had the opportunity to become acquainted with Israel and Palestine firsthand about 15 years ago. He is the author of Blessed are the Peacemakers: A Palestinian Christian in the Occupied West Bank *and has been involved in many follow-up activities. He has visited Israel and Palestine six times with an eye to both biblical history and current peacemaking. The following reflections were prepared for Northwest Yearly Meeting's "Peace Sabbath" and used with the author's permission.*

1. European Jews were likely the most persecuted people in the history of the world, culminating in the unbelievable horrors of the Holocaust. Think how we would feel if Quakers in America were so victimized. The Jews deserve a place to live peacefully.

2. The Old Testament and Revelation suggest that Israel will play a significant role in the return of Jesus. Should we be a part of that prophecy's fulfillment?

3. 800,000 people lost their homes because the United Nations gave half of Palestine to the new nation of Israel. Think how we would feel if the Jews had been given the northwestern United States and we were the ones who were driven from our homes.

4. Since 1967 Israel has disregarded UN mandates and built settlements (Jew-only communities) in the small areas of Palestine the UN had reserved for Palestinians. They constantly harass each other, but Israel can enforce its power, and does, making it very difficult for the

Palestinians. How would we react if we were the victims?

5. Israel is a tiny Jewish nation in the midst of hostile Arab nations, some of which want to drive Israel into the sea. Wouldn't we feel that the long history of victimization was continuing?

6. The United States, the world's most powerful nation, is extremely one-sided, supporting Israel even when it disobeys God's and human laws.

Naturally, out of this has come much bitterness and protracted fighting. Before the 20th century the tiny Jewish minority in Arab lands was generally well treated, far better than in Europe. The change came when between 1920 and 1948 nearly a million Jews from Europe freed themselves from oppression by returning to biblical Palestine/Israel and became a dominating power.

How do we pray? We must "pray for the peace of Jerusalem." We must pray for justice on both sides, for empathy that helps each understand why the other hurts. We pray that Americans will gain better understanding and be more balanced.

In brief, we pray that God's hand will overrule, even in lands dominated by non-Christians. Specifically, right now, let's pray that Israel will do more to trust the Arab League's conditional promise of 2002 to accept Israel as a nation. Pray that the Palestinians can rein in their more radical elements. Pray for the US President and Secretary of State to be honest brokers for peace. Finally, pray that US actions in the Muslim world will become a cause for peace rather than a lightning rod spreading terror.

Can Any Good Come out of Nazareth?

By Max Carter
Guilford College

Some of the best falafel in Ramallah comes from the Nazareth Restaurant, which sits just a few blocks from the Friends meetinghouse and the Friends Girls School. During our annual volunteer work in Ramallah at the Meeting, School, and Friends International Centre, our groups often visit the restaurant for some delicious local cuisine.

Omar Abu Daher, a 22-year old member of one of the security forces loyal to the Palestinian Authority President, must have agreed with our assessment of the Nazareth's food. He, too, dined there one May afternoon in 2007. As he prepared to eat a late lunch, Israeli soldiers dressed as Palestinians, their armored jeep camouflaged as a Palestinian delivery truck, entered the restaurant, took aim, and assassinated Omar in broad daylight.

Accompanied by a caravan of other Israeli vehicles, they drove back out of town along the main street of Ramallah. Within minutes, the area was cleaned up, shoppers again filled the streets of the bustling town, parents picked up their children from school, and life continued as if normal.

This *is* normality today in the Occupied Palestinian Territories, even as it is in Israel. Unspeakable violence such as suicide bombings, "extra-judicial" assassinations, Qassam rocket fire, and F-16 missile attacks emanate from Palestinian and Israeli sides, leaving lives destroyed, property mangled, and optimism for a permanent peace in tatters.

Max L. Carter is director of the Friends Center at Guilford College in Greensboro, NC. Used with permission of author.

The violence is justified as resistance, security, pre-emption, retaliation, or even as the will of G-d or Allah, whichever name is invoked. And it is not the only brutality imposed upon people. Aside from the constant fear and anxiety for many, there are home demolitions, land confiscations, travel restrictions, and various laws that are used to deny full rights to people. Palestinians cite the cruelty of Israel's "separation fence/wall" and checkpoints. Israelis cite the anti-Jewish threats and harangues from politicians, clergy, and common citizens.

What positive role can we hope to play as visiting Friends in the region – especially when those visits are for only a few weeks at a time? Is there anything that we can contribute to peace?

The Ministry of Presence

Our hosts in Israel and Palestine tell us that we must continue to come. Especially with the decline in tourism since the outbreak of the 2000 *Intifada*, those who take the time and perceived risk to visit are deeply appreciated. Time and time again, we are told that our presence reminds them that they are not forgotten; that somebody still cares; that there is still someone who wants to listen to their story.

During one trip, we visited with Rabbi Arik Ascherman of Rabbis for Human Rights. As we were taken into his tiny, cluttered office in West Jerusalem, we passed posters with his likeness and Hebrew inscriptions that we could not read. With a disarming smile, the rabbi shared with us that they were samples of posters plastered all over the city. The Hebrew words beneath his likeness were, "Wanted: Dead or Alive." His work with other Israeli and Palestinian peace partners had brought not only the risk of prison – but also of death at the hands of his fellow citizens.

Our time with him, short as it was, helped express that he was not alone in his struggle, that others would be "holding him in the Light" as he pursued the difficult work of peacemaking.

The Ministry of Communication

Especially with the present travel restrictions in Israel and Palestine (Israeli civilians are forbidden by law to enter the West Bank and Gaza; Palestinians have a very difficult time getting travel permits from the Israeli authorities), face-to-face contact between Israelis and Palestinians is very limited. Often we find ourselves the *de facto* go-betweens, communicating what we have seen and heard on one side with contacts on the other. Sometimes we can only plant seeds and hope for the best, even when the initial response is not encouraging.

In the summer of 1988, during the first Palestinian *Intifada*, I was in Ramallah listening to the excited talk of Palestinians forging the then radical call for a two-state solution, mutual Israeli/Palestinian recognition, and a future together. I shared this new vision with a group of Israeli soldiers on patrol, and one responded, "Oh, no. It will never work. Give the Palestinians an inch, and they will take a mile. They will drive us into the sea." Later sharing the same vision with a group of young Palestinians in a nearby village, I was told, "Oh, no. It will never work. Give the Israelis an inch, and they will take a mile. They will drive us into the desert."

Today, however, the aspirations for a two-state solution are held by the majority of Israelis and Palestinians.

Equally important is the work of conveying "back home" what we have seen, heard, and experienced. Being able to express the thoughts and feelings of common people from either side of the conflict adds an important alternative perspective. One person with whom we meet each year when we return to the States is our Congressional representative. Over a span of ten years, we have seen his views on the situation change incrementally. The change in understanding of others is often far more dramatic.

The Ministry of Mediation

Sometimes we find ourselves in situations where we are involved directly in conflict mediation. On one memorable occasion we toured civilian Palestinian homes damaged by an Israeli incursion the night before. As we observed the pockmarked stone and shattered windows, the young mother of the house, Nadia, confronted us: "And you call *us* the terrorists! I hope all Americans burn in hell!" Noting that the military hardware that had nearly killed her and her family had been made in the USA, she unleashed her wrath on us.

In response, we listened, expressed our sympathy, and determined after leaving her that we must provide funds to help repair the home. Our gesture of empathetic listening and concrete action resulted in Nadia's seeking us out a few days later to thank us with little tokens of appreciation: olive wood Christian symbols given to us American Quakers by a Palestinian Muslim.

On another occasion, our very presence caused a group of soldiers to stop kicking and beating a young man they had stopped on the street. We provide what many in the peace movement there call "the grandmother effect." There are things that even a hardened soldier will not do if his/her grandmother is watching – or a group of international observers.

These are the most important contributions that I feel we make on our trips. Of course, we do give many hours of volunteer work, on occasion offer up advice on strategies for responding to the conflict, and not infrequently provide much needed comic relief with cultural and linguistic gaffes. In the grand scheme of things, our offerings are quite minimal; on one scale, matters have only worsened during the years we have been visiting. Violence such as that witnessed at the Nazareth Restaurant is a common occurrence. But in small ways, and in individual lives, our presence, our care, and our witness make an impact.

The Ministry of Those Beside Whom We Serve

One other area, though, is even more important. We become changed persons ourselves through our experience in the region. We change not only in our growing knowledge of the situation and deepening understanding of the complexities of the conflict; we change through the ministry of those Israelis and Palestinians forging a "normal" life in the midst of the troubles. We develop the strength to share our perspective with sometimes hostile audiences through the inspiration of their determination. We maintain hope against all evidence to the contrary through the "long patience" demonstrated by those living the conflict daily. We refuse to give in to bitterness through the example of those who have lost so much – yet maintain their conviction that God demands love, justice, reconciliation, forgiveness, and peace.

Until her death in 2006, Violet Zaru was the source of some of our greatest inspiration. Born to a Ramallah Quaker family in the early years of the British Mandate in Palestine, Violet was in the early years of her professional life when the 1948 war brought the establishment of Israel and Jordanian occupation of the West Bank. She served the last years of her teaching career under the Israeli occupation that began in 1967, and she lived her last ten years under the flag of the Palestinian Authority. Never in her life was she the citizen of an independent state, able to enjoy unfettered travel, or not have cause to fear for her life or the safety of her property. Yet there was no more transcendently hopeful and loving person on earth. Even in retirement, she dedicated much of her efforts to serving the five-year-old children in the Friends Play Centre in the Amari Refugee Camp. Her constant refrain to these traumatized children was that God loved them; that there were people of many nationalities and religions around the world who loved them, too; and that God was their strength and protection —not weapons.

When Jesus announced the onset of his ministry from the synagogue in Nazareth, he emphasized that he was to "...bring good news to the poor...proclaim release to the captives...and recovery of sight to the blind...let the oppressed go free...proclaim the year of the Lord's favor." (Luke 4:18-19 NRSV)

The excellence of the falafel coming out of the Nazareth Restaurant in Ramallah pales before this Good News — as does the temptation to despair that comes from the all-too-frequent violence that took the life of Omar Abu Daher while enjoying a sandwich at the restaurant. Jesus's own ministry of presence, communication, mediation, and accompaniment show that, indeed, something good can come out of Nazareth. And good can come out of our own small efforts, too.

Compassionate Listening in Israel/Palestine: A Jewish Quaker Perspective

by David Rush

Between May 25 and June 5, 2010, I joined with twenty-three other North Americans on a Compassionate Listening Project visit to Israel and the Occupied West Bank.

This journey was a great privilege. I think I learned a great deal, and I have some ideas for how peace might be advanced there, now that I better understand some of the impediments blocking the way to peace. Whether these impediments can be overcome is an open question; for the sake of the lives of both peoples, I do hope fervently that they can be.

Over the course of a very full two weeks our group met a spectrum of people, from hard-liners to active peace-makers on both sides. The perspectives and techniques of TCLP were very valuable; people opened up to us with unexpected trust and candor. All of our conversations were begun in a quiet, respectful way. Even as we got to hard questions about difficult issues, the trust that had been built allowed us to maintain a strong human thread. (Indeed, at times, it was inviting to lapse from our analytical stance in the face of a gracious response. At times we could lull ourselves even when receiving some

---

David Rush is a member of Friends Meeting at Cambridge (MA). He has served as clerk of Membership Committee, and served on Nominating, Finance, and Advisory Committees, and as Eva Koch Fellow at Woodbrooke Quaker Study Centre in Birmingham, England. He is an emeritus Professor at Tufts University. This article used with author's permission.

chilling information, if it was delivered with a smile.)

I spent a few days in Jerusalem just before the onset of the delegation, and had supper with one of my first public health students, now an emeritus professor at Hebrew University. He has done many international projects with colleagues in the neighboring countries and the occupied territories, and he was a very progressive left wing person when I last talked to him in the early 1970s. I was taken aback when he explained that he is not in the peace camp and is quite skeptical of the left-wing analysis of conditions in I/P. I shall return to him and his ideas.

I learned from our group's encounters that we are dealing with two wounded peoples, both of whom are committed to their respective historical narratives. Unfortunately, for both peoples they remain true and necessary, but one is incompatible with the other, and both depend centrally on the identity of victimhood. If peace is to be possible I believe it must be understood by each people how these narratives are cherished and are crucial to the psychological integrity of the other people, all on the path to ultimately transcending them. There are libraries full of books explicating these narratives, in more or less nuanced form; we probably don't have time to talk about them this morning, but can at a later time, if you wish. Needless to say, there is more than enough victimization, along with more than enough blame, in the histories of both peoples.

The glimmer of hope I believe I discerned on this trip is that, unlike the stories of the past, the current stories of these two peoples are *not neccesarily* incompatible, and if the past sins of the other are not to remain excuses for current intransigency, both Israelis and Palestinians need to work hard on changing these contemporary stories

My former student's story, and that of Amotz Asa-El [former editor of the *Jerusalem Post*], and an Israeli ex-diplomat with whom we met, is that the Palestinian leadership is duplicitous, that it speaks one story in

Hebrew and English, and a very different one in Arabic to the Palestinian masses; that the Palestinians see a two-state solution as an interim ploy to buy time, masking the ultimate goal of driving almost all the Jews (except the few "good" Jews who lived in Palestine say, in the 1920s and before) from Palestine. I heard a recent talk by Lawrence Wright, one of *The New Yorker* writers on the Middle East, who said that Hamas teaches blatant hatred in its schools; the PA probably does better, but not much better. (Certainly Israeli Jews teach their own story in their schools, neglecting that of the Palestinians; but what is being taught in Gaza goes far beyond bias; I, as a Jew, and all of us, as Americans, are keenly aware that hate speech is a powerful weapon, whoever uses it.) However, all three of these Israelis stopped short of addressing Israel's faults: the other side's misbehavior seemed, in their minds, to have limited Israel's responsibility for its own. Specifically, they did not address the presence and function of humiliation of an occupied people.

There are many Palestinian stories, just as there are many Israeli ones. A central theme in what we heard was that the occupiers, particularly the more militant settlers, seem to make it a policy to harass and humiliate the Palestinians; often the army is cited as well. (There has been a major reduction in the number of checkpoints in the West Bank, with reported increased economic activity and prosperity there, as attested to by *The Economist* and other sources. No militant Palestinians we met would agree that this is the case.) This humiliation is particularly hurtful in a culture in which shame, dignity and honor are so central. In strong parallel with Arab duplicity seeming to absolve Israelis from attending to some of their own faults, the tales of humiliation seem to be used to justify the Palestinians in not addressing their own part in stalling further reconciliation.

Let us for the moment allow that both these complaints are justified. What I realized is that, unlike the historical narratives, they are not mutually contradictory. Both could be true. And both peoples and their leaders not only could work to address the grievances of the other but, to my mind, must do so if peace is to become possible.

I am convinced that peace cannot come about before trust and confidence are built on both sides, something to which communication on a personal level is important. Each group needs to be able to see and acknowledge the suffering of the other. Both need to be accepted as human beings, as potential partners. The Palestinians must convince the Israelis that their peace efforts are sincere, and not just a tactic for achieving the ultimate goal of domination and expulsion; the Israelis need to understand that humiliation of Palestinians does not serve any useful purpose, but rather poisons any effort at reconciliation. (Portraying and treating the Palestinian as less than human does, however, serve the purposes of the right-wing government, and undermines the Israeli peace camp.) Our government needs to keep up its efforts on both sides to better the conditions for peace.

One of the tragic ironies of the moment is that before the Oslo accords Israelis could visit anywhere in the occupied territories, and Palestinians had easy access to Israel. As a step towards statehood, the PA gained administrative control over parts of the West Bank, especially the cities, and Israelis were forbidden free access to these areas, while Palestinians without Jerusalem residency could no longer enter Israel without official permits. This was meant to be an interim arrangement, but has become, since 1993, the way things are. Thus, one of the essentials for peace, interchange at the personal level between Israelis and Palestinians, while still possible, has become very difficult.

I believe that the Boycott/Divestment/Sanctions movement hurts the chances for peace. While the deaths on the Turkish flotilla have led to some relief from the embargo on Gaza, the entire episode underscores what most Israelis believe: "The world hates us, and our best chance for safety lies in a strong military, with a militaristic government." Ironically, this undermines the credibility and strength, such as it is, of the Israeli peace movement. I believe that efforts such as barring Israeli academics from scholarly publications and conferences gives Netanyahu thousands more votes in any subsequent election. I also believe that that scolding (which is, after all, shaming) is one of the least effective ways of getting people to act on their best motives. I am further convinced that any time a "peace" group (whether Jewish, Quaker, Christian, secular or whatever) shares a platform or agenda with those who oppose the legitimacy of the existence of Israel, in whatever cause, whether in the name of justice for Palestinians, post Zionism, anti-Zionism, or the so called one-state solution, it is yet another nail in the coffin of a peaceful solution, since it only further convinces many Israelis that the outside world is implacably opposed to their ongoing existence, and they had better hunker down and be as close to an armed colossus as possible—in other words, elect an implacable right-wing government. It also helps the Palestinians believe that they are making progress in reaching their goals, when the goal of peace is more likely being sabotaged. If we want an Israeli government that might take risks for peace, we on the outside should do all we can do to support the Israeli left. On the contrary, the Christian Zionists support the Israeli right, and the actions of the foreign so-called peace groups that treat Israel as a pariah state have exactly the same effect of undermining those in Israel that are not only the best hope for peace, but maybe the only hope.

About the right of return: soon after I returned we heard Arik Ascherman, head of Rabbis for Human Rights, respond to a very strong challenge on the right of all Palestinians to return to their pre-1948 homes. Ascherman gave what seemed to me a very thoughtful, nuanced response. He said he could never tell others to forgo their rights, to give up what is justly theirs. But in present conditions, Palestinians could maintain all their rights, or could choose to give up this one in order to have the chance of peace. Full right of Palestinian return is a non-starter for Israelis, which you can better understand if you imagine that all the refugees of the world's wars, including, for example, the Native Americans, were to be given such a right.

Pretty much everyone I have spoken to agrees that we now know what 99% of a peace agreement will look like, if one is to be achieved. It will be like the Geneva Accords: two states; 1967 borders, with swaps; East Jerusalem as the Palestinian capitol; and a symbolic right of return, with adequate compensation for those who will not be able to return. Sari Nusseibeh, one of the past PLO negotiators has said that single issues cannot be settled sequentially but that an agreement, almost certainly painful for both sides, but one that each side can ultimately live with, should be presented as a referendum to both peoples simultaneously. They each can then choose: you can have this entire package, or an endless status quo: violence now, and violence down the generations.

I am further convinced that much of the American left, secular and religious, has not learned to distinguish between being peacemakers and being warriors for justice. Peacemakers, and mediators in general, must be able to speak credibly to both sides of a conflict, to have at least the appearance of impartiality. Partisans, or warriors, may be fighting for justice for the oppressed, but we should not be fooled into thinking that one can do both. I believe that is impossible.

Finally Kitty suggested that I clarify my Zionism, my conviction that the State of Israel should be allowed to exist. I do not think all Jews can or should make Aliyah, that is, that we should all go to live in Israel. But my reading of two millennia of Christian behavior towards the Jews (and of more recent Muslim anti-Judaism) makes a Jewish homeland seem to me urgently necessary. America is atypical: American Jews have never been so safe or secure as we are here, today. But America is not the only place in the world, and these wonderful conditions might not last forever, even here. So long as only a few Christians feel obliged to repent for the past treatment of the Jews, so long as only a few Christians do not feel obliged to teach that the polemic against their fellow Jews by the Gospel writers (particularly the Gospel of John, the "Quaker Gospel") was a response to a particular time and place and not evidence of deicide, so long as the Pope can reverse *Nostre Aetate* and reinsert the Good Friday prayer for the conversion of the Jews, that is how long a safe haven for Jews in danger need exist.

Current AFSC Work in Israel/Palestine

In the aftermath of World War II, AFSC gained experience resettling refugees and displaced persons, and was asked by the United Nations to organize relief efforts for Palestinian Arab refugees in the Gaza Strip. This continued until the United Nations Relief Works Agency began operations on May 1, 1950. From its initial engagement with refugees in Gaza, AFSC has been committed to peacebuilding as well as relief efforts.

Today, AFSC, through its Palestinian staff and partners in Gaza, the West Bank and East Jerusalem, supports young people and their communities to enable them to marshal local resources that can directly meet pressing humanitarian, social and educational needs.

Over the past eight years the AFSC Palestine Youth Program has worked with over 4,000 young people, offering them the opportunity to use their talents and develop their skills to undertake projects that they themselves have identified in their local community. In this project AFSC works in partnership with universities, youth organizations and the Palestinian Ministries of Youth and Education and the United Nations (UNRWA).

Shortly after the end of Israel's "Operation Cast Lead" assault on Gaza in January 2009, AFSC provided emergency humanitarian assistance to hospitals and clinics and to agencies in Gaza feeding orphaned and displaced children. AFSC works with former Youth Program participants and other partner organizations to help families to repair damaged homes using as much as possible locally available materials not subject to the continuing Israeli and Egyptian blockade of the Gaza Strip.

For more about AFSC work in this region, see afsc.org/office/palestine.

Congressional Briefing: Israelis and Palestinians Demand Peace in Gaza

by Tim Sallinger

MARCH 8, 2010: WASHINGTON, DC—Concerned citizens and Congressional staffers convened on Capitol Hill March 8 to hear the riveting stories of two people with deep ties to the Israeli-Palestinian conflict.

Laila El-Haddad, a Palestinian from Gaza, lives in Maryland with her children and husband, a Palestinian refugee denied the right to return to his homeland. Her parents currently live in Gaza.

Two seats down from El-Haddad sat Elik Elhanan, an Israeli former IDF soldier. In 1997 his 14-year-old sister was killed when two Palestinian suicide bombers blew themselves up in central Jerusalem.

The two speakers had a common, peaceful message. Both demanded that Israel end its occupation of the Palestinian territories, and that the U.S. cease its military aid to the government of Israel.

"The impact of military aid to Israel is terrible, is disastrous for the entire region," Elhanan said. "[It] is responsible for the fact that we are dying for such a long time. And when I say 'we,' I talk about all the people who die from the actions of my government, be they Israeli or Palestinian."

AFSC organized the panel, sponsored by Interfaith Peace-Builders and the U.S. Campaign to End the Israeli Occupation. The entire event can be viewed on YouTube at www.youtube.com/watch?v=GLxSG8qm4Mg.

Miryam Rashid, director of the AFSC's Middle East program, said it brought a unique perspective to Washington.

AFSC material used with permission of author and AFSC.

"Our government shows such little understanding of the impact of U.S. foreign policy on peoples' daily lives," Rashid said. "Members of Congress, administration officials, U.S. citizens—everybody should see the briefing."

El-Haddad spoke first, describing freedom of movement within Gaza. Military checkpoints and separation walls in the Gaza Strip "do more than simply inconvenience Palestinians," she said. "They paralyze life and livelihoods."

The situation in Gaza is very important to the Palestinian writer, who fears for her family's safety. On her blog at www.gazamom.com, she described getting phone calls from her parents during the 2009 Israeli bombing of Gaza.

"When the bombs are dropped around them, they send me a quick note to inform me of what happened before running to safety. I am still not sure where 'safety' is; and neither, I think, do they. In Gaza, there is no 'safe.' And there is nowhere to flee to, with the borders closed, the sky and sea under siege."

Elik Elhanan is a co-founder of Combatants for Peace (CFP), a group composed of both Palestinian and Israeli ex-fighters who decided to lay down their arms and seek a nonviolent end to the conflict and an end to the Israeli occupation.

The former soldier provided insight into how prevalent political outlooks among Israelis are shaped by U.S. foreign policy. Military culture is deeply rooted in Israeli society, he said.

"Israel is an army with a state, rather than the other way around. And the military is still the most important social fact in Israeli life."

From an early age, Israelis are taught that the oppression of Palestinians is a "necessary evil," that Israel must defend itself from its enemies, he said.

"As long as [there is] this delusion that only power can maintain Israel...our fight is an uphill fight. This delusion will go on as long as you keep financing it."

APPENDIX

Resources for Interfaith Peacemaking and Dialogue

BOOKS ON INTERFAITH

Sandy and Jael Bharat. *A Global Guide to Interfaith: Reflections from Around the World.* O Books: Washington, 2007. A comprehensive look at the interfaith movement from a global perspective, with stories, illustrations, and useful information.

John B. Cobb Jr. and Ward M. McAfee, eds. *The Dialogue Comes of Age: Christian Encounters with Other Traditions.* Minneapolis: Fortress Press, 2010.

Ranya Idliby, Suzanne Oliver, and Priscilla Warner. *The Faith Club: a Muslim, a Christian, a Jew—Three Women Search for Understanding.* New York: Free Press, 2006. Includes advice on how to start a faith club and a reading group guide. A fascinating story and a practical guide.

Rebecca Kratz Mays, ed. *Interfaith Dialogue at the Grassroots.* Philadelphia, PA: Ecumenical Press, 2008.

Stuart M. Matlins and Arthur J. Magida, eds. *How to Be a Perfect Stranger: The Essential Religious Etiquette Handbook,* 3rd Edition (Paperback). Skylight Paths Publishing, 2003.

Jim Pym, *The Pure Principle: Quakers and Other Faith Traditions.* Sessions of York, 2000.

Leland Steward, ed. *World Scriptures.* From the Scholar's Desk: Boliver, MO, 2006. Selections were compiled in cooperation with faith groups represented and include an extraordinary diversity, from Taoist and Hindu to Scientology and Science of Mind.

Allison Stokes. *Shalom, Salaam, Peace.* New York: United Methodist Church, 2006. Used in Methodist study groups, this is an excellent resource.

Patricia A. Williams, ed. *Universalism and Religions.* Quaker Universalist Reader #2, 2007.

ARTICLES AND PAMPHLETS ON INTERFAITH

Marigold Bentley."Interfaith—now more than ever" *Quaker News*, winter 2005.

Sallie King, *Friends and Other Religions.* Quaker Press of FGC, 2003.

Elizabeth Nesbitt, *Interfaith Pilgrims.* Quaker Books, 2003.

Carol Murphy, *Many Religions, One God*, Pendle Hill Pamphlet #150, 1966.

Douglas Steere, *Mutual Irradiation*, Pendle Hill Pamphlet #175.

Dan Seeger, *Sharing our Faith.* Quaker Press of FGC, 1991.

Margot Tennyson, *Friends and Other Faiths*, Quaker Home Service, 1992.

ISLAM

Mohammed Abu-Nimer, *Nonviolence and Peace Building in Islam: Theory and Practice.* University Press of Florida: Tampa, Florida, 2003.

Akbar S. Ahmed, *Islam Today: A Short Introduction to the Muslim World.* Taurus: London, 2001. A lucid, readable account by an outstanding Muslim scholar.

Abdullah Yusuf Ali, *The Meaning of the Holy Qur'an.* Amana: Beltsville, Maryland, 2001. A classic work by an

Indian Muslim scholar, with extensive notes and explications necessary for a serious reading of the Qur'an.

Karen Armstrong, *Islam: A Short History*. Modern Library: NY, 2002. Insightful and sensitive introduction to Islam by a former nun who is well respected in the Muslim community.

Tariq Ali, *The Clash of Fundamentalisms: Crusades, Jihads and Modernity* . Verso: London, 2003.

Reza Aslan, *No god but God: The Origins, Evolution, and Future of Islam*. New York: Random House, 2005.

Geraldine Brooks, *Nine Parts of Desire: The Hidden World of Islamic Women* . Anchor Books: NY, 1995.

Carl W. Ernst, *Sufism: An Essential Introduction to the Philosophy and Practice of the Mystical Tradition of Islam*. Shamballa: Boston, 1997.

Hassan Hathout, *Reading the Muslim Mind*. American Trust Publications: Plainsfield, Indiana, 1995. A thoughtful reflection on Islam by an Egyptian-born physician, scholar, speaker, poet and ethicist who is regarded as one of the great spiritual teachers of Islam in America today.

Asma Gull Hasan, *American Muslims: A New Generation*. Continuum: New York, 2001. A lively and thoughtful book by a young American Muslim woman who describes herself as a "Muslim feminist cowgirl." A must-read for anyone who wants to know what life is really like for a Muslim in today's America.

Tarif Khalidi, ed. and translator, *The Muslim Jesus: Sayings and Stories in Islamic Literature*. Harvard University Press: Cambridge, 2001.

Anthony Manousos, *Islam from a Quaker Perspective*. Friends Bulletin: Torrance, CA, 2002.

Michael Sells, *Approaching the Qur'an: the Early Revelations*, Ashland: White Cloud Press, 2007. A Quaker scholar who taught at Haverford College (now at the

University of Chicago), Sells explores the poetry and music of the Qur'an which is essential to understanding its meaning. This book comes with a CD containing powerful recitations of the Qur'an by male and female Qur'an reciters.

Marston Spreight, *God is One: The Way of Islam.* Friendship Press: New York, 2001. An excellent introduction to Islam by the Director of the Office on Christian-Muslim Relations of the National Council of Churches. Contains a detailed study guide for a six-week course intended to help Christians deepen their understanding of the history, culture, and religion of Muslims.

Gisela Webb, ed. *Windows of Faith: Muslim Women Scholar-Activists in North America.* Syracuse University Press, 2000.

JUDAISM, ISRAEL/PALESTINE AND FRIENDS

Claire Gorfinkel, *I Have Always Wanted To Be Jewish And Now, Thanks To The Religious Society Of Friends, I Am.* Pendle Hill Pamphlet, 2000.

Patricia Edwards-Konic, *Enduring Hope: the Impact of the Ramallah Friends Schools.* Friends United Press, 2008.

Rabbi Michael Lerner. *Healing Israel/Palestine: A Path to Peace and Reconciliation.* North Atlantic Books, 2003. This book applies a compassionate listening approach to the conflict, an effort to hear and respect the stories on both sides. "The first step in the process of healing is to tell the story of how we got where we are in a way that avoids demonization," he writes. So he relates the history of Zionism and the state of Israel in a way that acknowledges both the rights and the wrongs of Jews and Palestinians alike.

When The Rain Returns: Toward Justice and Reconciliation in Israel and Palestine (AFSC, 2005). A study highlighting Quaker responses to the Israeli-Palestinian conflict.

LISTENING/COMMUNICATION SKILLS

Carol Hwoschinsky. *Listening with the Heart: A Guidebook for Compassionate Listening* . Published by the Compassionate Listening Project. (compassionatelistening.org)

Kay Lindahl. *Practicing the Sacred Art of Listening: A Guide to Enrich Your Relationships and Kindle Your Spiritual Life.* Skylight Paths Publishing, Woodstock, VT, 2003. (http://www.sacredlistening.com)

Kay Lindahl. *The Sacred Art of Listening: Forty Reflections for Cultivating a Spiritual Practice.* Skylight Paths Publishing, Woodstock, VT, 2003.

Anthony Manousos, ed. *Compassionate Listening and Other Writings by Gene Hoffman, Quaker Peacemaker and Mystic.* Friends Bulletin: Torrance, CA 2003.

VIDEO

Ruth Broyde Sharone, *God and Allah Need to Talk.* A documentary about interfaith work in the LA area after 9/11 by (see filmsthatmatter.com)

ECUMENICAL AND INTERFAITH PEACEMAKING

Douglas Gwyn, George Hunsinger, Eugene F. Roop, and John Howard Yoder, *A Declaration on Peace: In God's People the World's Renewal Has Begun.* Scottdale, PA: Herald Press, 1991. This book was sponsored by the Historic Peace Churches/FOR Consultative Committee as a contribution to ecumenical dialogue on the centrality of peace witness to Christian faith.

Robert Herr and Judy Zimmerman Herr, eds. *Transforming Violence: Linking Local and Global Peacemaking.* Scottdale, PA: Herald Press, 1998. This book was sponsored by the Historic Peace Churches/FOR Consultative Committee as a contribution to the Programme to Overcome Violence, predecessor to the Decade to Overcome Violence.

Margot Kässman, *Overcoming Violence: The Challenge to the Churches in All Places.* Geneva, Switzerland: WCC Publications, 1998. A WCC document about the Programme to Overcome Violence and intended as a resource for the Decade to Overcome Violence.